FIRST, FOR THE DURATION

THE STORY OF THE EIGHTH ALABAMA INFANTRY, C.S.A.

Linda L. Green

HERITAGE BOOKS
2008

HERITAGE BOOKS
AN IMPRINT OF HERITAGE BOOKS, INC.

Books, CDs, and more—Worldwide

For our listing of thousands of titles see our website
at
www.HeritageBooks.com

Published 2008 by
HERITAGE BOOKS, INC.
Publishing Division
100 Railroad Ave. #104
Westminster, Maryland 21157

Copyright © 2008 Linda L. Green

All rights reserved. No part of this book may be reproduced or transmitted in any form or by any means, electronic or mechanical, including photocopying, recording or by any information storage and retrieval system without written permission from the author, except for the inclusion of brief quotations in a review.

International Standard Book Number: 978-0-7884-4553-8

Table of Contents

Prologue:	Setting the Stage	iii-v
Chapter One:	Getting Organized	1-6
Chapter Two:	Baptism By Fire	7-14
Chapter Three:	The Peninsula Campaign	15-29
Chapter Four:	Second Manassas to Sharpsburg	30-45
Chapter Five:	Fredericksburg to Chancellorsville	46-56
Chapter Six:	Gettysburg and Its Aftermath	57-67
Chapter Seven:	The Winter of Uncertainty and a Spring of Struggle	68-80
Chapter Eight:	Petersburg, the Siege of No Relief	81-92
Chapter Nine	The Long Road to Appomattox	93-99
Epilogue		100-102
Index:		103-110
Appendix A:	Roster of the Men Who Served	111-151
Appendix B:	The Surrender Roster—Paroles	152-156
Appendix C:	Prison Roster—Ft. Delaware	157-171
Appendix D:	Alternate Designations, Assignments and Battles	172-174
Appendix E:	Transcribed Company Notes	175-197
Appendix F:	Transcribed Field and Staff Notes	198-203
Appendix G:	Bibliography	204-210

PROLOGUE:
SETTING THE STAGE

WAR!!! It has finally come after years of being on the brink of armed conflict. The Southern states were seceding from the Union. And, Alabama joined three of her Southern sisters—South Carolina, Mississippi, and Florida—by voting 61 to 39 on January 11, 1861 to adopt the Ordinance of Secession. On Monday, February 4, 1861, a convention of the seceded states met in Montgomery, Alabama. This was the first session of the Provisional Congress of the Confederate States of America. With this meeting, a roller coaster of events was set in motion. On February 8, 1861, the convention unanimously adopted the Provisional Constitution of the Confederacy. On February 9, Jefferson Davis of Mississippi was unanimously elected Provisional President with Alexander Stephens of Georgia as Vice President. By the 18th of February, 1861, Jefferson Davis has been inaugurated in front of the state capitol in Montgomery. And, on February 20th, the Provisional Congress authorized the President to make contracts in order to buy and manufacture the materiel of war. The Confederate Congress also authorized a domestic loan of $15 million dollars.

Events continued on the fast roller coaster toward war. By March 4, 1861, the Confederate Congress had adopted the Stars and Bars as its flag and it first flew over the Alabama State capitol, which was also serving as the Confederate capitol. On March 9, 1861, the Confederate Congress authorized the issuance of treasury notes of up to a million dollars. By March 13, Alabama had ratified the Provisional Constitution. On March 16, when the Confederate Congress adjourned, Jefferson Davis had a functioning cabinet to carry on the affairs of the new government.

April 11, 1861, Confederate forces under the command of General Pierre Gustave Toutant (P.G.T.) Beauregard demanded the surrender of Fort Sumter in Charleston Harbor, South Carolina. And on the 12th day of April 1861, Confederate forces fired on Fort Sumter. WAR!!! It had finally come.

New recruits on both sides had been stirred to arms with emotional oratory. They expected a quick battle of a few days with hard fighting and a triumphal return. Everything would be over in a matter of days.

By April 17, 1861 attention in Alabama was focusing on the volunteering and organizing of the militia. Alabama's young men flocked to the colors of the Stars and Bars willingly as Alabama began organizing units and officering them in a somewhat haphazard manner. The ideals for which the war was being fought held glamour, courage and fascination for the idealistic young men for dreams of glory were as yet untouched by the deadly reality of the coming conflict where so many of Alabama's young men would perish defending their lands and homes and kinfolk. States' Rights and slavery were not issues for a majority of these young men who served Alabama and the South so gallantly. All too soon they would realize the war would drag on far longer than either side expected. Federal and Confederate soldiers would spend most of their time fighting heat, cold, mud, dust, loneliness and boredom. Those who raced to the call to arms on both sides were no more prepared for the realities of war than the shock of actual combat. But Confederate troops quarreled less amongst themselves or their leaders versus junior and senior officers (the ruling caste) whose rampant individualism would be a major factor in Southern defeat. They bore their hardship, which exceeded that of any other group, North or South, with less complaint than the top dogs, partly because they were more habituated to deprivation, suffering and sorrow. In addition, Southern soldiers were deeply religious and concerned for the welfare of their families and the education of their children. This also accounted for the higher desertion rates among the Southern soldiers.

In addition, most Confederate volunteers had never ridden a train. While riding in boxcars, they knocked holes in the sides for ventilation and sightseeing. With their heads sticking out, they sang and yelled. To the onlookers, the soldiers reminded them of chickens in a poultry wagon. Many soldiers were killed when they fell from the tops of the coaches where they had climbed. The practice was forbidden by officers but the independent thinking Confederate soldier paid no heed to the order. The idea of exciting times ahead—aided and abetted by the free flowing liquor—made the journey's risk tolerable.[1]

NOTES

[1] McClelan, Baily George, I Saw the Elephant, Company D, 10th Alabama, edited by Norman E. Rourke, Shippensburg, PA: White Mane Publishing Co., Inc., 1995, 10, hereinafter cited as Rourke, Elephant.

John Anthony Winston
Ex-Governor of Alabama
First Colonel Eighth Alabama Infantry
Photo Courtesy of Alabama Department of Archives and History

CHAPTER ONE:
GETTING ORGANIZED

Ten companies, separately raised, and traveled to Richmond, Virginia, would be formerly organized on the 10th of June 1861 as the Eighth Alabama Infantry Regiment. Of the ten companies, five were from Mobile, two were from Perry County, one from Dallas County, one from Coosa County, and one from Butler County. All of the men in these ten separate companies signed up for the duration of the war (a three year enlistment as no one thought the war would last that long). Thus, the Eighth Alabama was the FIRST, FOR THE DURATION.[1]

Captain Young L. Royston formed the Alabama Rangers. This unit was tendered to and received into the service of the Confederate States on May 8, 1861 for the duration of the war. The company received marching orders on May 16th to proceed from its rendezvous point in Perry County, Alabama to Richmond, Virginia. The Rangers were assigned to the newly forming Eighth Alabama Infantry Regiment as Company A.

The "Governor's Guard" from Perry County was offered to the Secretary of War in Montgomery on May 13, 1861. The company arrived in Richmond on the 23rd and went into camp at the Fairfield Race Course. On May 27th, it was mustered into the Confederate States service after which the company was sent to Gloucester, Virginia. By June 14, 1861, the "Governor's Guard" had joined eight other Alabama companies forming the Eighth Alabama Regiment. The "Governor's Guard" officially became Company B.

The "Greenville Guards" were formed in Butler County in the fall of 1860. In January and February of 1861, the "Guards" spent six weeks in Pensacola, Florida assisting Florida troops in taking possession of the U. S. Navy Yard and forts at the mouth of Pensacola Bay. The "Guards" did not learn much about soldiering because there was no fighting. The Navy Yard had been abandoned. The Federal troops had taken refuge in Fort Pickens. This fort was deemed too strong to attack at this time of the year. The "Guard" had the usual experience of being undrilled and undisciplined volunteers, complained about rations, duties imposed without need, and general restiveness under restraint and, of course, dislike of "fine airs" by petty officials. On returning from Florida, the "Guards" were discharged from their service to the State of Alabama, and many of the officers resigned. Those who remained asked Hilary A. Herbert to take charge of the company. He did so assuming the rank of Captain, reorganizing the "Guards" and offering the unit to the State of Alabama on May 10, 1861. In late May, he was directed to take his company, which had not been mustered in to service to Richmond, Virginia. The "Guards" camped for a day and a night in Montgomery. The people there were ablaze with enthusiasm and lavish in their hospitality. Among the refreshments distributed to the troops were liquors in great abundance. After that, Captain Herbert cut off liquor supplies because so many of the troops became drunk.[2]

The uniform of the "Greenville Guards" was grey with red trimmings. The red was used to designate artillery, but the "Guards" knew nothing about that. Each original member of the unit paid for his own uniform. All new recruits did not have uniforms. But these were soon supplied by the Patriotic ladies of Greenville, who presented the "Guards" a company flag. The ladies also gave the "Guards" brightly colored haversacks with long tassels. But these gay trappings were highly ornamental and were not practical for battle.[3]

The trip from Montgomery to Richmond was a long and slow one as the South did not have standard gauge railroad track and many times troops changed trains several times. This was the first war in which trains were used to move troops. The first change for the "Guards" was at West Point, Georgia on the Chattahoochee River. Captain Herbert had difficulty in containing his men, who at this point had not been formerly mustered into service and he had no real authority over them. At West Point, the troops were put on flat cars. The sun was hot, many were still drunk, and there was no water. Finally the train stopped to let the troops get some water after Captain Herbert threatened the engineer with commandeering his train. Herbert had a soldier in his unit that had worked for the railroad before the war.[4] In Covington, Georgia, the train again stopped where Captain Herbert was presented a bouquet of flowers by the girls attending a school there. Girls everywhere crowded the car, bringing the troops flowers and refreshment. The blood of the battlefields was far from the minds of these young men as the train proceeded to Richmond.[5]

Shortly after reaching Richmond, the "Greenville Guards" were mustered into the service of the Confederacy. The "Guards" were notified that with eight other companies then encamped around them and one already at Yorktown, they would be formerly organized into the Eighth Alabama Regiment as Company F. No field officers had as yet been assigned for the Eighth Alabama so the captains of the nine designated companies soon held a conference and proceeded to elect from their own number, a colonel, a lieutenant colonel, and a major. Herbert, let it be know, he wasn't interested in one of the regimental positions, was selected as the one of the three to visit President Davis and ask that those selected be appointed. Mr. Davis received the three officers, but the decision had already been made for the regimental positions of the Eighth Alabama Regiment.[6]

The "Hamp Smith Rifles" were organized in Mobile on May 6th, 1861, and mustered into Confederate States service on June 5th, 1861 in Richmond. Their travel experiences were similar to those of the "Greenville Guards." This unit was allotted to the Eighth Alabama Regiment as Company E.

The Alexander Stephens Guards were organized in Mobile and accepted into service on May 18, 1861 and arrived in Richmond, Virginia May 27th, and

HILARY A. HERBERT

Courtesy of U.S. Naval Historical Center

mustered into Confederate States service on the 28th and on June 13, 1861 joined the newly forming Eighth Alabama Infantry Regiment as Company C.

The "Independent Blues" of Selma, Alabama were formed in Dallas County by Thomas Smith and reported to Richmond where they were mustered into Confederate States service. By May 21st, 1861, the unit had been allotted to the Eighth Alabama Regiment as Company D.

The "German Fusiliers" were formed by John P. Emerich (Emrich) in Mobile. The unit was accepted into Confederate States service and ordered to Richmond on May 25th. They did not leave until May 30th as they were being outfitted with uniforms, knapsacks, cartridge and cap boxes. They arrived in Richmond June 5th, were mustered into service on June 8th and ordered to Yorktown, Virginia, where they were allotted to the Eighth Alabama Regiment as Company G.

The "Mobile Independent Scouts" were organized in Mobile on May 17th by William W. Mordecai. The unit was mustered in to Confederate States service at Richmond, Virginia June 8th, 1861. It was then allotted to the Eighth Alabama Regiment as Company H.

Then there were the "Emerald Guards" organized by Patrick Loughry in Mobile May 20th, 1861. They left for Richmond June 3rd and arrived on June 8th. They were immediately mustered into Confederate States service and ordered to Yorktown. Arriving in Yorktown on June 12th, it was allotted to the Eighth Alabama Regiment as Company I.

Not much is known about the unit that became Company K. It was formed in Radfordsville, Coosa County, Alabama May 25th, 1861. By May 27th, it had arrived in Montgomery. By May 31st the unit left Montgomery, arriving in Richmond June 4th. It was mustered into the Confederate States service on June 9th and left Richmond for Yorktown on June 12th. There it joined the newly forming Eighth Alabama Regiment as Company K.

The Field and Staff organization of the Eighth Alabama Regiment was organized June 12th, 1861. The original field officers were Colonel John A. Winston of Sumter County Alabama; Lieutenant Colonel John W. Frazier, a native of Tennessee; Major Thomas E. Irby, a South Carolinian who had recently moved to Dallas County, Alabama and had become a prominent politician. Irby had also seen service in the Mexican War. The Regimental Quartermaster was J. A. Robbins of Dallas County, Alabama.

Colonel John Anthony Winston became the first commander of the Eighth Alabama. He was born in Madison County, Mississippi Territory (Alabama) in 1812. He was a former governor of Alabama. Ex-governor Winston was introduced to President Davis by John J. Pettus, Governor of Mississippi. Winston was seeking a fighting place in this war. It was on Pettus' recommendation that Winston was given command of the Eighth Alabama for he had no prior military experience. Winston was confirmed December 13th, 1861.[7]

Winston was a strict disciplinarian and exacted a full discharge of duty from all under his command. Winston was decidedly a strong character. As governor, he had from his frequent vetoes won the nickname of John Anthony Veto Winston. He was a man of great will power who often exercised it. Intellectually he was a man of great point, though his English was often bad— perhaps intentionally. He was a martinet and absolutely without tact in dealing with "volunteers" who as a rule knew nothing about discipline and were slow to see the necessity of it. Added to the Colonel's want of tact in dealing with his men, he knew nothing about drill and he was too old to learn, or rather, too proud to sit down and study carefully military tactics. Winston did know the value of discipline and every order he issued he intended should be obeyed. Regimental drills were at first always conducted by Lieutenant Colonel Frazier, a West Pointer. (Frazier later transferred to the 28th Alabama, became a brigadier general in 1861 in command of the Cumberland Gap in Tennessee, where having been surrounded, he surrendered himself and his command as prisoners of war. So who was the martinet?) Winston commanded in but one important battle and deported himself in a very soldierly manner. He resigned soon after the Battle of Seven Pines on June 16th, 1862, due to chronic rheumatism.[8]

Colonel Winston was succeeded by Young L. Royston (formerly commander of Company A) on June 16th. Royston, having been promoted to Major, then to Lieutenant Colonel due to deaths on the staff, was not promoted to Colonel of the Eighth Alabama. Royston stood about six feet seven inches tall and was straight as an arrow. He was such a shining target that in 1862 at the Battle of Frazier's Farm an enemy marksman brought him down with a wound that kept him away until the spring of 1863. He returned in time to join the regiment at the Battle of Salem Church on May 3rd, 1863. There another enemy marksman picked him off with a shot that permanently disabled him just as the battle was beginning. While Royston was recovering from his wounds at home, he and others started a letter writing campaign seeking a brigadier general's position. But that did not come and he was retired September 20th, 1864 as an invalid officer. He would serve as Lieutenant Colonel at Selma on November 20th, 1864 in Alabama State Reserve Unit No. 93.[9]

Major Irby was born in South Carolina, but for many years had been a resident of Dallas County, Alabama. He died early in the war at the Battle of Williamsburg in the spring of 1862.[9]

Then there was Thomas Phelan, the adjutant, who was the son of the Honorable J. D. Phelan of the Alabama Supreme Court. He was raised in Perry County, Alabama. And, he too did not make it through the war having been killed during the Battle of Gaines Mill in the spring of 1862.[11]

With a regimental staff in place on June 10th, 1861, the Eighth Alabama was now organized to fight. But, there would be months of skirmishes, trench warfare, and incessant drilling, before the regiment would be baptized under fire.

NOTES

[1] Eighth Alabama Infantry, Research Library, Antietam Visitors Center, National Park Service, Sharpsburg, Maryland, hereinafter cited as Antietam Visitors Center.

[2] Grandfather's Talks, Hilary Abner Herbert Papers, Southern Historical Collection, Chapel Hill, North Carolina: University of North Carolina, 107, hereinafter cited as Herbert, Grandfather's Talks.

[3] IBID, 108.

[4] IBID, 109.

[5] IBID.

[6] IBID, 110.

[7] Papers of John Anthony Winston, Governor of Alabama, Montgomery, Alabama: State Archives, hereinafter cited as Winston Papers.

[8] IBID; Evans, Clement A., editor, Confederate Military History Extended Edition, Wilmington, NC: Broadfoot Publishing Co., 1987 reprint of the Confederate Publishing Company edition of 1899, 857-858.

[9] Herbert, Grandfather's Talks, 111.

[10] IBID, 112.

[11] IBID.

CHAPTER TWO:
BAPTISM BY FIRE

From mid June 1861 until the following spring, the Eighth Alabama made several marches from the Yorktown area to the vicinity of Hampton and Newport News. At Yorktown, the regiment came under the command of Major General John B. Magruder. In August part of the regiment marched off to the Hampton area to reconnoiter the vicinity, where it observed the burning of Hampton. General Magruder had learned that Union General Benjamin F. Butler had plans to use the town for runaway slaves. Magruder ordered the town burned. After this, the regiment performed garrison duty and built fortifications until early October when it moved to Big Bethel for a skirmish. Men of the regiment boasted of how they would fight the Yankees, most of this bluster was to cover the fear they felt. This isn't to say that they were cowards. Their enemy counterpart was having the same feelings and expressing the same brags about how Johnny Reb would be beaten back. For most, however, they were more nervous than fearful. Many concealed their nervousness by joking and light conversation. But it was all a sham, as their brow glistened with perspiration, their stomachs knotted and breathing became difficult. They were about to kill or be killed, and no amount of joking could remove that sick feeling.[1]

On October 3rd, 1861, the organization of the Army of the Peninsula under Major General Magruder included the Fifth Brigade composed of the Eighth and Thirteenth Alabama Regiments under Colonel Winston. The brigade was assigned to the Yorktown area. Between November 6th and December 2nd, 1861 Federal intelligence showed the Eighth Alabama commanded by Colonel Winston with about one thousand men near Big Bethel Church. The skirmish at Big Bethel was a victory for the Confederates. After the skirmish, the Army of the Peninsula was actively employed in constructing defenses at Gloucester Point and Yorktown along the line from the Warwick River to Lee's Mill. Watching and skirmishing with the enemy was a daily occurrence, but Confederate troops kept enemy troops within their own entrenchments at Newport News and Fortress Monroe. The Virginia peninsula became a drill ground and training school for a part of the army that was to become famous as the Army of Northern Virginia.[2]

At Harwood's Mill, nine miles from Yorktown, the Eighth Alabama began building its winter quarters. The regiment also spent time drilling, clearing woods, creating entrenchments, and dragging artillery upon the breastworks. The soldiers had a great deal of picket duty while in winter quarters. Some nights, a picket would have to be relieved about every fifteen minutes as his post was always some yards away from any warming fires. In the absence of houses, when brush was attainable, the soldiers would build screens between the fire and the wind, arranged so as to form a brush tend with the side next to the fire open and about five feet high and the other side closed from the ground to the top. The soldiers would use the brush if no straw was available for bedding. They would wrap up in their blankets with their feet toward the fire. The men were in good spirits despite the weather. Many had lost blankets, shoes and other personal belongings during the marches to Newport News and Hampton and later skirmishing at Big Bethel.[3]

Every day the soldier faced the unseen enemy of disease. Most of it was the result of unsanitary camps and doctors who did not have the means or methods of sterilization. In addition, the rural background of most of the men did not protect them from the gathering of large groups in confined spaces. As a result, they were exposed to communicable diseases such as measles, chicken pox, mumps, and whooping cough. Measles was the worst of the illnesses the men of the Eighth Alabama encountered. And food was no less a culprit of poor health and rampant disease. The southern soldier was fed unsanitary, vermin-ridden food. Much of the sickness was caused by rancid beef.[4]

For months there was sickness in the camps of the Eighth Alabama, especially among the farm boys who had all their lives been accustomed to more or less regular hours for work. Irregular hours, resulting from guard/picket duty, exposure to the night air, and the exceptionally hard work of digging trenches, brought on diarrhea and measles. Some even caught the whooping cough. But, during the first six to eight months, rations were sufficient and Confederate money was "as good as gold."[5]

Bad weather conditions forced Magruder to leave Winston's Eighth Alabama at Harwood's Mill. Magruder's reports indicated the Federals could not advance either because of the bad state of the roads. The Eighth Alabama remained in winter quarters at Harwood's Mill, except when called out for outpost duty and some small skirmishing, until April 3rd, 1862, when Union General George B. McClellan's Federal troops began advancing up the Virginia peninsula.[6]

According to the roster of the Army of the Peninsula, Magruder had a force of about eleven thousand and this "thin gray line" interposed the only barrier between the great Federal Army and the Confederate capitol now in Richmond. The Eighth Alabama was ordered to fall back to take up a position at Wynn's Mill between Yorktown and the James River. Confederate troops fell back slowly until they reached their lines at Yorktown on the west bank of the Warwick River. Along the Warwick River were two grist mills, (Wynn's and Lee's) located three to eight miles south of Yorktown. The defense at Yorktown consisted of bastioned earthworks, enveloping the town, connected by a covered way with two strong redoubts (Nos. 4 and 5) on high ground south of Yorktown. A line of rifle pits was constructed on the west bank of the Warwick River from Yorktown to Lee's Mill. The two dams located between Lee's Mill and Wynn's Mill were thrown across the Warwick causing the lowlands to flood to a depth of two to five feet. Between Redoubt No. 5 and Wynn's Mill, the Confederate line was held with men at intervals of twenty feet. The weak points in the defensive line were the two flanks resting on the York and James Rivers.[7]

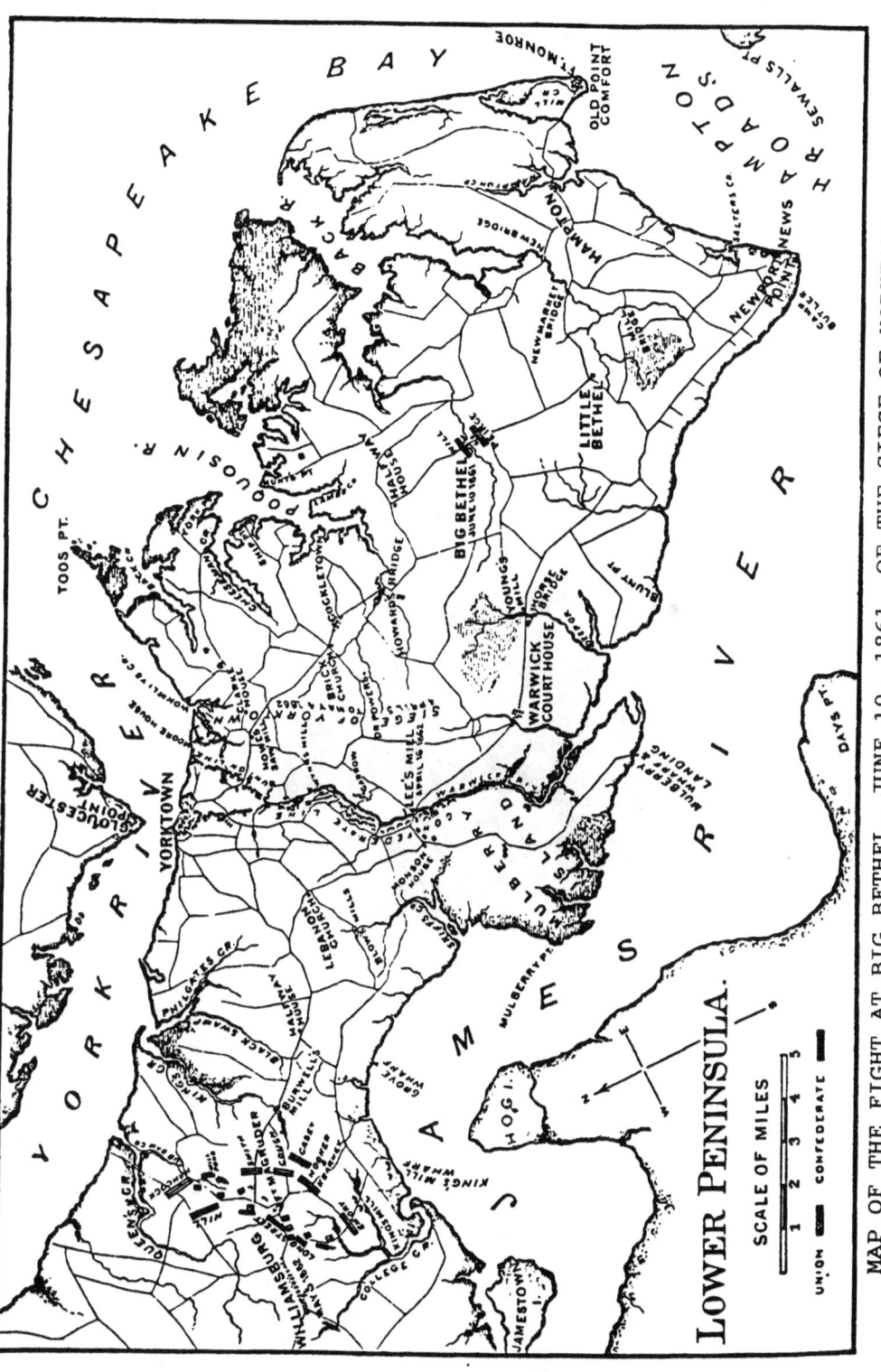

MAP OF THE FIGHT AT BIG BETHEL, JUNE 10, 1861, OF THE SIEGE OF YORKTOWN, APRIL 5 TO MAY 4, 1862, AND OF THE BATTLE OF WILLIAMSBURG, MAY 5, 1862.

Major General John B. Magruder, C.S.A.
From a Photograph

During the three weeks the Eighth Alabama was at Wynn's Mill, Lieutenant Colonel Frazier resigned, Major Irby was promoted and Captain Royston was promoted to Major. The adjutant, Thomas Phelan, was elected captain of Royston's old Company A. At Wynn's Mill, Royston, before his promotion, with his own company and Captain Cleveland's company of the Eighth Alabama and three companies from a Georgia regiment in General Richard Pryor's Brigade, was ordered to move to the front to reconnoiter the position of the enemy. A portion of the enemy lines and breastworks were marked by a dense forest and undergrowth of pine. Royston led those companies a mile down the enemy's line within range of their fire, drove in their pickets, and captured part of their camps with considerable provisions and other needed stores. This effort made known to the Confederate command staff the character and extent of the enemy's fortifications and the number of batteries up front.[8]

On the morning of April 5th, 1862, McClellan's army appeared in front of the Confederate lines and opened fire with artillery. Confederate artillery responded. Colonel Winston was commanding at Wynn's Mill with three regiments, a small battalion and two well posted batteries. Confederate troops appeared to be in good spirits according to Union intelligence reports. Baptism by fire was now a reality. Here, the Eighth Alabama first heard the whistling of bomb shells. Federal sharpshooters kept up a brisk fire on the right wing of the Eighth. For several days, Federal troops made continuous demonstrations along the front, but no serious attempt was made to break the lines until April 15th. At that time, Federal troops assaulted Dam No. 2 about a mile to the right of Wynn's Mill. The Federal troops were repulsed with considerable Confederate losses. Thus did Magruder's little army of about eleven thousand keep at bay a Federal force ten times their number.[9]

Magruder's army held for three weeks when reinforcements began arriving from General Joseph E. Johnston's Army of Northern Virginia on the 10th of April. He assigned Major General Magruder to the right wing, and the Eighth Alabama bid their leader farewell. Although he had compelled his troops to dig, and marched their socks off, the soldiers learned from their experiences and regarded Magruder with affection.[10]

The organization of Confederate forces as of April 30th, 1862 showed Major General John B. Magruder commanding the Army of the Peninsula on the right wing of the Army of Northern Virginia. Major General James P. Longstreet commanded the center, and Major General D. H. Hill commanded the left. At this point, the Eighth Alabama Regiment was still under the command of Colonel John A. Winston with about eight hundred in the regiment, which was part of Pryor's Brigade under Longstreet. Pryor also had the Fourteenth Alabama, the Fourteenth Louisiana, and Macon's battery. The total strength of Longstreet's force was nearly fourteen thousand. Brigadier General Cadmus M. Wilcox had the Ninth Alabama, the Tenth Alabama, and the Eleventh Alabama, with the Nineteenth Mississippi and Stanard's battery.[11]

Federal troops began to entrench for siege and build redoubts for heavy guns, keeping an artillery fire on Confederate positions almost daily. The Confederates worked diligently day and night, strengthening their positions. This continued until May 3rd, when Johnston decided to abandon the peninsula. Magruder opposed this action because eastern Virginia and eastern North Carolina would fall under Union control.[12]

During the siege, the men of the Eighth Alabama were exhausted from the heavy duty and incessant watching. To add to their discomfort, a cold windy rain fell most of the time. On the night of May 3rd, Confederate forces evacuated their position. The Confederate army marched away from Yorktown and the muzzles of McClellan's cannon. All night the Confederates marched on muddy roads, shoving mired artillery and wagons. The retreat continued on the fourth of May through Williamsburg. Johnston instructed Longstreet to send a brigade to relieve the troops in the breastworks east of the town. Generals Richard Anderson's and Roger A Pryor's two small brigades and two batteries went back through Williamsburg. The troops filed in to their positions just as the rainfall increased to a heavy downpour and continued through the night. By the morning of May 5th, the rain had subsided to a drizzle when Federal skirmishers appeared through the woods.[13]

Colonel Winston, who had been very sick during the siege, was temporarily replaced by Lieutenant Colonel Irby. General Anderson's South Carolinians manned a bastion beside the road that had been previously constructed by Magruder (Fort Magruder). General Pryor's troops were scattered among the redoubts and rifle pits on either side of Fort Magruder. Irby was directed to divide the regiment into four battalions which were detached to guard different portions of the line. Captain Herbert commanded Companies F and G, Captain Nall in charge of Companies K and B at the Fort Magruder earthworks, Major Royston in command of Companies C, E, and H. Lieutenant Colonel Irby had Companies A, D, and I. The first Battalion under Irby and the Second Battalion under Royston were intended to hold the strong points and were also held as Corps Reserve. The Federal troops closed in and there was heavy skirmishing. Anderson sent a courier to Longstreet asking for reinforcement. Longstreet directed Brigadier General Cadmus Wilcox and Ambrose P. Hill with their brigades to the front. The two commands extended Anderson's right flank where the Federals under Brigadier General Joseph Hooker were pressing the attack. Later Brigadier General George E. Pickett's brigade entered the fight. Longstreet ordered an attack by Wilcox and Hill supported by Pickett and two regiments from Pryor. The Southerners advanced across the muddy ground into woods where the fight escalated. Artillery from both sides and the sound of heavy musket fire could be heard for miles. The Confederates pushed forward, shoving the Federal infantry. By five o'clock in the afternoon of May 5th, Federal troops were testing the Confederate left. General Jubal Early's brigade led Hill's division in an attack that resulted in a slaughter as his Virginians fell under heavy Federal fire. Hill ordered more soldiers up, which only added to the casualties. After the battle had been underway for sometime, Irby became impatient at the inactive duty and led his battalion out of the fortifications he had been ordered to hold. He was met by overwhelming numbers and as he had no support, he was compelled to fall back. The sharp fighting lasted several hours with considerable losses on both sides. It was here that Lieutenant Colonel Irby was killed.[14] Irby's battalion did not break. It held against a New Jersey regiment of Union General Daniel Sickles' brigade. Captain Patrick Loughry took command. He held the position assigned to him by Brigadier General Richard H. Anderson until ordered to fall back that night.[15]

Bad weather continued to plague both sides. The roads were wretched and food was not a luxury to be had at this point. Irby's battalion, now led by Loughry, now came under the control of Brigadier General George Pickett, as the battalion was in his sector. General Pickett, on learning of Irby's death, ordered his body carried from the field. The Second Battalion under Royston continued to occupy the fortified position on the right, when he was ordered to the extreme left to reinforce other units of the Eighth at Fort Magruder. Soon after Royston's arrival, the Federal troops were repulsed.[16]

Confederate forces now began pulling back to Williamsburg. Williamsburg afforded strong defensive positions. It occupied a high plain between the York and the James Rivers. At Williamsburg, Longstreet ordered up reinforcements, and in short order a section of artillery along with three fresh brigades arrived to push Union General Joseph Hooker back with the loss of his cannon and heavy casualties[17]

The battle of Williamsburg, a minor rear guard action, exerted a heavy casualty toll—over a thousand Confederates and nearly twice as many Federals lay dead in the mud. During the battle of Williamsburg, the Eighth Alabama lost one hundred fifty men out of one thousand nearly half of all that were lost out of Pryor's brigade.[18]

Even though the Federal troops were repulsed at Williamsburg, the Army of Northern Virginia continued to pull back to Richmond. The Confederate withdrawal resumed later the night of May 5th. The march was even worse than the earlier ones because the recent rains had made the roads almost impassable. McClellan's Army followed at a snail's pace. Williamsburg was left in Federal hands. When the Federals took possession of Williamsburg, they burned the College of Williams and Mary. Federal troops (the Army of the James), held the lower peninsula of Virginia for the duration of the war. On May 6th, 1862, General Johnston sent a General Order to Generals Longstreet, D. H. Hill, and General J. E. B. Stuart congratulating their troops in repulsing the Federal attacks at Williamsburg on May 5th, 1862.[19]

Following the battle of Williamsburg, the Eighth Alabama was commanded by Colonel Young L. Royston. Royston replaced Colonel Winston, when he resigned due to ill health. The regiment was now allocated to the Brigade of Brigadier General Cadmus Marcellus Wilcox under Major General James Longstreet. The regiment was transferred to the vicinity of Mechanicsville a few miles northeast of Richmond in preparation for more battles on the upper peninsula. On May 15th, Johnston's army crossed the Chickahominy River, the last natural barrier between Richmond and the Federals. McClellan advanced up the peninsula leisurely. Federal troops repaired the bridges burned by the retreating Confederates.[20]

The organization of the Army of Northern Virginia commanded by General Joseph E. Johnston near Richmond as of May 21st, 1862, included the First Division commanded by Major General G. W. Smith. The Second Division Commanded by Major General James Longstreet which included A. P. Hill's Brigade, Pickett's Brigade, R. H. Anderson's Brigade, Wilcox' Brigade, Raleigh Colston's Brigade, and Pryor's Brigade. The Third Division was commanded by Major General J. B. Magruder. The Fourth Division was commanded by Major General D. H. Hill. The cavalry brigade was commanded by Brigadier General J. E. B. Stuart with reserve artillery commanded by Brigadier General William H. Pendleton.[21]

The new commander of the Eighth Alabama Regiment's Brigade, Cadmus Marcellus Wilcox, was born in Wayne County, North Carolina May 29, 1826. Then the family moved to Tennessee when he was a young boy of two. He studied at Cumberland College in Nashville and in 1842 was appointed to the United States Military Academy at West Point, New York. On graduation in 1846, he participated in the Mexican War. In 1852, he was assigned as an instructor of military tactics at West Point. He remained there until 1857, when due to ill health, he was sent to Europe on a twelve month furlough. On his return he published a work on rifles and rifle firing. He also translated and published a work on the evolution of infantry as practiced in the Austrian army. He was then ordered to the New Mexico territory in 1860, while still in New Mexico, he learned of the secession of Tennessee. He resigned from the army and headed for Richmond, where he was commissioned Colonel of the Ninth Alabama Regiment on July 9th, 1861. He became a Brigadier General October 21st, 1861, and a Major General August 9th, 1863.[22]

Wilcox, with his brigade now in Mechanicsville, was postured for a series of battles on the upper peninsula. To President Davis, Johnston appeared reluctant to wage war, to give battle and risk defeat. President Davis replaced Johnston after he was wounded at the end of May with General Robert E. Lee who would command the Army of Northern Virginia to great Glory to the end of the war.[23]

Brig. Gen. Cadmus M. Wilcox
(National Archives)

NOTES

[1] Grandfather's Talks, 115-116.

[2] IBID, 113.

[3] IBID, 115.

[4] IBID.

[5] IBID, 116.

[6] IBID, 119; Eighth Regiment Alabama Volunteer (Infantry), Author Unknown, Introduction and Edited by William Stanly Hoole, Montgomery, Alabama 1866, Confederate Regimental Series No. 10, Confederate Publishing Company: University, Alabama, 1985, 15, hereinafter cited as Hoole, Unknown.

[7] Hoole, Unknown, 16; "Short History of the Eighth Ala Regiment" by LTC Hilary A. Herbert, 1864, Orange Courthouse Virginia, Hilary A. Herbert Papers, Southern Historical Collection, Chapel Hill: University of North Carolina, 2-5, hereinafter cited as Herbert, Short History.

[8] Hoole, Unknown, 15.

[9] IBID, 116; Winston Papers.

[10] IBID; Grandfather's Talks, 123.

[11] Hoole, Unknown, 15-16.

[12] IBID, 16.

[13] IBID, 16-17; Sorrel, G. Moxley, Recollections of a Confederate Staff Officer, edited by Bell Irvin Wiley, Jackson, TN: McCowat-Mercer Press, 1958, 60-61.

[14] Grandfather's Talks, 124-125; Hoole, Unknown, 16-17; Herbert, Short History, 6-7.

[15] War of the Rebellion: A Compilation of the Official Records of the Union and Confederate Armies, Washington, 1901, Series 1, Vol. IV, 668-670; Series 1, Vol. IX, 37; Series 1, Vol. XI, Part 1, 226-268, 586-588; Series 1, Vol. XLI, part 2, 137, hereinafter cited as OR.

[16] Herbert, Short History, 6-7.

[17] IBID; Hoole, Unknown, 16.

[18]IBID, 17.

[19]IBID, 14-16.

[20]OR, Series 1, Vol. XI, part 2, 486-487; OR, Series 1, Vol. XI, part 3, 532; OR, Series 1, Vol. XXVII, part 2, 288, 333.

[21]OR, Series 1, Vol. XI, part 3, 648, 652.

[22]OR, Series 1, Vol. XXVII, part 2, 618-621, 775; Hoole, Unknown, 17; Herbert, Short History, 9.

[23]Chestnut, Mary Boykin, A Diary From Dixie, edited by Ben Ames Williams, Boston, MA: Houghton Mifflin Co., 1949, 175.

CHAPTER THREE:
THE PENINSULA CAMPAIGN—
SEVEN PINES, GAINES' MILL, AND FRAZIERS' FARM

Union General George B. McClellan, following General Joseph E. Johnston's retreat from Yorktown through Williamsburg, found he could not attack Johnston's army on the south side of the Chickahominy, or besiege Richmond, without also crossing to the south side of the Chickahominy River. He also had to protect his own base of supplies on the north side of the Chickahominy at White House on the Pamunkey Branch of the York River and at West Point on the main York River. McClellan was thus placed in a position to have to divide his forces. In doing this, a river and its swampy banks, which were subject to frequent flooding, split his forces.

SEVEN PINES

By May 24th, 1862, parts of McClellan's army had crossed the Chickahominy pushing forward on the Williamsburg Road to Seven Pines (also called Fair Oaks), a crossroads name for the loblolly pines at the junction. Two of the five Federal corps roughly thirty thousand men, crossed the repaired bridges to the south side of the river. McClellan had the three other Federal corps on the northern banks of the river.[1]

Johnston hoped to formulate a plan of attack to prevent McClellan from linking up with Union General Irvin McDowell who was at Fredericksburg. Then, Confederate General James Ewell Brown (J.E.B) Stuart brought information that Confederate General Stonewall Jackson had routed Union General Nathaniel Banks at Winchester, Virginia. This caused Lincoln to recall McDowell closer to Washington to protect the capitol.[2]

Stuart's information altered the strategic situation along the Chickahominy. With McDowell's threat temporarily removed, Confederate commanders could become more aggressive. Johnston decided, however, to wait for General Benjamin Huger's division to arrive from Petersburg before finalizing his plans.[3]

Confederate General Daniel H. Hill reconnoitered along the Williamsburg Road toward Seven Pines. He found the entire Federal Third and Fourth Corps were south of the Chickahominy, but no Federals were on the Charles City Road south of Seven Pines. He informed Johnston around noon on May 30th, and Huger's division arrived at about the same time. Johnston now acted. He and Longstreet worked late into the night on the plan of attack. Johnston gave Longstreet two divisions (D. H. Hill's and Huger's) plus Longstreet's own for the attack. The responsibility for implementing and executing the assault was Longstreet's. Johnston was convinced that the two Federal corps south of the

Chickahominy were vulnerable. If Federal reinforcements could be cut off across the river, then two fifths of McClellan's army could be isolated and crushed.[4]

Johnston's plan followed the roads. D. H. Hill's division was to lead the attack on the Williamsburg Road, driving toward Seven Pines where the Federal divisions of Brigadier Generals Silas Casey and Darius Couch were located. General Longstreet was to move up on General Hill's left by Nine Mile Road to Fair Oaks, converging on the Federal right flank and preventing reinforcements from crossing the Chickahominy. On Hill's right was Huger's division which would come down the Charles City Road, securing the Confederate right. General Gustavus W. Smith's division under Brigadier General Chase Whiting would support Longstreet, and General John B. Magruder's command was to remain in reserve. Johnston committed twenty three of his twenty seven brigades to the offensive. Only General A. P. Hill's newly organized division, opposite Mechanicsville would have no role to play in this operation. Johnston would use nearly forty two thousand of his seventy four thousand troops in this attack.[5]

After nightfall on May 30th, another thunderstorm hit the area with heavy rain and lightning. Conditions were miserable. The Chickahominy continued rising and flooded the bottom lands. By daylight, a dense fog had settled around the woods of Seven Pines.[6]

By one o'clock on May 31st, Huger was not within sight of Hill. Longstreet, due to a misunderstanding, had taken Smith's road away, and then Huger's, and had himself produced the delay that he and Johnston were to stress in their reports later as causing a problem in the execution of the battle. Brigadier General Wilcox stated in his report of the action that he was at the junction of the Charles City Road and Williamsburg Road by three thirty in the afternoon. He then received orders to move three brigades—his own, Raleigh Colston's and Roger A. Pryor's on the Charles City Road in the rear of Huger's division, but this order was then modified; and the three brigades were ordered to precede Huger's. Then having passed Huger's troops, the march continued for a short time, when orders again came to counter march to the Williamsburg Road and follow in the read of the advancing troops. Wilcox had retraced his route, when an order again came to about face and march down the Charles City Road, and thus keep abreast of the firing on the Williamsburg Road, Again, orders were received in writing to move across the Williamsburg Road, following country roads and paths through the woods and fields. This maneuver was slow as the land between the two roads was low and sometimes waist deep in water. It was nearly five in the afternoon when the column reached the Williamsburg Road. At this point, Wilcox' troops entered the fight on May 31st. Later, Wilcox reluctantly yielded to an order to withdraw under cover of darkness.[7]

The Confederates had fought under terrible conditions—waist deep in water with sticky-holding mud at the bottom; thickets and dense woods and impenetrable briars. These soldiers had enthusiastic courage and tremendous

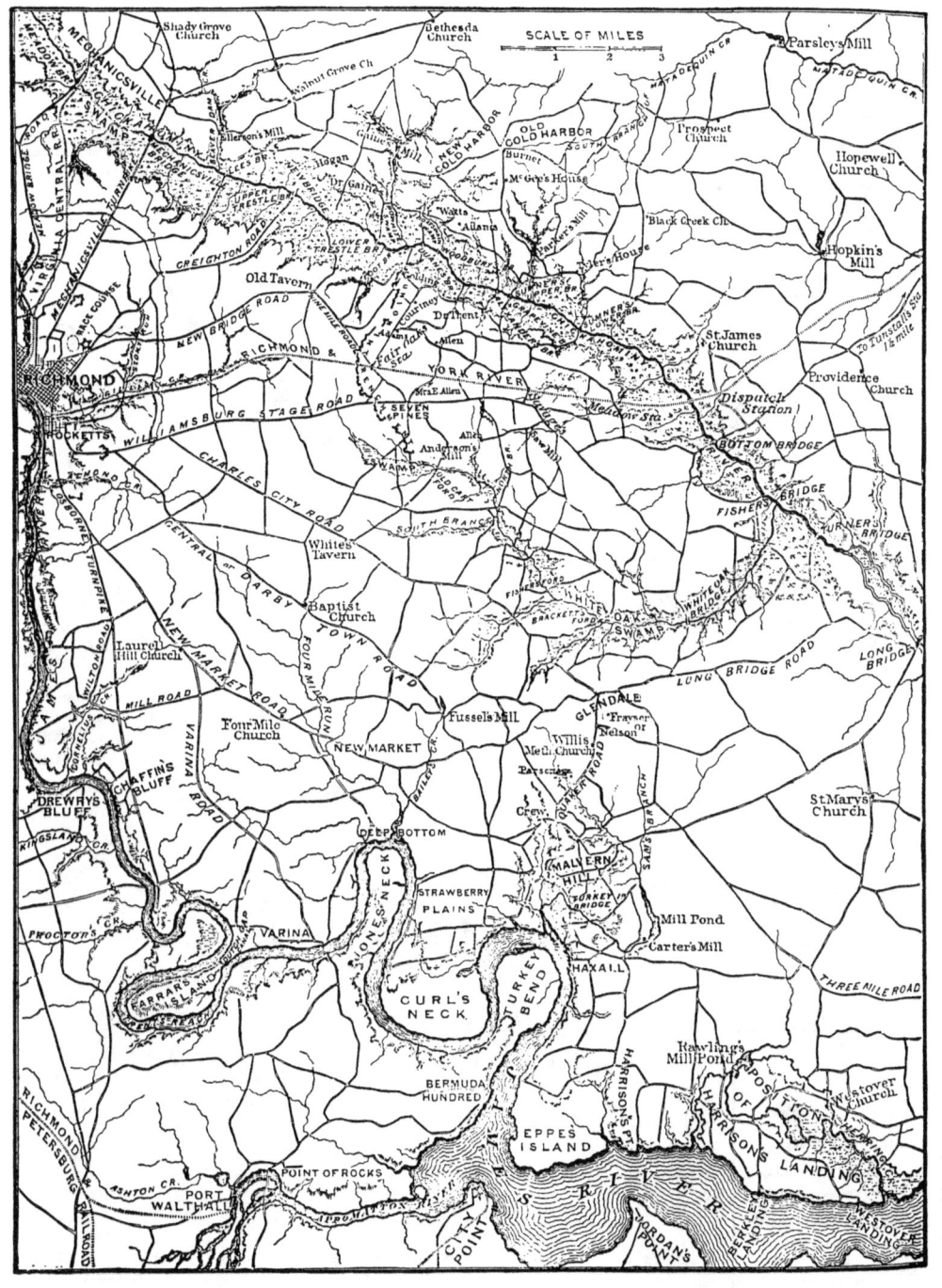

REGION OF THE SEVEN DAYS' FIGHTING
Map Taken from The Official Military Atlas of the Civil War

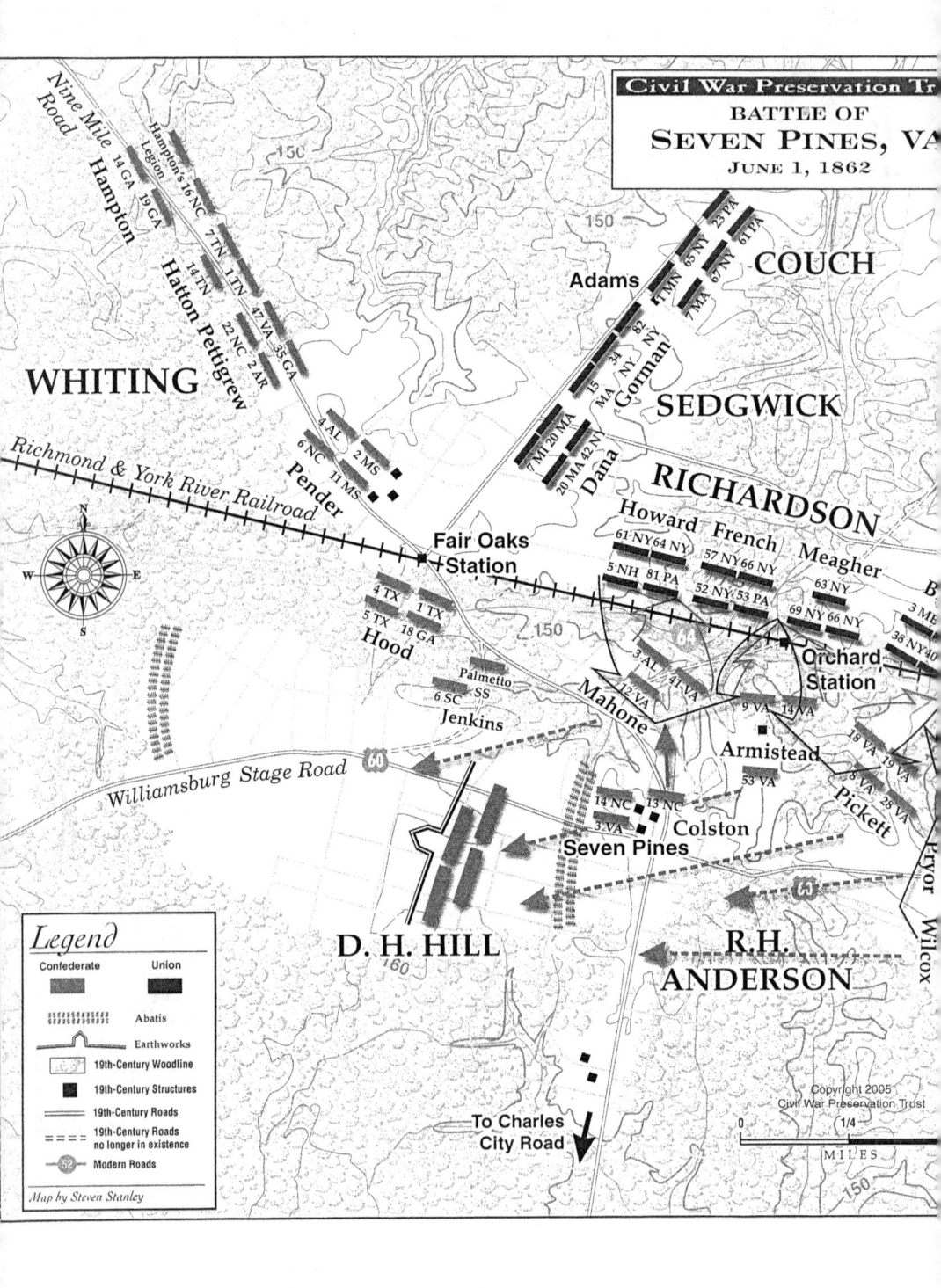

confidence in their leadership. Obviously, when only five brigades whip one and a half corps behind field works in a stand up fight, the whole was a deed of heroism.[8]

Johnston's fine offensive scheme foundered and no major military objectives were gained (the destruction of McClellan's army). Seven Pines was a waste of life and a great disappointment. The action of May 31st had ended without any decisive results, except that the Federals had been driven from their original position at Seven Pines and had formed new lines north of the Richmond—York River Railroad. The Confederates had taken up new positions in front of them and would be ready to resume the fight the next day. It took the Confederates sometime to sort themselves out in the pine forest with its dense underbrush, to get rationed and arranged for the coming fight. They built blazing fires from the pine knots scattered all about to dry their clothing and blankets, but this light aided the Federals in reinforcing their lines north of the railroad. It was nearly midnight when the Confederate army was put in order and the dead were being buried and the wounded being cared for. On the evening of May 31st, General Johnston had been badly wounded. Major General Gustavus S. Smith became the commander on the field for a few hours. General Robert E. Lee assumed command shortly after noon on June 1st, 1862 of what was to become the Army of Northern Virginia.[9]

General Roger A. Pryor's brigade did not take part in the action of May 31st, except to have marched all day long and finally it bivouacked a few hundred yards to the rear of Wilcox' brigade. Pryor's brigade helped repulse a serious attack on June 1st. The fighting was renewed early in the morning but the brigade didn't move forward until shots were already being exchanged by pickets.[10]

Colonel Winston, commanding the Eighth Alabama of Pryor's brigade, halted his regiment about three quarters of a mile from where there was a break in the fighting. The regiment stood on line awaiting orders. The orders finally came! The regiment moved forward by the right flank. But Winston had not put out any flankers as he did not suspect the enemy was any nearer than those engaged toward the front. The regiment crossed a boggy bottom. The Federals, concealed by woods, suddenly fired a deadly volley from the right. The regiment gave way toward the left, in some confusion, until it had gone some fifty five yards when it rallied and returned the enemy's fire. The Eighth was placed on the left of the Ninth Alabama of Wilcox. The Federal fire seemed to be moving further to the left. The remainder of Pryor's brigade was extended to the left. The Eighth Alabama now received assistance from the Fourteenth Alabama which was to its right flank when ordered were received to fall back. Major Hilary Herbert had been wounded, his horse shot from under him, and he was captured.[11] Losses of the regiment on June 1st, 1862 were 131 killed, wounded and missing. During the action between May 31st and sunset of June 1st at the battle of Seven Pines, the Eighth Alabama lost several other officers—Captains Leonard F. Summers and

Patrick Loughry, and Lieutenant Joshua Kennedy.[12] Pickett, Pryor and Wilcox having received orders to fall back chose to stay until the assault was repulsed.[13]

Wilcox and Pryor finally withdrew. Pickett stayed several hours longer, and retired only the "the Yankees ceased to annoy him." Being pursued by the enemy, the Confederates experienced some losses. But the enemy did not pursue across the open field. The Confederates fell back until finally by ten o'clock that night they had moved back to their camps near Richmond.[14]

Besides the good effect of driving the enemy back with heavy losses "we have made superior soldiers of several brigades that were entirely fresh and unreliable." These troops took 347 prisoners, ten pieces of artillery, five thousand small arms, one garrison and several regimental standards.[15]

Colonel Winston resigned on June 16th because of very bad rheumatism. The command of the regiment fell to Young L. Royston, about the same time, the regiment was transferred from Pryor's brigade to Wilcox' brigade composed thereafter entirely of Alabamians.[16]

GAINES' MILL

When the great battles around Richmond commenced, although the Eighth Alabama moved several times it did not become engaged until the battle of Gaines' Mill, June 26-27, 1862. Here the Federal front line occupied a constructed work of fallen timber at the end of a ditch at the bottom of a hill where Dr. Gaines' house was located. The ditch was about six feet wide and from three to four feet deep. About a hundred yards in the rear of this line and on top of the hill was a second line of fortifications, manned by infantry and artillery.[17]

General Stonewall Jackson, coming from his Valley campaign and joining the Army of Northern Virginia, was to initiate the attack at three o'clock in the morning on June 26th by moving to Pole Green Church, three miles northeast of the Federal position behind Beaver Dam Creek and to notify General A. P. Hill when the movement was complete. By eight o'clock, Longstreet's and Hill's troops were in position on the plateau above the Mechanicsville Bridge upstream, and A. P. Hill's brigades rested before the Meadow Bridge. All were waiting for General Hill to cross the bridge, which was the signal that Jackson had closed on the Federal flank. The formation was complete and everything was in place for the attack, but General Lee, who was on the field with President Davis, directed it should be delayed until word was received from Huger and Jackson. By three o'clock in the afternoon, artillery that was supposed to be Huger's was heard and Longstreet ordered his artillery to open fire. Hill still had no word from Jackson. His patience ended and he went forward on his own initiative across the Chickahominy River. By four o'clock there was still nothing definite from Huger or Jackson. Longstreet pressed the attack. Federal pickets scattered from the oncoming Confederates, racing through the streets of Mechanicsville. When

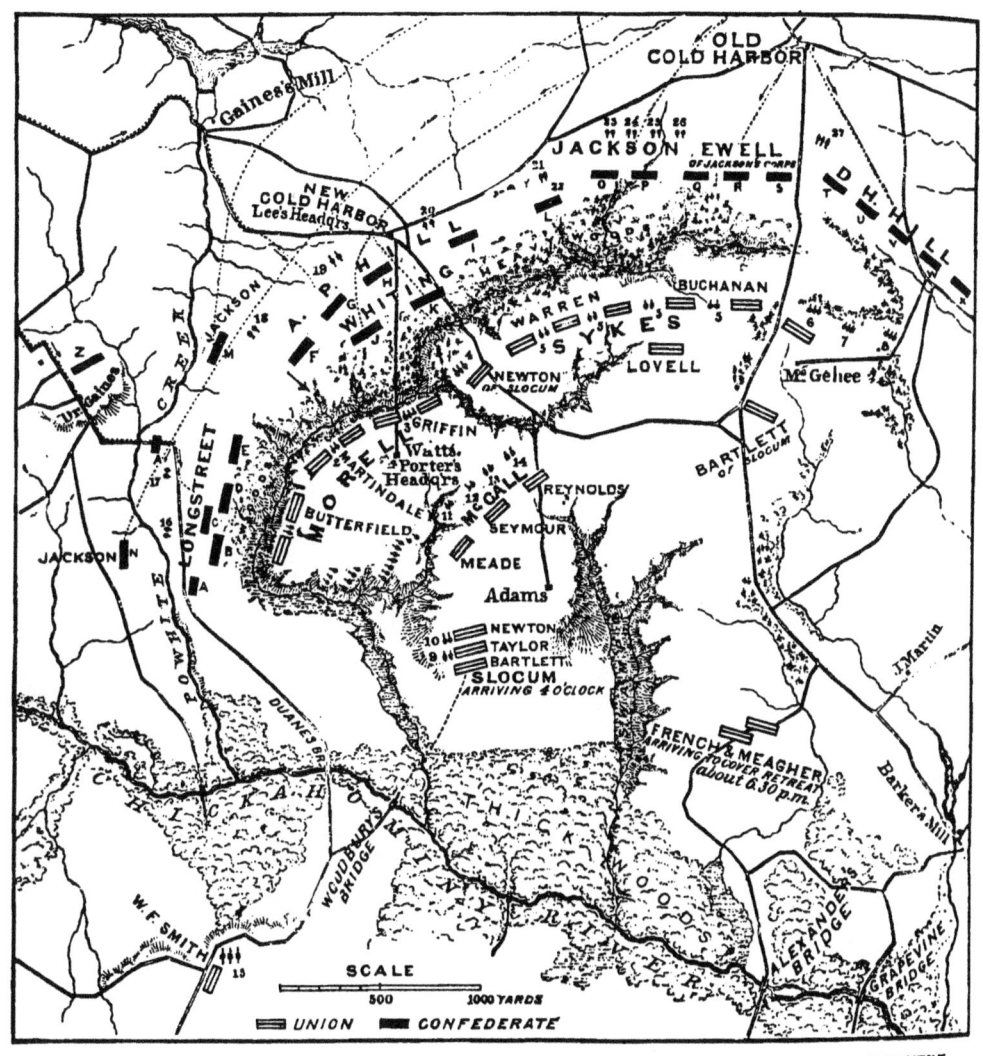

MAP OF THE BATTLE-FIELD OF GAINES'S MILL, SHOWING APPROXIMATELY THE POSITIONS OF INFANTRY AND ARTILLERY ENGAGED. (THE TOPOGRAPHY FROM THE OFFICIAL MAP.)

Longstreet and D. H. Hill saw the Federals fleeing through the town, they started their troops forward. General Lee found A. P. Hill had advanced without Jackson. Where was Jackson? Lee had no choice but to allow A. P. Hill to continue with the attack. Some of Hill's units pressed forward under heavy fire only to be blown back. Other regiments struggled through the swamp, met a wall of flame, and retreated.[18]

Lee ordered Longstreet to create a diversion on the Federal left to relieve pressure on A. P. Hill. About five o'clock, Longstreet sent Wilcox with his three brigades forward. Wilcox commanding the 4th Brigade, Pryor commanding the 5th Brigade, and Featherston commanding the 6th Brigade on the left were ordered to advance. Pickett's brigade was to make a diversion on the left of Wilcox's three brigades. General Richard H. Anderson's brigade was divided, part supporting Pickett's direct assault, the other portion guarding the right flank of the brigades under Wilcox. General Kemper's brigade was held in reserve with the arrival of General Whiting's division on the field. The conflict raged with unabated fury until after dark, neither party gaining ground, Federal cannon continually raked Wilcox' three brigades. He continued to move forward against the Federal batteries with the exception of the Eighth Alabama which had become entangled with Pryor's brigade and halted on the left. The remaining regiments encountered a terrible fire from the guns and infantry on each side of the Long Bridge Road. Without halting a moment, the troops dashed upon the batteries at the double quick in magnificent style, no longer in ranks, but holding together well and cheering, but not stopping to fire. No battlefield can boast more gallantry and devotion. The toughest fighting was encountered by Wilcox', Pryor's and Featherston's brigades. They skirmished all day, under a most annoying artillery barrage. They were the first, too, to make the assault and receive the terrible fire of infantry from the enemy's lines. The Federal left was forced back, and the Federal position was partially turned. Several Federal batteries and many prisoners and regimental standards fell into Confederate hands. This Confederate success came at a heavy price and the ranks were so reduced that the advance on the enemy's second line of defense drove the Confederates back with the Federals retaking the batteries. Confederate survivors fell back into the woods.[19]

The Confederates regrouped and moved forward again regaining the Federal battery. Confederate losses were greater than Federal losses, but the telling fire of the Confederate infantry on the Federal lines as they retired thinned the Federal Ranks so rapidly that Federal dead soon outnumbered Confederate dead. The Federals counter attacked again. The Confederates again fell back in some confusion, leaving their dead to mark their line of battle.[20]

Where was Jackson? Why had he not attacked when he was supposed to? His troops were in bivouac between Pole Green Church and Hundley's Corners, approximately three miles from the battle. His three divisions had spent the previous night at Ashland, fourteen miles away. Although Jackson ordered the march for two thirty in the morning, his troops did not start until eight o'clock, some five hours after he was supposed to contact General A. P. Hill's brigades. He gave no reasons or excuses for the delay in his troop movements.[21]

At dawn on June 27th, the enemy opened fire and continued for more than an hour, throwing shot and shell into the camp of Wilcox brigade, without causing serious inconvenience or inflicting any loss. Wilcox moved his brigade about half a mile across and open field and down the Chickahominy River to support Generals Pryor and Featherston. Arriving, Wilcox found them on the crest of a ridge in pine woods; in front of them was a ravine through which a small stream ran parallel to the Mechanicsville turnpike. The stream was impracticable for infantry. The enemy, in rifle pits and behind trees on the crest of the hill, was delivering a well directed brisk fire.[22]

Halting at the rear of Pryor and Featherston, Wilcox directed a company of the Eighth Alabama be deployed as skirmishers into the woods skirting the Chickahominy River to the right, and the Tenth Alabama was moved to the front and right of the positions of Pryor and Featherston. Neither the skirmishers nor the Tenth met any of the enemy. A battery of artillery was ordered into the position on the ridge when Featherston and Pryor came under the fire of enemy sharpshooters. The Confederate battery opened with a fire of shot and shell upon the Federals. Captain Anderson, of Wilcox' brigade, commanded the artillery, which soon dispersed the Federal troops.[23]

Wilcox, Pryor, and Featherston received orders to advance down the Chickahominy River. They had to construct a bridge for the artillery to cross the river. Axes, spades and nails were furnished by one of the batteries and a detail from the Eighth Alabama constructed the bridge. In less than 30 minutes a previously destroyed bridge was rebuilt, and the brigades and batteries crossed the river quickly and safely. The brigades were then ordered to advance in line of battle. Wilcox was on the right with three regiments in line of battle, one near the Chickahominy River, and the fourth in the rear, and Pryor's brigade was on the left.[24]

Wilcox' brigade passed Dr. Gaines' house, where the occupants said the Federals has just left and were in the line of woods just beyond the house. Wilcox entered the woods, and descended for about two hundred yards, crossed a stream, then ascended a steep hill for about five hundred yards, and emerged into an open field not having met the enemy. There his troops found a large deserted enemy camp, in which they found forage, bacon, flour in small quantities, and boxes of valuable medicines and surgical instruments. The Federals had fallen back so rapidly that they burned and destroyed most of the supplies they could not move. Wilcox' troops pursued steadily until one o'clock in the afternoon when the Federals were discovered strongly posted near Powhite Creek. The three brigades under Wilcox advanced to the edge of the creek to reconnoiter the enemy and ascertain his strength. It was soon found that the Federals were there in full force. Wilcox halted his troops in position to await the arrival of additional troops.

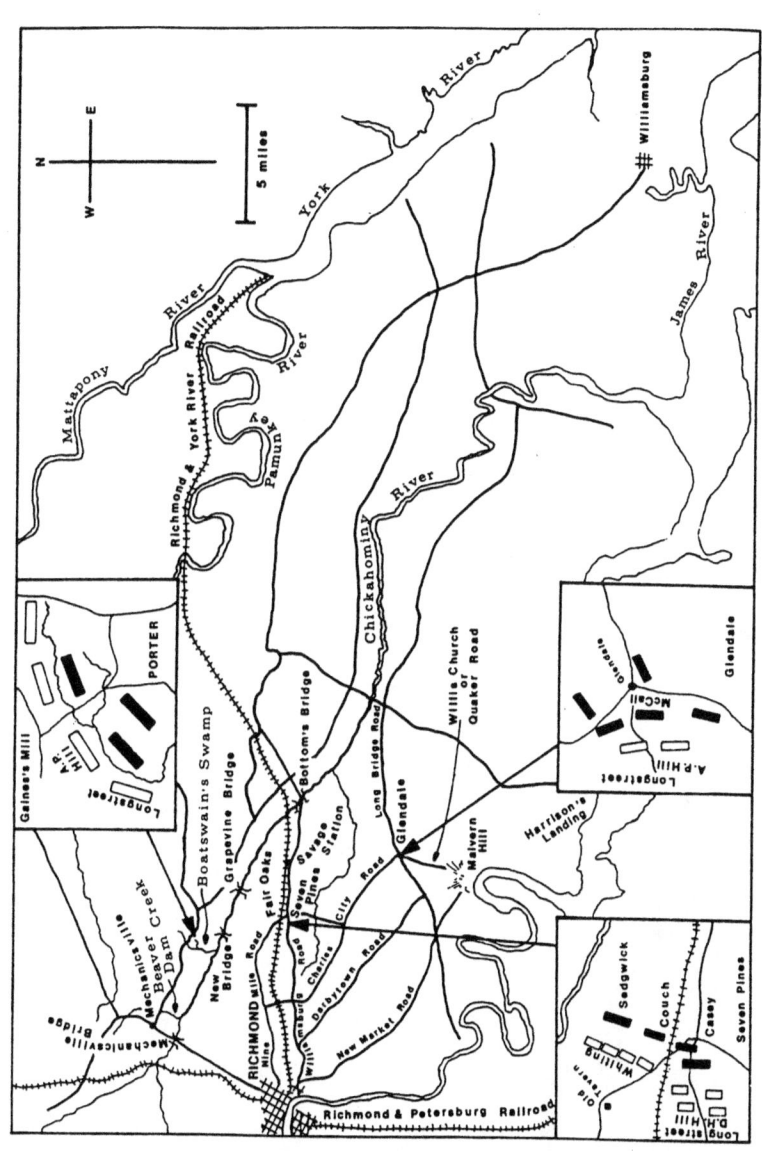

PENINSULA AND SEVEN DAYS' CAMPAIGNS, MAY-JULY 1862
Map Taken from The Official Military Atlas of the Civil War

Troops were seen off to Wilcox' left flank and in front, and not knowing whether they were friend of foe, Wilcox waited quietly. Wilcox soon determined the troops were part of Jackson's forces, Ewell's division. Wilcox again began to move forward, his brigade still on the right with Pryor to the left. Wilcox' troops again entered some heavy woods opening again into another field. There they halted for a short time before moving off by the left flank about a mile and there joined up with Featherston's brigade. Wilcox continued to advance, following the road leading through the heavy pine forest in which the enemy was supposed to be located.[25]

The Alabama brigade had now advanced from Mechanicsville about six miles. Federal skirmishers were seen to the front and Confederate troops halted. Instructions were to engage the skirmishers but advance no further and not enter a general engagement. General Pryor put out skirmishers, and firing for a short time, the enemy's skirmishers withdrew. Federal artillery then began to fire heavy rifled guns from a hill beyond the Chickahominy River, which was beyond the range of Confederate artillery. The Confederate artillery was moved to the rear. Federal skirmishers now reappeared. They would fire and fall back behind the crest of the hill. The Confederates were now told that if enemy skirmishers continued to reappear on the left, that they should be driven and followed to their supports, and that the three brigades should be ready to attack. Pryor advanced against the skirmishers, who soon fell back over the crest of the hill. Pryor's regiment pursued. Reaching the crest of the hill in pursuit of the enemy, Pryor's troops came in full view of the enemy position and came under heavy musket fire, thus revealing the fact that the enemy was there in strong force. Pryor withdrew to the rear and down a ravine toward his support and away from the enemy's infantry fire. The Federals did not follow.[26]

Wilcox now advanced. The first line of attack was about a hundred yards to the front and composed of the Tenth and Eleventh Alabama. The line moved forward under a perfect hail storm of shot, shell, and Minnie balls. So terrific and destructive was this fire, that the first line, though it advanced bravely, was compelled to give way; the second line, however, continued to advance exposed also to the enfilading fire of batteries across the Chickahominy River. The Tenth and Eleventh Alabama were formed in the line of battle below the crest of the hill from which Pryor had withdrawn. Pryor's brigade, except the Second Florida, formed to Wilcox' left. Wilcox' Eighth and Ninth Alabama were to the rear of the Tenth and Eleventh Alabama regiments, and Featherston was in the rear to support both Pryor and Wilcox. Wilcox' three brigades advanced along a ravine, where they were partially protected from enemy fire. After regrouping, they moved forward rapidly over a field of some eight hundred yards in an admirable order and preserving their alignments perfectly. Ascending the crest of the hill they came in full view of Federal troops, and were instantly met by a heavy and destructive fire from infantry within less than one hundred yards. The Confederates now rushed toward the enemy, and the conflict began with an ardor and determination that could not fail to inspire the utmost confidence in those that witnessed it and nothing could surpass the valor and impetuosity of those men of Pryor's and Wilcox' brigades. Enemy musket fire was heavy and poured into the Confederate troops like a rain of fire. The Confederates were exposed to three lines of Federal fire and yet they continued to advance. There was a slight halt and some wavering and a few men gave way, but the second supporting line of the Eighth and Ninth Alabama regiments continued forward movement. In spite of brush, briars and ditches, and under this concentrated and dreadful fire, the Eighth and Ninth Alabama drove the enemy's first line back to its second line of defense. And, charging the heights drove the Federal troops from their second line. This truly was a hazardous charge, no place for fancy drilled holiday soldiers. The Eighth moved forward firmly, steadily and in good order. Bombs, canisters, grape shot, and Minnie balls rained destruction on their ranks, but boldly and defiantly they moved forward. Friends were falling, precipices were being climbed, deep ditches being crossed, and breastworks bristling with bayonets were to be overcome. All this had to be achieved under a heavy fire from the front, flanks, and rear, yet undismayed, the Eighth steadily advanced, every officer and every private seemed inspired by the desperate duty.[27]

Wilcox' troops pressed on with unabated fury. The Federals, with but a few yards between themselves and the Confederates, were shaken and began to yield. The Federal troops broke and fled in confusion, leaving the Eighth and Ninth Alabama masters of the strong position known as Gaines' Mill. The Confederates, full of confidence, rushed forward; and, the enemy was driven from his rifle pits, through the nearby woods, and finally into the open fields. Now for the first time, cheers could be heard from the Confederate troops as they drove the enemy from his strong positions.[28]

The struggle was a desperate one from the time the Confederates were ordered to advance until the end of the fight about three hours later. During all this maneuvering for attack, the Confederate troops were under a brisk enfilading fire of artillery from the Federal batteries of rifled cannon from the heights beyond the Chickahominy River. All the Confederate troops behaved admirably under this fire, no confusion or disorder was perceptible in their ranks.[29]

Confederate losses up to this time were severe, but now the enemy was made to suffer. No longer screened by his breastworks or standing timber, the Federal soldiers were slaughtered. Confederates had no difficulty in chasing them in all directions. Confederate fire was extremely precise. The numbers of the enemy's dead in regular lines marked in some places very distinctly where the line of their different regiments had been formed. The enemy, in yielding, lost his battery of Napoleon guns. Many prisoners were taken. The Confederates continued to pursue being stopped only by nightfall. The victory was complete. The Federals had been repulsed and pursued at every point.[30]

The heaviest losses in a single brigade were those of Cadmus Wilcox of Longstreet's division. In this bloody encounter, the Eighth Alabama had numbered less than four hundred. They lost one hundred forty nine killed and wounded. When the missing was added, the total was not one hundred sixty three. Casualties among the officers of the Eighth Alabama included Captain Thomas Phelan, Lieutenants C. M. Maynard, Lane, and August Jansen. The dangerously wounded included Captain Hannon, Lieutenants McHugh, McGrath, and McLaughlin who later died of wounds. One aggregate of killed, wounded and missing for Wilcox brigade was five hundred eighty four out of a force of one thousand eight hundred fifty. Lieutenant Colonel Young L. Royston, commanding the Eighth, was with the regiment during the entire engagement, and commanded it with great courage and good judgment. The gallant Colonel Royston was everywhere in the hottest of the fire stimulating, urging and leading his command forward. This was a glorious victory, but it had been dearly won. Almost one half of the Eighth Alabama had been killed or wounded and only fourteen commissioned officers were left unhurt. The losses sustained by the Eighth Alabama, already weakest in numbers, were evidenced by the severity of the battle in which it was engaged. One June 28th, 1862, the Eighth Alabama regiment began burying the dead and collecting arms.[31]

McClellan was apparently retreating to the protection of his gunboats on the James River. Longstreet's division recrossed the Chickahominy River at New Bridge, and massed near Richmond on the Darbytown Road. On Sunday, June 30th, Longstreet camped near the ground where the battle of Frazier's Farm would be fought.[32]

FRAZIER'S FARM

Federal defenses were not as strong as they were at Gaines' Mill, but they did have a high ridge to their advantage. The burden of the battle of Frazier's Farm fell to Longstreet and A. P. Hill with no support from Jackson. The Eighth Alabama was now quite small. Around three o'clock in the afternoon of June 30th, 1862, the Eighth Alabama advanced with the brigade (the Eighth on the left), through an open field for about four hundred yards.[33] At Frazier's Farm, Wilcox had perhaps the hardest fighting of the day in the face of two valiantly defended Federal batteries. Once, when his orders conflicted, he halted his advance, but when the day was over his record was as good as any brigadier, though his loss had been ghastly. Just before the advance, an officer (supposed to be a general's aide) came down the line ordering the troops to give way to the left. The Eighth began moving to the left which created a gap of about two hundred yards between it and the next regiment to the right. On the left was a body of uncleared thickets and undergrowth in which a heavy Federal force was concealed.. The woods had strangely been overlooked by Confederate commanders in their planning of the attack. The result was that the Federal troops rained a deadly fire in to the brigade and the Eighth Alabama being closest, suffered more than any other regiment in the brigade. The fire from the front was from six pieces of artillery and a heavy infantry barrage. The command "Forward!" no sooner fell on the ears of every man, when the most heroic, desperate and bloody hand to hand fighting occurred.

The battle was long and furious. Wilcox' brigade rushed forward across an open field toward the Federal batteries. Colonel Royston moved the Eighth Alabama forward. Many of the regiment who emerged from the woods had their lives snuffed out by "iron missiles hurled from those blazing cannons." Without a halt or a waiver, in the face of belching cannon and a solid line of leaden hail from a double line of infantry, the Alabamians charged into the blasts of the cannons, yelling and firing. Advancing steadily under heavy fire, losing men at every step, the regiment came within thirty yards of the Federal battery driving the enemy gunners back. Here the Alabamians were determined to conquer or die. The enemy's first line of infantry too gave way, but now their reserve came up. The Federals counter attacked with their fresh reserves. And again, the fighting was hand to hand. The thinned exhausted Confederates could advance no further. They were flanked on their left and the enemy poured a most deadly oblique fire into the regiment. Each side, in turn, was compelled to give ground. At one time, the Eighth was left almost alone in front of the enemy. They were ordered to fall back, but were soon reinforced by the Palmetto brigade, under General Evans which rushed in with a demonic yell. With renewed courage, the Alabamians regrouped and moved forward again. By now the Eighth Alabama was reduced to about one hundred eighty men.[34]

The charge of the Alabamians of Wilcox' brigade for the two, six gun batteries shed honor on the entire command. Royston fell dangerously wounded in the head and hip. Before the battle was over, the Eighth Alabama had lost seventy four of its one hundred eighty men.[35]

The Federals brought up more reinforcements retaking the battery, only to have the Alabamians rally and force them back again. But, Wilcox' men could not endure the musket fire and pulled back into the nearby woods from which they had originally advanced. The cannon stood abandoned, neither side able to secure the prizes. Captain Cleveland took command of the Eighth, a mere handful of men now. He ordered them to attack, but though he made a valiant effort, the Eighth Alabama was unable to carry the Federal position. Sergeant Harris had the flagstaff severed in his hands by a musket ball, but he was uninjured.[36]

With ammunition exhausted by sunset, Wilcox pulled his brigade back two hundred yards and remained there until nine o'clock in the evening, when it was withdrawn from the field as fresh troops arrived in sufficient force. The total loss of Wilcox' brigade in killed, wounded, and missing was four hundred seventy two, a loss proportionately greater than in the engagement of June 27th.[37]

At the close of the day the regiment was encamped near Richmond under the command of Captain Cleveland. The scene at the field hospital on the night of June 30th was heart rending. The groans and intense agony of the torn and bleeding bodies of comrades was enough to make one shudder. General Wilcox passed among the hundreds of wounded and dying heroes wringing his hands and weeping. He was heard saying, "My poor boys! My poor boys!"[38]

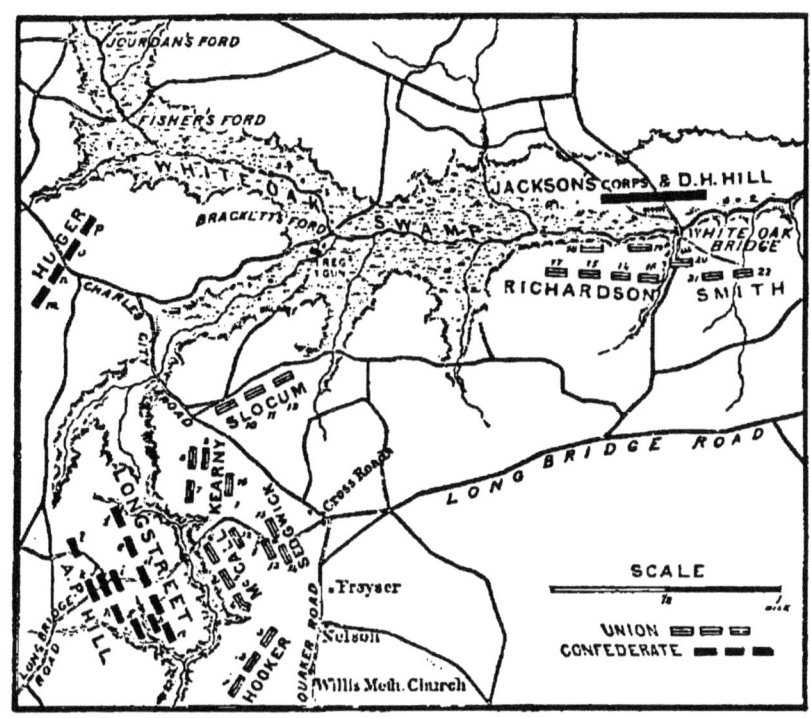

BATTLE OF FRAYSER'S FARM, JUNE 30, 1862
Map Taken from The Official Military Atlas of the Civil War

June 30th was the crisis of McClellan's retreat. The Confederate forces were now within striking distance of his rear and on his flank. Miles of his trains blocked the roads.[39]

Longstreet's and Hill's divisions remained in reserve on the Long Bridge Road. The Eighth Alabama was held in reserve during the battle of Malvern Hill and did not actively participate. So severe had been its losses in previous battles, that its numbers were not more than that of a company much less a regiment. The regiment remained encamped until the beginning of what was called the Maryland campaign starting with Second Manassas. Just before the beginning of this campaign, Major Herbert had been exchanged and took command of the Eighth Alabama. Now, new recruits began arriving daily strengthening the Eighth Alabama.[40]

The Seven Days campaign, as it came to be called, altered the course of the war in Virginia. With a masterful strategy of concentration and turning movements, Lee removed the immediate danger to Richmond and gained the strategic initiative. For a week, with little to eat and without a change of clothing, Lee's men displayed the fighting spirit that would soon make them one of the finest armies in American military history.

To the Confederates, the Seven Days campaign became an operation of missed opportunities. Inaccurate maps, inadequate staff, organizational flaws within the army and the difficult terrain crippled Lee and his commanders' efforts in offensive operations. At critical movements, subordinate officers failed Lee. Forced to refashion tactics, Lee hurled his divisions against Federal troops in defensive positions. The result was the loss of a fourth of his army. Within Lee's army the blame for the missed opportunities centered upon Jackson. Jackson's troops made up twenty three percent of the army's total, but incurred less and six percent of the loss. Longstreet and A. P. Hill's troops suffered the most in proportion, with Cadmus Wilcox brigade sustaining the heaviest unit losses, mostly at Frazier's Farm.[41]

After the Seven Days battles, the guns fell silent on Virginia's peninsula, but the Federal army was still there and not too far from Richmond at that. McClellan had failed to take Richmond despite his greatly superior numbers. Lee, after having driven the Federals from near Richmond, failed to destroy or seriously cripple McClellan. Lee was criticized both for making costly assaults on Malvern Hill and for clearly faulty management of the battle.

Under General Order 64 which was issued August 10th, 1864, numerous personnel of the Eighth Alabama were placed on the Roll of Honor. In the battle of Williamsburg: Private William A. Duke, Company A; Private J. R. Philips, Company C; Corporal William H. Powell, Company D; and, Private James Ganavan, Company I. At the battle of Seven Pines: Sergeant Frank Williams,

Company A; Private W. A. Hall, Company B; Private J. B. Tallen, Company C; Corporal Eli Shortridge, Company D; Private John H. Deaton, Company E; Private George W. Lee, Company F; Private Charles Hippler Jr., Company G; Private John Caney, Company I; and Private J. D. Garrison, Company K. At the battle of Gaines' Mill: Corporal Samuel L. Cochran, Company A; Private R. T. Bush, Company B; Private John G. Shields, Company C; Private W. E. Donoho, Company D; Sergeant J. B. Milner, Company F; Third Sergeant C. F. Walker, Company G; Sergeant W. H. McGraw, Company H; Private Hugh McKewn, Company I; and, Private John W. Griffin, Company K. And, at the battle of Frazier's Farm: Sergeant Joseph Jackson, Company A; Corporal H. M. Howard, Company B; Private Robert Geddes, Company C; Private J. P. Whelan, Company D; Fourth Sergeant G. Schwartz, Company G; Private J. Smith, Company G; and, Private John Lynch, Company I. Paperwork during the war was very slow when it came to identifying valorous actions, reports of actions and casualty lists.[42]

NOTES

[1] Herbert, Grandfather's Talks, 125.

[2] OR, Series 1, Vol. XI, part 2, 502-509; OR Series 1, Vol. XI, part 3, 648-652.

[3] OR, Series 1, Vol. XI, part 2, 980-985; Papers of James Ewell Brown Stuart, San Marino, CA: The Huntington Library.

[4] OR, Series 1, Vol. XI, part 1, 1075-1076.

[5] OR, Series 1, Vol. XI, part 2, 980-985; Johnston, Joseph E., "From Manassas to Seven Pines," Battles and Leaders of the Civil War, Vol. 2, New York: Castle Books, 1956, 202-219.

[6] IBID, Herbert, Grandfather's Talks, 125.

[7] Hoole, Unknown, 17; Grandfather's Talks, 126; Longstreet, General James, "Battle of Seven Pines—Report of General James Longstreet," Southern Historical Society Papers, Millwood, New York: Kraus Reprint Co., 1977, Vol. III, 227-281.

[8] Hoole, Unknown, 18.

[9] Herbert, Short History, 7 ½; Smith, Gustavus W., "Two Days of the Battle of Seven Pines (Fair Oaks), Battles and Leaders of the Civil War, Vol. 2, New York: Castle Books, 1956, 220-228, hereinafter cited as Smith, Two Days, BLCW; Wert, Jeffrey D., General Longstreet, New York: Touchstone Books, 1993, 121-122, hereinafter cited as Wert, General Longstreet.

[10] Hoole, Unknown, 18; Smith, Two Days, BLCW, 237.

[11] Herbert, Grandfather's Talks, 126-133.

[12] Hoole, Unknown, 17; Confederate Records, Eighth Alabama Infantry Microfilm, Field and Staff Notes, Washington, D. C.: National Archives, hereinafter cited as F&S Notes.

[13] Hoole, Unknown, 17.

[14] IBID; Barnwell, Robert W., "The Battle of Seven Pines," Confederate Veteran, Vol. XXXVI, No. 2, February 1928, 58-61; Alexander, E. P., "Records of Longstreet's Corps, Army of Northern Virginia, The Seven Days Battles," Southern Historical Society Papers, Vol. I, January to June, 1876, 66.

¹⁵Herbert, Short History, 8-9.

¹⁶Herbert, Grandfather's Talks, 9; Hoole, Unknown, 17.

¹⁷Herbert, Short History, 9; OR, Series 1, Vol. XLXI, part 2, 1217; OR, Series 1, Vol. XLVI, part 1, 1273; Freeman, Douglas Southall, Lee's Dispatches Unpublished Letters of General Robert E. Lee C.S.A. to Jefferson Davis and the War Department of the Confederate States of America 1862-1865 from the private collection of Wymberley Jones deRenne, of Wormsloe, Georgia, New Edition, New York: G. P. Putnam's Sons, 1957, 18-19, hereinafter cited as Freeman, Lee's Dispatches.

¹⁸Hoole, Unknown, 18; OR, Series 1, Vol. XI, part 2, Wilcox Report of July 21, 1862; Hill, Daniel H., "Lee's Attacks North of the Chickahominy," Battles and Leaders of the Civil War, Vol. 2; New York: Castle Books, 1956, 347-362; Freeman, Lee's Dispatches, 19.

¹⁹OR, Series 1, Vol. XI, part 2, Wilcox Report of July 21, 1862; Hoole, Unknown, 19; Law, E. M., "On the Confederate Right at Gaines' Mill," Battles and Leaders of the Civil War, Vol. 2, New York: Castle Books, 1956, 363-365; Wert, General Longstreet, 136-137, 139.

²⁰IBID, Demott, John D., "The Cause of the Silent Battle," Battles and Leaders of the Civil War. Vol. 2, New York: Castle Books, 1956, 365.

²¹Herbert, Short History, 4.

²²OR, Series 1, Vol. XI, part 2, Wilcox Report of July 21, 1862; Hoole, Unknown, 18-19; Hill, Daniel H., "McClellan's Change of Base and Malvern Hill," Battles and Leaders of the Civil War, Vol. 2, New York: Castle Books, 1956, 383-395, hereinafter cited as Hill, McClellan's Change, BLCW.

²³IBID; Hogan, N. B., "Gaines' Mill," Confederate Veteran, Vol. VI, No. 12, December 1898, 567-568.

²⁴IBID; Williams, Major. J. H., "Wilcox' Brigade at Gaines' Mill," Confederate Veteran, Vol. VIII, No. 10, October 1900, 443-444.

²⁵OR, Series 1, Vol. XXI, part 1, 539; OR, Series 1, Vol. XXVII, part 2, 618-621, 775; Wert, General Longstreet, 140.

²⁶IBID; Herbert, Short History, 5' Hill, McClellan's Change, BLCW, p. 385-391.

²⁷OR, Series 1, Vol. XI, part 2, Wilcox Report of July 21, 1862; Patterson, Edmund DeWitt, Yankee Rebel The Civil War Diary of Edmund DeWitt Patterson edited by John G. Barrett, Knoxville, TN: University of Tennessee

Press, 2004, originally printed in 1966 by the University of North Carolina Press, 29-30, hereinafter cited as Patterson, Yankee Rebel.

[28] IBID; Herbert, Short History, 6-7; Patterson, Yankee Rebel, 36.

[29] Herbert, Short History, 11.

[30] OR, Series 1, Vol. XI, part 2, Wilcox Report of July 21, 1862.

[31] Herbert, Short History, 11; OR, Series 1, Vol. XI, part 2, Wilcox Report of July 21, 1862.

[32] Hoole, Unknown, 19; Wert, General Longstreet, 140-141.

[33] IBID; Longstreet, James, "The Seven Days Battles Including Frayser's Farm," Battles and Leaders of the Civil War, Vol. 2, New York: Castle Books, 1956, p. 396-405.

[34] Herbert, Short History, 12; OR, Series 1, Vol. XI, part 2, Wilcox Report of July 21, 1862; Hogan, H. R., "Battle of Frazier's Farm—A Correction," Confederate Veteran, Vol. I, No. 11, November, 1893, 333-334; Patterson, Yankee Rebel, 47.

[35] Hoole, Unknown, 19-20; Herbert, Short History, 13; Wert, General Longstreet, 142-143; Patterson, Yankee Rebel, 48

[36] OR, Series 1, Vol. XI, part 2, Wilcox Report of July 21, 1862; Patterson, Yankee Rebel, 48.

[37] Hoole, Unknown, 19-20.

[38] Herbert, Short History, 14; OR, Series 1, Vol. XI, part 2, Wilcox Report of July 21, 1862.

[39] Hoole, Unknown, 19-20; OR, Series 1, Vol. XI, part 2, Wilcox Report of July 21, 1862.

[40] OR, Series 1, Vol. XI, part 2, Wilcox Report of July 21, 1862.

[41] IBID.

[42] OR, Series 1, Vol. XI, part 2, 994.

CHAPTER FOUR
SECOND MANASSAS TO SHARPSBURG

By July 23, 1862, General Lee had completed the reorganization of the Army of Northern Virginia into two corps. Major General Thomas (Stonewall) Jackson commanded one corps and Major General James P. Longstreet commanded the other corps. Longstreet's Corps began its distinctive career as it came through Thoroughfare Gap to participate in the fighting at Second Manassas. He brought to the plains of Manassas a corps which consisted of: one division commanded by Brigadier General James L. Kemper; a second division under Brigadier General Cadmus M. Wilcox; a third division under Brigadier General D. R. Jones; a fourth division commanded by Brigadier General John B. Hood; and a fifth division commanded by Major General R. H. Anderson; an artillery brigade under Colonel J. D. Walton; and, an artillery battalion under Col. Stephen D. Lee. There was also other miscellaneous batteries.[1]

The Eighth Alabama, still under Pryor in Wilcox' division, remained encamped near Richmond until August 10, 1862 by which time its ranks had been strengthened by new recruits. In addition, some who had only been slightly wounded and were being discharged from hospitals, began returning to the regiment.[2]

The regiment left Richmond for Gordonsville on August 11th. From Gordonsville, it marched with Longstreet's Corps toward Manassas. The regiment was marching north to meet a threatened attack by Union General John Pope from the Rappahannock River.[3]

Longstreet crossed the Rapidan River at Racoon Ford on August 20th and bivouacked for the night within a few miles of Kelly's Ford on the Rappahannock. Early on August 21st, three brigades under Wilcox (his own, Pryor's and Featherston's) marched toward Stevensburg, and then took the road to Kelly's Ford. The engagement at Kelly's Ford, involved Featherston's, and Pryor's brigades. Meanwhile, to the south along the Rappahannock, Longstreet's command skirmished with Federals and had exchanged artillery fire.[4]

By midday on August 26th, Lee had decided Pope was pulling back from the Rappahannock River. Although Lee did not know whether Pope had learned of Jackson's movement, he summoned Longstreet to his headquarters. Lee warned Longstreet to march as soon as possible to join Jackson and gave Longstreet the selection of the route.[5]

SECOND MANASSAS

The battle of Second Manassas began on August 26th, and ended on September 1st, 1862 with the last fighting at Chantilly, Virginia. Late on the 26th

Longstreet's twelve infantry brigades and sixteen artillery batteries began fording the Rappahannock at Hinson's Mill. After crossing, the Confederates bivouacked.

Since the night of August 26th, when Pope learned of Jackson's seizure of Bristoe Station, Pope's supply base, the Union commander had been searching for the elusive Southern commander and his "foot cavalry." On the morning of August 27th, Pope abandoned his Rappahannock River line and ordered a convergence of all his corps against Jackson. Pope had six corps under his direction at this time.[6]

Under cover of darkness, Jackson headed westward, filing into position behind a wooded ridge near the town of Groveton, north of the Warrenton Turnpike. All his units were in place by midday on the 28th. To Pope, the Confederates had seemingly vanished until late on the afternoon of the 28th when Jackson attacked. In a vicious engagement, Jackson lost 1300 men including Richard Ewell and Isaac Trimble, who were seriously wounded.[7]

On August 27th, Longstreet had detoured General Wilcox through the Hopewell Gap to flank the enemy from the eastern end of Thoroughfare Gap. After a tedious, fatiguing, rather difficult march, the Gap was reached at ten o'clock in the evening. Hopewell Gap is about three miles from Thoroughfare Gap. He passed through Hopewell Gap sighting no enemy troops. General Wilcox' division rejoined Longstreet about midday on August 29th from the Hopewell Gap. Wilcox' division of three brigades settled in the line of march behind Hood and Evans on the Confederate left. Except for Hood's men, the Southerners relaxed. They were footsore, weary, and thirsty.[8]

Longstreet completed disposition of his troops on the Manassas plains. Now the Confederate front covered roughly three miles, divided almost equally between Jackson and Longstreet. Jackson's line to the north offered an excellent defensive position; Longstreet's line to the south had no natural strengths but was more like a platform from which to launch an attack. The woods concealed Longstreet's ranks. If the Federals stumbled into the ground between the two wings, Lee could snap the blades together like a great pincer movement, slicing the enemy's ranks into pieces. By a strategic maneuver, Lee had placed his army in one of the greatest tactical opportunities of the war.[9]

To the north, the clamor of battle escalated as Jackson's defenders clung to an embankment against a series of Federal assaults. About three thirty in the afternoon, the enemy's infantry were seen emerging from a woods upon an open field of battle. The woods and field were in front of Jackson's extreme right and to the left and near Featherston's brigade of Wilcox division. Seeing the advance, Wilcox moved his own regiment closer to support Pryor and Featherston. The first Federal line advanced in fine style across the open field. There was but little to oppose them, except pickets and skirmishers until they reached a small rise where they came face to face with Jackson's line and came under intense short range fire. The enemy hesitated for an instant, recoiled slightly, and then continued their advance. The Eighth Alabama sustained its dearly earned reputation for invincibility. Its numbers again being respectable, the Eighth delivered a destructive fire in to the Federal troops which covered the ground with the gay and tinseled uniforms. At some points, the fighting was hand to hand, muzzle to muzzle, vicious and deadly. The final Federal attack crashed into Jackson's left. The grand onward march of victorious standards amid the booming of cannon and the rattling of small arms, and the frequent and sometimes manful attempts of the enemy to stay the tide, were all plainly to be seen on the plains of Manassas. The Eighth charged, the enemy fled, and the bullet torn flag of the regiment again floated in victory. Then, a second enemy infantry line came from the woods on to the field. Confederate artillery opened fire on this second line. The Federals were caught out in the open. This barrage checked the enemy advance. As the shells and spherical cases would burst over, in front and near them, their ranks broke, hesitated, and often scattered. This artillery fire alone, broke regiment after regiment, and drove them back into the woods. Confederate reserved were ordered up, both infantry and artillery. Wilcox ordered Featherston to close in behind the enemy's first line attacking Jackson to cut off their retreat. The order was given, three times and in the most positive peremptory manner, but it was not obeyed. At length, the front line of the enemy, sadly thinned by the close fire of Jackson's men, broke and fell back in disorder. Jackson's troops pursued. Featherston and Pryor joined in the pursuit.[10]

At Second Manassas, Major Herbert saw more of this battle than any previous battle. The Eighth Alabama of Pryor's brigade was in reserve and constantly moving from right to left and back again such as might be needed at crucial points in the conflict. Marching from point to point this way, over the field which was a succession of plateaus, the regiment was frequently exposed to a fire which they could not return, but were witnessing everywhere the discomfort of the enemy. It was always more or less demoralizing to troops to be exposed to fire without the opportunity to return fire, but the effect of the shells whizzing about and of fragments that struck the lines of the Eighth Alabama was all counteracted by the grandeur of the spectacle they all witnessed on the field to their front.[11]

Now Federal artillery opened fire, Wilcox ordered his brigades to halt and reform, having become disorganized during pursuit of the enemy. His command was being swept by brisk Federal artillery fire. His men were only slightly protected by a small ridge to their front. This fire was born by these men with great coolness, no disorder or embarrassment being perceptible. Wilcox formed his three brigades in line of battle and at right angles to the Warrenton Turnpike. Here the Eighth Alabama did not form a portion of the first line, but was kept within supporting distance so as to be able to reinforce such portion of Wilcox lines as might need assistance.[12]

Jackson asked Longstreet for help. About one o'clock in the afternoon, on Longstreet's side of the field (to the right of Jackson or on the south side of the

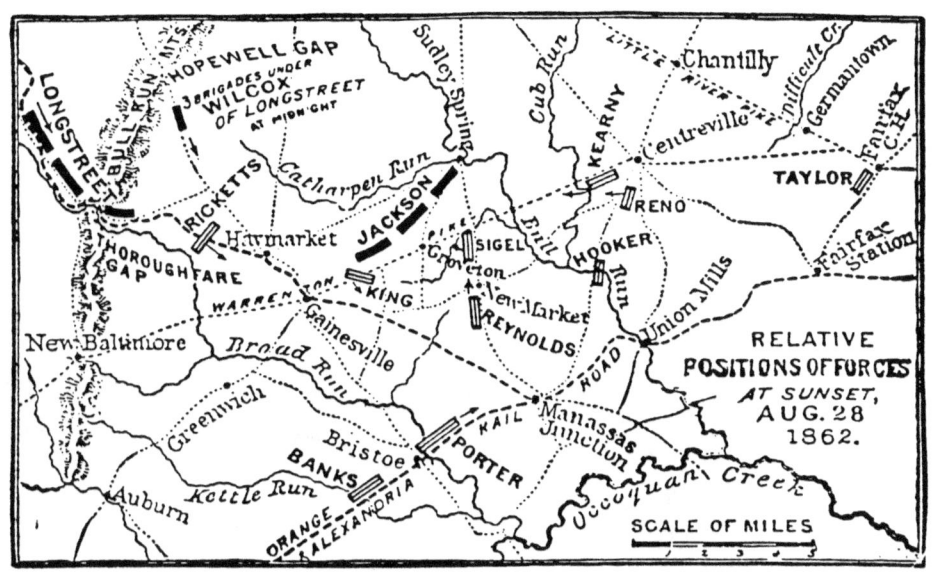

Map Taken from The Official Military Atlas of the Civil War

field), Longstreet's artillery initiated an artillery duel that lasted most of the day with Federal batteries near Groveton. Part of General Wilcox' artillery was used. But, Wilcox' artillery company was short of men due to sickness, and a detail from the Eighth Alabama was assigned to the artillery. At times, the Federal infantry and artillery were plainly visible moving in different directions, both the right and left of the Warrenton Turnpike.[12]

Reconnaissance by Lee and Longstreet, meanwhile, confirmed the Federal force on the right flank consisted of at least one corps. When their meeting adjourned, Longstreet returned to his lines. His units needed realignment. He reorganized his lines, closed the gaps, and shifted a few brigades. Wilcox' division was shifted to the right behind D. R. Jones brigade, but no serious attack was made and after firing a few shots, the enemy withdrew.[14]

At four thirty in the afternoon of August 29th, Wilcox with his three brigades moved to the right side of the Warrenton Turnpike near the Manassas Gap Railroad. The Federals maintained a defensive position, and their skirmishers exchanged constant fire with the Confederate infantry.[15]

By sundown, Wilcox was ordered back to the turnpike, and then forward to support General Hood, who had become engaged with the enemy inflicting severe losses. Longstreet had designated Hood's division as the column of direction and cautioned him not to outpace his support. The objective was Henry Hill. Hood advanced followed by D. R. Jones, with the hope of severing Pope's retreat route. With this change of Wilcox' position, the division was exposed to heavy Federal artillery fire. Not knowing where General Hood actually was, Wilcox continued his advance in the direction of the heaviest fighting. As he continued his advance, his division was caught in an enemy cross fire, but the distance was so great for the musket fire, that only a couple of soldiers were wounded. Although the Eighth Alabama did not fire a shot on this day, they were, nevertheless, severely galled, being very frequently recipients of favors intended for the front line. The Eighth had seventeen killed or wounded that day.[16]

Hood advanced at six thirty in the evening. The Confederates emerged from the woods, plunged down a slope and drove toward Groveton. Within minutes, they collided with two brigades of Union Brigadier General John Hatch's division. Believing the Confederates had retreated, Pope had earlier directed General Irwin McDowell to pursue them toward Groveton. The job had been given to Hatch. Instead of finding a retreating foe, Hatch's men ran into Hood's veterans. The collision stunned the Federals who quickly formed a rough line of battle. The combat rapidly lost its form in the evening hours. The Confederate forces shoved the Federal troops back. They seized one cannon and several battle flags in the confusing struggle. Men flailed at each other with muskets and bayonets. It became so dark that one flag could not be distinguished from another, nor the Federal soldiers from Confederate soldiers. By eight o'clock in the evening, most of the fighting had subsided.[17]

The day of August 30th, 1862, opened as a clear and bright one, with the two armies ready for renewed conflict. The position of Lee's two wings was unchanged except that he had massed thirty six guns under Colonel Stephen D. Lee on a hill in the center of his lines, where the lines of fire led down the center of a depression followed by Young's Branch and threaded by the Warrenton Turnpike leading through the midst of the Federal lines to the Stone Bridge over Bull Run Creek. The brigades of Longstreet from the center southward were those of Wilcox, Hood, Kemper, and D. R. Jones. Anderson was held in reserve on the Warrenton Turnpike in the rear. Longstreet was basically to support Jackson in this battle.[18]

By sunrise on August 30th, pickets began to fire; at times quite rapidly. The enemy could be seen relieving their skirmishers. The firing between skirmishers continued throughout the day. The Federals advanced as if the fate of the army hung in the balance, and it did. Men fell in clusters. Longstreet directed infantry brigades toward the struggle. Before seven o'clock in the morning, General Roger Pryor's brigade (including the Eighth Alabama), was placed in line at right angles to the turnpike, with an open field extending to the front more than a mile. The open field had a succession of valleys and hills. Featherston's brigade was in line on Pryor's left and extended so far left as to be in contact with the extreme right of Jackson's First Division. Wilcox' own brigade was in the woods to the rear of the center of the line occupied by the other two brigades. This Second Battle of Manassas was truly a magnificent spectacle. The great expanse of open country permitted much more of it to be seen. For the next four hours, Longstreet's veterans fought magnificently. Like a great hammer they pounded the Federal defenders in a series of blows—first Hood, then Evans, Kemper, Jones, and Wilcox. The combat flowed across Young's Branch and onto the bloody crest of Chinn Ridge to the climax at Henry Hill. By the time Wilcox' division arrived; most of the struggle was over. Both Wilcox and Hood conferred and agreed that they were too far forward of the Confederate lines and could be easily flanked if they did not pull back. The brigades were pulled back after both Wilcox and Hood conferred with Lee and then Longstreet. This was one of the finest counterattacks of the war. That Longstreet's troops did not ultimately succeed in destroying the Federal army can be attributed, in part, to the failure of Jackson to lend assistance. When Longstreet charged, Lee sent a message to Jackson to protect Longstreet's left flank. For reasons unexplained, Jackson did not move forward until nearly six o'clock in the evening, near two hours later. By then his delay had allowed the Federals to enfilade Longstreet's units with artillery.[19]

At Second Manassas, Pope's Army of Virginia was beaten, but not defeated. McClellan's feeble attempts to send support to Pope also failed, perhaps intentionally as he personally hoped Pope would fail. Rain fell during the night of August 30th discomforting the sleeping and tormenting the wounded. There was nothing left for Pope to do except withdraw in humiliation.[20]

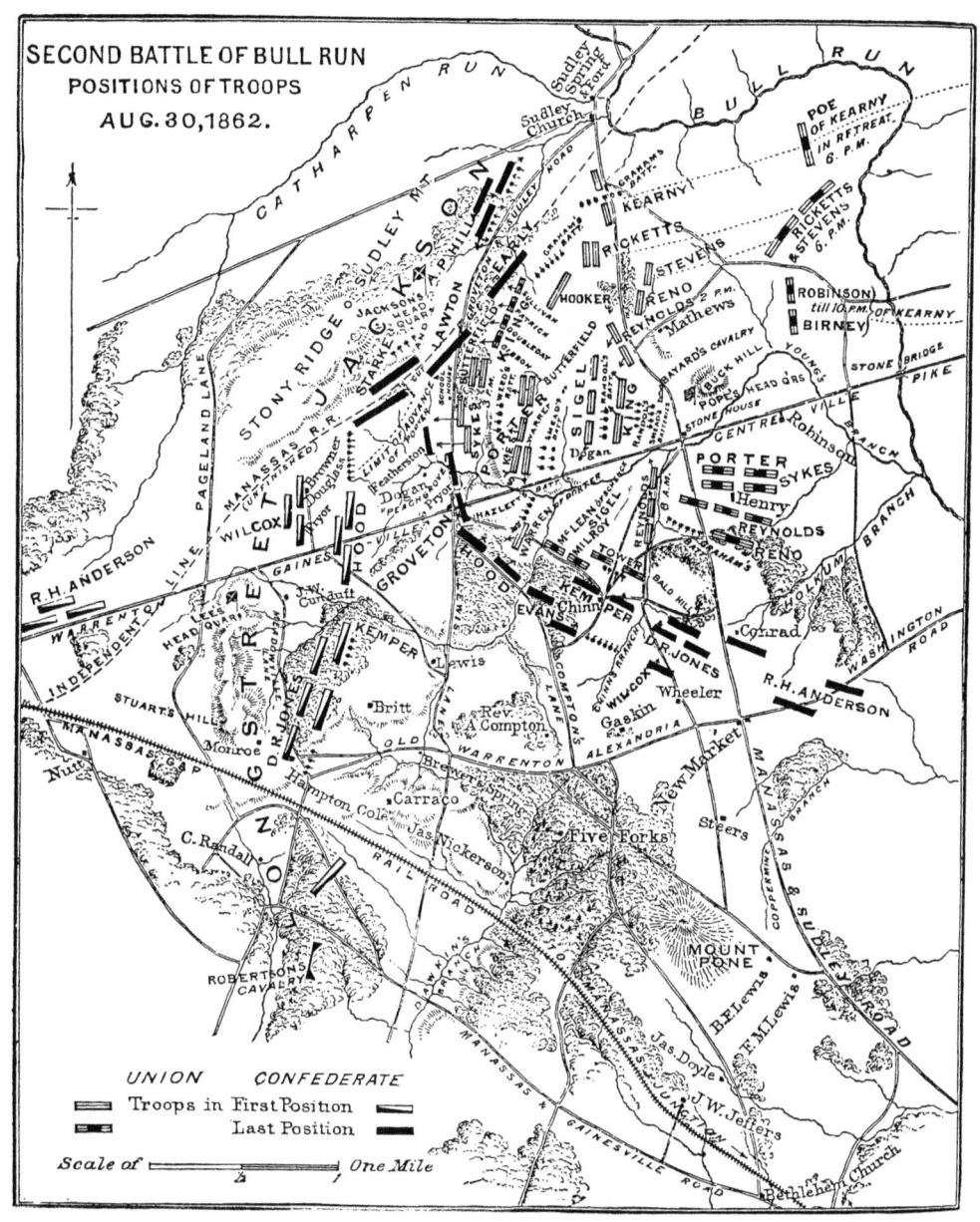

FIRST AND LAST POSITIONS IN THE FIGHTING OF AUGUST 30TH 1862
Map Taken from The Official Military Atlas of the Civil War

On August 31st, Pope gathered his beaten Army of Virginia on the Washington side of Bull Run Creek at the heights of Centreville. The heavy rain threatened to render Bull Run Creek impassable and impeded not only Confederate movements, but also Federal troop movements. Despite the weather and the mud, Lee stirred his army hoping to intercept Pope's retreating forces between Centreville and Washington. Longstreet remained on the battlefield to cover the burial of the dead and removal of the wounded. It was a pathetic scene after the battle to see so many dead men lying on the ground, shot, torn, and so badly disfigured and swollen largely beyond their natural size. Some lying on the field were still breathing, yet were unconscious of their sufferings. On August 31st, Second Manassas was over for the Eighth Alabama.[21]

The relative strength of Longstreet's Corps at Second Manassas was about eight thousand five hundred as of July 20th, 1862. Total Confederate strength was approximately fifty four thousand under Lee. General Wilcox reported he had three hundred thirty killed, wounded, or missing in his division. He pointed out in his report of October 11, 1862 on the action of August 30th, 1862 that none of the regiments in his own brigade were commanded by an officer higher in rank than that of major—Major J. H. Williams of the Ninth Alabama, Major H. A. Herbert of the Eighth Alabama, Captain J. C. C. Sanders of the Eleventh Alabama, and Major John H. Caldwell of the Tenth Alabama. The Eighth Alabama lost an aggregate of 70 killed and wounded between Thoroughfare Gap, the Rappahannock, and Second Manassas.[22]

In one month, Longstreet's Corps had marched two hundred miles on little more than half rations, and fought nine battles and skirmishes. His corps had captured nearly as many men as it had in its ranks, besides taking arms and other munitions of war in large quantities. Longstreet's command incurred more casualties in the four hour counterattack than Jackson's did during two days of fighting.[23]

General Orders No. 64 dated August 10th, 1864, identified some personnel of the Eighth Alabama Infantry for the Roll of Honor. Those listed for Second Manassas were Captain R. Murphy of Company A, and Private James Jennings of Company I. No others in Wilcox brigade were mentioned. Wilcox, himself, was mentioned in Lee's report to President Davis saying that "he (Wilcox) unhesitatingly and swiftly moved his troops to threatened points. His movements were executed with commendable zeal and ability."[24]

The victory at Second Manassas opened the path for an invasion of Maryland. Lee informed Davis that his army was not ready for such an invasion. It needed shoes, clothing, and food. The march to Manassas outraced the commissary wagons. There was a general lack of ammunition, supplies, and animals which also concerned Lee. But, Lee went on to propose that some supplies could be purchased in Maryland. Longstreet endorsed Lee's proposal for an invasion of northern territory. Longstreet felt that army could forage for its needs in Maryland rather than continuing to strain the resources of the Virginia farmers. But, regardless, the men needed time to regain their strength even though the strategic situation indicated an offensive thrust beyond the Potomac could be beneficial. Opportunism characterized Lee's operations.[25]

HARPER'S FERRY

After the Second Battle of Manassas, Lee again reorganized the Army of Northern Virginia. Now Lieutenant General James P. Longstreet, recently promoted, commanded the First Corps. In the First Corps there were five divisions. The division of Major General Richard H. Anderson consisted of the First Brigade of Brigadier General Wilcox (Eighth, Ninth, Tenth, Eleventh, and Fourteenth Alabama Regiments); Second Brigade of Brigadier General William Mahone (Sixth, Twelfth, Sixteenth, Forty-first, and Sixty-first Virginia); Third Brigade under Brigadier General Winfield S. Featherston (Twelfth, Sixteenth, Nineteenth, and Second Battery all from Mississippi); Fourth Brigade under Brigadier General A. R. Wright; and, the Fifth Brigade under Brigadier E. A. Perry. There was the division of Major General Lafayette McLaws, followed by Major General George E. Pickett's Division. Pickett's division consisted of the First Brigade under Brigadier General Richard B. Garnett; Second Brigade under Brigadier General Lewis A. Armistead; Third Brigade under Brigadier General James L. Kemper; Fourth Brigade under Brigadier General Micah Jenkins; and, Fifth Brigade under Brigadier General M. D. Corse.[26]

The First Corps of the Army of Northern Virginia also had the Division of Major General John B. Hood of Texas. The First Brigade was under Brigadier General J. B. Robertson; Second Brigade under Brigadier General E. M. Law; Third Brigade under Brigadier General George T. Anderson; and, Fourth Brigade under Brigadier General Robert Toombs of Georgia. There was also the division of Brigadier General Robert Ransom Jr., which included Ransom's own Brigade, Cook's Brigade, and reserve artillery which included the Washington Artillery of Col. J. B. Walton and the Alexandria Battery of Lieutenant Colonel E. Porter Alexander (later General)[27]

Part of General Lee's rationale for the Maryland campaign and the Harper's Ferry operation was his assessment of the Federal army following its defeat at Manassas. Lee believed the Federal troops were disorganized and demoralized. And, when he learned that McClellan was again in command, he calculated the enemy's pursuit of the Confederate advance would be slow and cautious. Lee's plan was also predicated on the tactical vulnerability of Harper's Ferry. If the Confederates could seize the high ground, the Federal garrison of approximately twelve thousand troops was doomed. By eliminating the Federal force at Harper's Ferry and by moving his army behind the mountain ranges west of Frederick, Maryland, Lee could secure a supply line into the Shenandoah Valley and advance into Pennsylvania, while drawing the Federal Army of the Potomac farther from the capitol at Washington and its base of supply.[28]

On September 3rd, 1862, Longstreet, sent six brigades under Major General Anderson, which included the Eighth Alabama Regiment, to cooperate with Major General McLaws in the assault on Maryland Heights and Harper's Ferry. The Eighth took up a position and occupied the road leaving from Harper's Ferry through Pleasant Valley. The Eighth Alabama crossed into the valley through Crampton's Gap and left a force to guard the pass. This force was later overpowered on September 13th. The Eighth Alabama now had impassable mountains to their right and left, the narrow pass to their rear in under enemy control and to their front was Harper's Ferry.[29]

By September 4th, 1862, Lee's Army of Northern Virginia was crossing the Potomac River near Leesburg. The Confederates were on their way into Maryland. Come September 6th, Jackson was in Frederick, Maryland. The Federal garrison at Harper's Ferry and Martinsburg had been cut off from Washington.[30]

McClellan was reorganizing the Army of the Potomac and the Army of Virginia into one large army basically eliminating the Army of Virginia for now. By September 7th, the Federal Army of the Potomac began to move northward from Washington, protecting the capitol and Baltimore. He did not know the emeny's plans or whereabouts. Also by September 7th, The First Corps of the Army of Northern Virginia had completed its crossing of the Potomac.

Meanwhile, the Eighth Alabama, on detached service to McLaws, found the approach to Harper's ferry was protected by Bolivar Heights and Loudon Heights. The enemy had fortified and occupied both Heights. The river in front of the town could not be crossed except by the bridge which was held by the enemy. Such was the situation for the Eighth Alabama for nearly two days, everyone friend and foe alike, besieged, cooped up, hemmed in and apparently at the mercy of each other. The salvation of the Eighth Alabama and other regiments under Anderson depended on the capture of Harper's Ferry.[31]

On September 9th, 1862, at Frederick, General Lee issued orders for future operations—Special Orders 191 called for Jackson to march his three divisions to Harper's Ferry by recrossing the Potomac upstream from the town, then turn eastward and seal off the western approaches to the town; other troops were sent to Crampton's Gap. Much of Longstreet's Corps was to go on to Boonsboro, Maryland. Lee projected Harper's Ferry would fall by September 12th, thus his split army could reunite at Boonsboro or Hagerstown, Maryland. By September 12th, Jackson was converging on Harper's Ferry.[32]

In the meantime, General McLaws captured Maryland Heights and turned the cannon against the town. Jackson took the Bolivar Heights on the Virginia side and south of the town, General Walker occupied Loudon Heights, and had other troops thundering in the rear of Harper's Ferry. On the morning of September 15th, the rumor spread through out the lines of the Eighth Alabama like an electric flash that Harper's Ferry had surrendered. The Confederates netted over eleven thousand prisoners, seventy three cannon, thirteen thousand small arms, roughly two hundred wagons and a stockpile of supplies at a loss of only a couple of hundred men.[33]

McClellan began pushing west toward the mountains beyond Frederick, Maryland. Lee had General Stuart and his cavalry off at South Mountain; and, other troops were nearby. Longstreet was near Hagerstown; Jackson was at Harper's Ferry. On the night of September 13th, Stuart learned of Lee's lost orders (found by Federal soldiers), and informed Lee that McClellan had his battle plan.[34]

On September 14th the left wing of McClellan's army under Major General William B. Franklin moved toward Crampton's Gap in an effort to relieve Harper's Ferry. If the Federal troops shoved through the gaps at South Mountain and Crampton's Gap, the disbursement of the Confederate army, the straggling, and the delay in capturing Harper's Ferry could combine to jeopardize Lee's entire Army of Northern Virginia.[35]

On September 15th, 1862, the Confederates at South Mountain were forced by McClellan's army to fall back to Sharpsburg, Maryland. Lee was in the process of concentrating his scattered forces at the small village in preparation for a withdrawal back across the Potomac. But hearing that Harper's Ferry had fallen, he reversed his plan, and established a line west of Antietam Creek.

Crossing the Antietam Creek on the morning of the 15th, Major General D. H. Hill's division and Longstreet's Corps were placed in line of battle between the stream and the village of Sharpsburg. A hard night's march had brought Jackson from Harper's Ferry and McLaws was enroute. Jackson left Major General A. P. Hill in charge of the capitulating Federal forces at Harper's Ferry.[36]

On the morning of September 16th, Wilcox' brigade was heading north to rejoin Longstreet. The Eighth Alabama marched through Harper's Ferry and halted about a mile and a half from it on the Virginia side. There the Eighth rested until near sunset, when they moved out toward Shepherdstown. The regiment was already much fatigued by the incessant picket duty and marching and countermarching. The march to Shepherdstown therefore was a trying experience for it was tramp, tramp, the whole night; mounted officers dozed on their horses; and, the men fell asleep at every momentary halt. There was nothing more agonizing than the effort to resist sleep when it was overpowering. The army was weakened with every mile it marched. Men left the ranks in droves, unable or unwilling to continue because of illness and exhaustion, compounded by the lack of food and shoes. They suffered from hunger, reduced in some instances to chewing tobacco to alleviate stomach pangs. Enlisted men and officers foraged for food, even plundered for food. In fact, the officer ranks had been so reduced that the officers still with their regiments were insufficient in numbers to stem the flood of stragglers and deserters.[37]

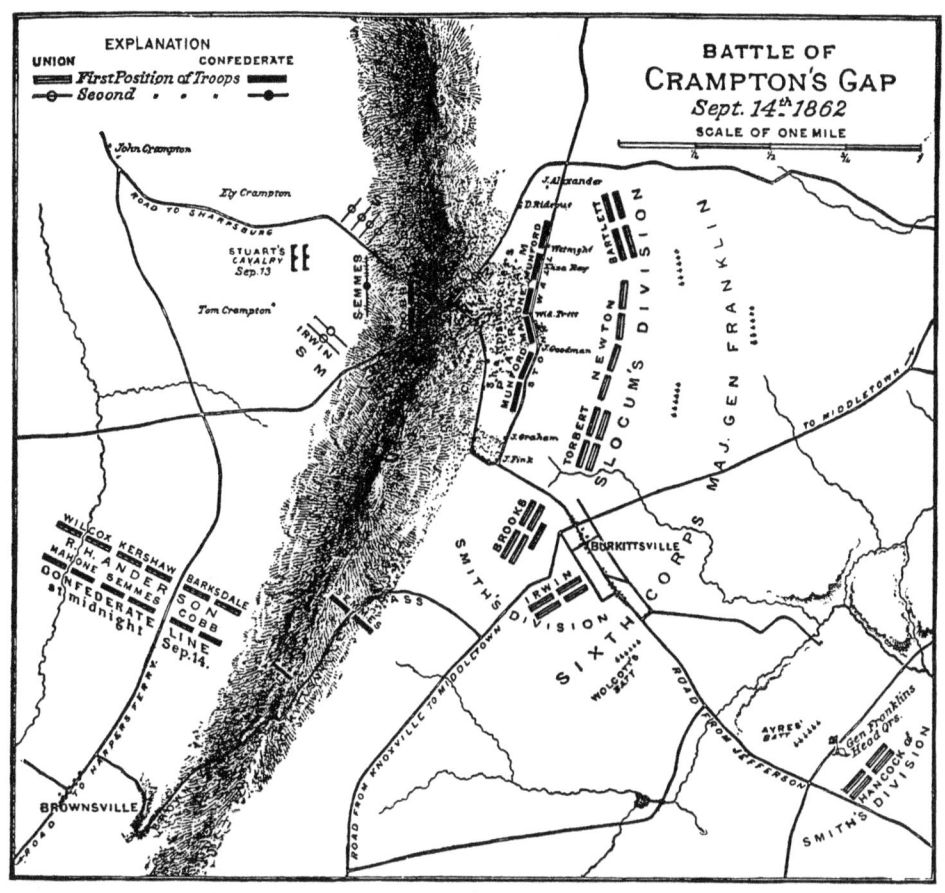

Map Taken from The Official Military Atlas of the Civil War

SHARPSBURG

Wilcox crossed the Potomac on a pontoon bridge at Harper's Ferry on September 16th. On the night of the 16th a gentle rain began falling after dark. Lee's Army of Northern Virginia was massing for battle. On September 18th, President Davis had signed into law an act authorizing the appointment of Lieutenant Generals and the creation of Army Corps ex post facto. Along the four mile Confederate line, many of the troops bedded down with hunger having had only ears of green corn and apples to eat during the day. On the 17th Wilcox's troops waded across the river at Shepherdstown to Sharpsburg. Each regiment had its own wagons, artillery, caissons, ammunition wagons, ambulances, etc., and halting now and then the march was tedious and worrisome. The Eighth Alabama arrived about seven o'clock in the morning on the field at Sharpsburg rejoining Longstreet.[38]

The battle of Sharpsburg had already started in the fog and early morning mist that shrouded the village around six o'clock when Union General Joseph Hooker's Federal troops charged southward along the Hagerstown Turnpike into Jackson's and Hood's troops. The cannonading that was heard was an indication of the trouble ahead. The Eighth Alabama stopped long enough to unload their knapsacks and blankets, and then made double quick time until they got near enough to the enemy's infantry to attack.[39]

Wilcox' own brigade was drawn up, the roll called, and then advanced toward the fight without halting long enough to even get water. Here again the metal of the Eighth Alabama was tested. Leaving Sharpsburg to their right, the Eighth made a detour to the left passing beyond the town and through open fields exposed for a half a mile to a withering fire of artillery. The Eighth Alabama's fight was chiefly near and to the right of Pfeifer's House in and for an apple orchard for which they fought off and on all day long. The ground did not offer much advantage to either side. Colonel Alfred Cummings, who was temporarily in charge of the brigade, was wounded in the beginning of the fight. Still marching by the right flank, the Eighth Alabama came within grape shot range of the enemy's batteries and small arms fire. They moved forward through a cornfield which sloped downward from the orchard and entered the fight. The fight grew ever more furious. Wilcox' brigade occupied the right center of the line with the Eighth on the right of the brigade. On the far right of the brigade was a gap in the line which was unoccupied.[40]

A heavy compact line of enemy infantry about one hundred twenty yards in front of the Eighth Alabama, poured a well directed fire into them which the Eighth answered with great efficiency. Sergeant Harris, the color bearer was wounded, and Corporal Ryan of Company E took up the colors and was then mortally wounded.[41]

Enemy batteries to the right and left at a forty five degree angles concentrated their fire with terrible accuracy. Wilcox' brigade was unsupported by Confederate artillery. As ammunition was nearly exhausted, the men began using the cartridge boxes of their dead and wounded comrades. The enemy's line in front of the Eighth Alabama wavered and portions of it broke. But, the Federal line was rapidly reinforced by fresh troops. The Eighth Alabama had no fresh troops to reinforce them.[42]

Wilcox' entire brigade was being pushed back by overwhelming numbers. Major Herbert ordered the Eighth to fall back. About three hundred yards to the rear, Major Fairfax, General Longstreet's "fighting aide" as the soldiers called him, was endeavoring to rally the troops who had fallen back before the Eighth was ordered to fall back.[43]

After dispatching Lt. McWilliams and two other men after ammunition, Major Williams and Major Herbert rallied about one hundred of the brigade and moved forward again. Major Williams of the Ninth Alabama was the ranking officer and took charge of the brigade. The brigade moved back over the little hill across which they had just retreated, but this time the brigade went with a whoop and a shout. The enemy was advancing through the cornfield. The brigade fired a heavy volley and the Federals scattered and retreated in great disorder. The brigade followed only a little way as their venture would be unsupported by artillery. The enemy had artillery on the front and right flank of the brigade. The Confederates were forced to withdraw again under heave Federal artillery fire. Major Williams had been wounded in this countercharge. Major Herbert was now the senior officer in the brigade.[44]

The brigade with the Eighth Alabama in the lead went forward again toward the apple orchard hill. Again, the enemy was attempting to cross the cornfield. And again, the brigade fired heavily into their approaching Federal lines and then charged. This time the enemy saw how few the brigade really had and they rallied forming behind the rock fence on the opposite ridge about one hundred yards away. Moving forward without firing, under a storm of hurtling shells and signing musket balls, the Eighth Alabama held up in the orchard. Major Herbert was moving from right to left among the line to encourage the men, telling them to aim carefully. The unequal fight was kept up until the Eighth Alabama began to gradually melt away under enemy fire. After a time, the Confederate line to the left of the Eighth began to fall back; and seeing that happen, Herbert ordered the Eighth to fall back and endeavored to keep them together in good order. However, enemy fire from the front and artillery fire across the flank from across Antietam Creek was so deadly that the men retreated in such disorder that one the brigade got over the hill to their rear, Herbert halted the colors. There were only eight men around the flag, most were the German Fusiliers. Others were not far away though. The regiment and the brigade soon rallied again. Two more color bearers went down. Sergeant Costello of Company G died of a Minnie ball to the head. Herbert himself had picket up the colors only

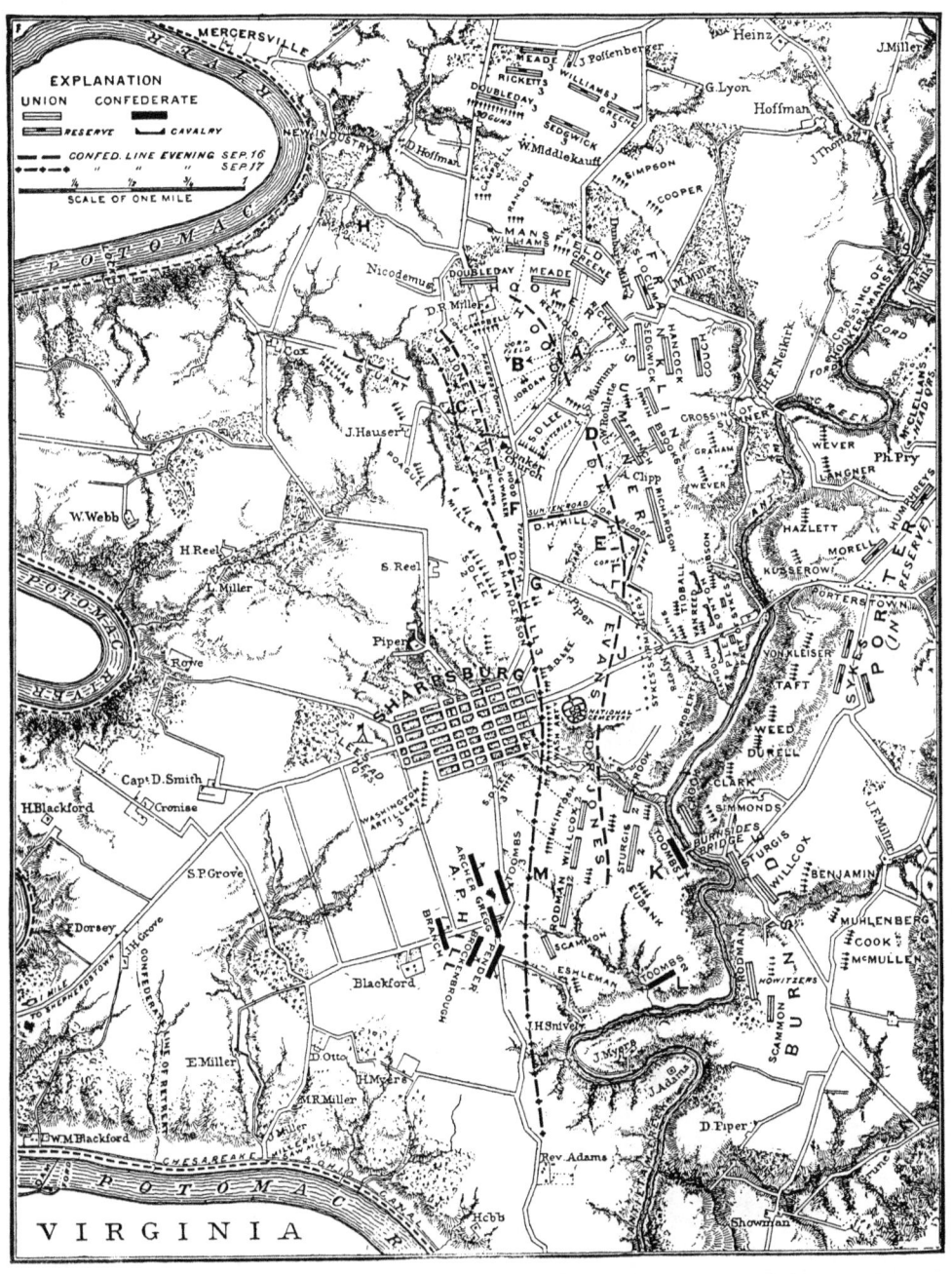

THE FIELD OF ANTIETAM
Map Taken from The Official Military Atlas of the Civil War

to turn them over to Sergeant G. T. L. Robinson of Company B, who was later wounded.[45]

The Federals did not attempt to occupy the disputed apple orchard until later in the evening. It was nearly sunset when A. P. Hill's division arrived from Harper's Ferry and came on the field to the right of Wilcox' brigade. The Federals made no further attacks against the Eighth Alabama's portion of the line, so the regiment was moved to support General Hill's left. The Federals now attempted to take the ground the Eighth had just taken over on the left. Brigadier General Phil Cook, commanding a brigade of Georgians and with whom Herbert was cooperating, saw this movement. He told Herbert to change his frontal position quickly to meet the Federal advance. The nature of the ground permitted the Eighth Alabama to shift positions without been seen.[46]

The Federal troops came confidently forward. The Eighth was in line just in from of the Federal advance, but concealed by the crest of a hill. When the enemy was within thirty yards of the Eighth Alabama, the men rose, fired and charged. The Federal troops fled in confusion, leaving the Eighth Alabama now in charge of the often disputed apple orchard. Thus, the battle of Sharpsburg along the portion of the line occupied by the Eighth Alabama infantry was over. Five main Federal drives had been halted with major losses. Nightfall found the Confederate army holding its position in the face of an overpowering enemy.[47]

The Eighth Alabama lost seventy eight killed and wounded out of its one hundred twenty. When the roll was called that evening only forty two answered the roll call. "Every man seemed to know how to die, but not to surrender." Casualties among Confederate infantry reached staggering proportions with the divisions of McLaws, D. H. Hill, J. R. Jones and Richard Anderson incurring the greatest losses. Wilcox' brigade was under Anderson.[48]

Several men of the Eighth Alabama were complemented for gallantry in Special orders from regimental headquarters: Lt. G. T. L Robinson later captain of Company B; Sergeant G. B. Gould, later First Lieutenant of Company F; Sergeant Brown, later Second Lieutenant Company D; Private L. P. Bolger of Company B, later Sergeant and killed at Gettysburg; Private M. J. McCloskie of Company G; Private James Regan of Company I; Private Peter Smith of Company G; Private Charles Roh of Company J; Private Herbert of Company H; and, Private John Callahan of Company C. General Orders No. 64 of August 10, 1864, listed ten personnel from the Eighth Alabama regiment for the Roll of Honor for their actions at the Battle of Sharpsburg: Corporal Davis Tucker of Company A; Sergeant Robinson of Company B; Private John Curry, Company C; Sergeant C. F. Brown of Company D; Sergeant T. S. Ryan of Company E; Captain J. R. Search of Company F; Fifth Sergeant James Costello of Company G; Private J. Herbert of Company H; Private James Ryan of Company I; and, Private Harris of Company K.[49]

Within a week the Army of Northern Virginia was encamped near Winchester, Virginia. Foodstuffs, clothing, footwear, and equipment began arriving from supply depots, but still not in the quantities required. The artillery had incurred serious losses, especially in Longstreet's Corps. The worst batteries were disbanded; their serviceable cannon and equipment were dispersed to other units.[50]

Lieutenant Colonel Royston returned from convalescent leave and took command of the regiment. The regiment moved from Martinsburg closer to the main body near Winchester, where it remained until October 30th, 1862. While there Royston was promoted to Colonel, Major Herbert to Lieutenant Colonel, and Captain Emerich (Emrich) to major, each with a date of rank back to June18th, 1862. So ended the Sharpsburg Campaign and with it McClellan was again removed from command of the Army of the Potomac.[51]

Lee was criticized for fighting the battle of Sharpsburg with nearly three to one odds against him and a deep river at his back, but Major Herbert of the Eighth Alabama believed it was Lee's only option to save Longstreet's Corps. The Confederates at Sharpsburg had repulsed one uncoordinated attack after another, and won a tactical victory. Lee's decision to fight and then retreat, however, gave the northern administration a political victory. Five days after the battle, President Lincoln signed the Emancipation Proclamation freeing the slaves in the rebellious states on January 1st, 1863[52]

The high spirits that had marked the beginning of the Maryland campaign faded into despair and sickness. Shoes wore out as the troops marched day and night on meager rations. Clothes stank from a month's unbroken wear. Blankets and tents were not available.

On October 30th, 1862, Wilcox' brigade marched from Winchester arriving at Culpeper Court House on November 3rd. At this point, General Wilcox learned that his brother had died leaving a widow and children. He felt responsible for them and wrote General Lee a note on November 12th asking to be released from the army. General Lee sent for Wilcox. After a short conversation, he convinced Wilcox the Army of Northern Virginia needed him even more. Anderson's division remained at Culpeper Court House until November 19th, when it marched off toward Fredericksburg for winter quarters arriving there on November 22nd, 1862.[53]

Lieutenant General Richard H. Anderson C.S.A.
From a Photograph

NOTES

[1] Longstreet, James. From Manassas to Appomattox. Memoirs of the Civil War in America. New York: Smithmark Publishers Inc., 1992, 156-158, hereinafter cited as Longstreet, From Manassas.

[2] Herbert, Short History, 114.

[3] Longstreet, From Manassas, 159; Freeman, Lee's Dispatches, 47.

[4] IBID; Wert, General Longstreet, 156-158.

[5] IBID, 160; Wert, General Longstreet, 163

[6] IBID; Wert, General Longstreet, 162-164; Freeman, Lee's Dispatches, 54.

[7] IBID, 167-171; Wert, General Longstreet, 166.

[8] IBID, 175, 180; Wert, General Longstreet, 168; Longstreet, Helen D., Lee and Longstreet at High Tide: Gettysburg in the Light of the Official Records, Wilmington, NC: Broadfoot Publishing Company, 1989, original copyright 1904, 177, hereinafter cited as Helen Longstreet. Lee and Longstreet.

[9] Herbert, Grandfather's Talks, 139; Longstreet, From Manassas, 184-185; Allan, Colonel William, "Relative Strength at Second Manassas," Southern Historical Papers, Millwood, New York: Kraus Reprint Co., 1988 Vol. VIII, 217-221.

[10] Longstreet, From Manassas, 187-190; Herbert, Short History, 15; Herbert, Grandfather's Talks, 140.

[11] Herbert, Grandfather's Talks, 138; Helen Longstreet, Lee and Longstreet, 177-179.

[12] Longstreet, From Manassas, 188; Helen Longstreet, Lee and Longstreet, 180.

[13] IBID, 191-198; Wert, General Longstreet, 169-170.

[14] IBID.

[15] IBID; Herbert, Grandfather's Talks, 139-140.

[16] Longstreet, From Manassas, 191-198; Wert, General Longstreet, 171.

[17] IBID; Wert, General Longstreet, 172-173.

[18] IBID; Herbert, Short History, 15; Wert, General Longstreet, 173.

[19] IBID; Herbert, Grandfather's Talks, 140; Wert, General Longstreet, 175

[20] Longstreet, From Manassas, 194; Wert, General Longstreet, 177.

[21] IBID, 192; Wert, General Longstreet, 178-180.
[22] IBID, 195; OR, Series 1, Vol. XII, part 2, 558.

[23] IBID, 191-198.

[24] OR, Series 1, Vol. XII, part 2, 558; OR, Series 1, Vol. XI, part 2, 994.

[25] Longstreet, From Manassas, 199-200; Wert, General Longstreet, 180.

[26] IBID, 202-203.

[27] IBID.

[28] IBID, 204-205; Wert, General Longstreet, 181.

[29] IBID, 206-207; Herbert, Short History, 16; Herbert, Grandfather's Talks, 141.

[30] IBID, 206-207; Wert, General Longstreet, 181.

[31] IBID.

[32] IBID, 203, 212-215; Wert, General Longstreet, 183

[33] IBID, 208.

[34] IBID, 203; Wert, General Longstreet, 187; Freeman, Lee's Dispatches, 64.

[35] IBID, 209-210.

[36] IBID, 210.

[37] Herbert, Short History, 17-18; Herbert, Grandfather's Talks, 143; Wert, General Longstreet, 185-186.

[38] Herbert, Short History, 18-19; Herbert, Grandfather's Talks, 144; Longstreet, From Manassas, 241; Helen Longstreet, Lee and Longstreet, 180-101.

[39] Herbert, Short History, 19; Longstreet, From Manassas, 241; Helen Longstreet, Lee and Longstreet, 184-186.

[40] IBID.

[41] Herbert, Grandfather's Talks, 147.

[42] IBID, 147-149.

[43] IBID.

[44] IBID, 149-152; Longstreet, From Manassas, 260-262; Herbert, Short History, 21.

[45] IBID; Herbert, Short History, 22.

[46] IBID, 20-22.

[47] Herbert, Short History, 23-25.

[48] Herbert, Grandfather's Talks, 152; Hoole, Unknown, 20.

[49] OR, Series 1, Vol. XI, part 2, 994.

[50] Herbert, Short History, 26; Wert, General Longstreet, 204.

[51] Hoole, Unknown, 21; Herbert, Short History, 25; Wert, General Longstreet, 202.

[52] Herbert, Grandfather's Talks, 152; Wert, General Longstreet, 202.

[53] Herbert, Short History, 26; Letter From General R. E. Lee to General Wilcox, dated 12 November 1862, R. E. Lee Papers, The Virginia Historical Society, Richmond, Virginia; Wert, General Longstreet, 203, 211.

CHAPTER FIVE
FREDERICKSBURG TO CHANCELLORSVILLE

Wilcox' brigade had been assigned the duty of protecting, throughout the winter, a line of the river for about three miles from Taylor's house near Fredericksburg to Scott's dam up river. The Eighth Alabama occupied about the center of this line, and was encamped on the hill south of and overlooking Bank's Ford. The regiment was in plain sight of the enemy. A battery of two guns, not more than three quarters of a mile off, could have fired a shell into their camp at any moment during the winter; so too the enemy's pickets and those of the Eighth occupying opposite sides of the river, could at any time have killed each other. But real soldiers on both sides knew that mere picket shooting helped neither side and was only murder. The Eighth Alabama was on the hill from late November 1862 to about June 1863, except for the Battle of Chancellorsville April 30th to May 6th, 1863.[1]

During the winter of 1862-1863, Lieutenant Colonel Herbert continually strengthened the regiment. The Eighth Alabama received about three hundred conscripts to fill its ranks from camps in Alabama. When the conscripts arrived, the battle hardened volunteer veterans of the regiment ridiculed them. Herbert attempted to make them feel at home and instill a spirit of patriotism in these new fellows. These men had come to join a regiment which had won as much a reputation as any other in the Army of Northern Virginia.[2]

As of December 20th, 1862, Wilcox' brigade including the Eighth Alabama was still in Anderson's Division under Lieutenant General Longstreet. So were Mahone's brigade, Featherston's brigade, Wright's brigade, and Perry's brigade. Also in the First Corps of the Army of Northern Virginia was McLaws' division which had troops from South Carolina, Georgia, and Mississippi, Hood's division with troops from Alabama, Texas, Georgia and North Carolina; Ransom's division of North Carolinians; and Pickett's division consisting of Virginians and South Carolinians[3]

FREDERICKSBURG

Union General Ambrose Burnside was determined to march to Richmond by way of Fredericksburg, but Lee beat Burnside to Fredericksburg by marching quickly from Culpeper Court House. The Confederates had marched east in a rainstorm. The roads from Culpeper to Fredericksburg had turned into a quagmire. Despite the bad conditions, Longstreet's divisions covered nearly forty five miles in three days. By November 22nd, four of his divisions were posed on the hills west of Fredericksburg. The Confederate lines extended from the river above Fredericksburg to Hamilton's Crossing, a distance of roughly six miles. Longstreet's troops held the front from Taylor's Hill on the left to beyond the valley cut by Deep Run. From there, Jackson's troops manned the woodland west of the Richmond, Fredericksburg and Petersburg Railroad. Beyond Jackson's right flank at Hamilton's Crossing, Stuart's cavalry and horse artillery were on the prowl. Longstreet's position behind the city embraced three hills: Taylor's, Marye's, and Telegraph (or Lee's as it was afterward known). Anderson's division held Taylor's Hill; Pickett's curled around Lee's hill; McLaws brigades covered Marye's Heights; and Hood's command lay across the valley of Deep Run. Ransom's two brigades were in reserve behind Anderson and McLaws'.[4]

The Federals had about a hundred pieces of artillery on Stafford's Heights just across the river. Wilcox' troops witnessed enemy activity in constructing batteries at various points on the heights beyond the river and on its banks. New batteries appeared daily, till at length, extending from a miles above Falmouth, the guns reached Fredericksburg, and on down the river about four miles.[5]

A thick fog blanketed the river on December 11th. By six o'clock in the morning the fog had lifted enough to reveal Burnside's troops constructing pontoon bridges across the Rappahannock River to Fredericksburg. By mid morning Federal guns on the east side of the river opened fire on the city.[6]

On December 12th, the Federal army crossed over the river under the smoke of the burning city and a dense fog. Nothing could be seen and nothing could be heard. General Lee stood on Lee's Hill and watched. Burnside had to fight. He could not stay in his present position without fighting. About ten o'clock in the morning, three heavy Confederate guns opened fire. Lee seemed to know the fog was lifting and the enemy would attack. The firing of the guns was an alert for all the Confederate soldiers. In less than ten minutes, the fog began to whirl upward and revealed an army of nearly one hundred thousand men in battle array.[7]

As the fog lifted, Wilcox moved his brigade to the front under cover of the forest and near the edge of an open field fronting the river and the town. On Wilcox' left was Dr. Taylor's house some one hundred fifty yards away, then extending to the right across the road to the right of Dr. Taylor's house leading to the town and then along the base of the hill. The woods to the right between the Eighth Alabama and where the fighting was going on were so thick that the real battle could not be seen.[8]

General Wilcox claimed that more artillery was being used by the enemy than he could remember from previous battles. He frequently counted as many as fifty shots per minute.[9]

The Federals under General Hancock made three assaults on Marye's Heights. The first two assaults resulted in Federals being slaughtered. The Federal guns were directed toward the Heights to destroy the stone wall. General Lee sent reinforcement and another battery of artillery. The third assault was even more formidable. The last Federal charge was Humphrey's division of Hooker's reserves. They were allowed to come within fifty yards of the Confederate lines. Then the Confederates rose up from behind the stone wall and delivered their withering fire and the batteries on the hill vomited double charges of canister. The first line melted, but the second came steadily forward, over the bodies of their comrades, but still no halt. The Federal lines continued to move forward. It was just pure butchery. Finally, the Federal formation was broken, torn to pieces, nothing left to rally, and the wreck of the Federal division fell back. The guns ceased at the stone wall and then the artillery on both sides became silent. The battle of Fredericksburg was indeed over now—a Confederate victory.[10]

The three Federal assaults on Marye's Heights were the most gallant, heroic and desperate of the whole war. Only Pickett's charge at Gettysburg would come close to surpassing what happened at Marye's Heights. Marye's Heights had born the brunt of the assault and there the slaughter was most deadly. Line after line of brave Federal soldiers had been cut one in one brave attempt after another to assault the position. The spectacle was simply awful. Blue coated dead were lying across each other, and for some two hundred yards the ground was so thickly strewn that it seems as if one could have walked a long way on the dead bodies without touching the ground.[11]

The Eighth Alabama regiment had been on the extreme left of the line. As a result very few were lost as they were not in the main attack. Featherston's and Perry's brigades had very heavy casualties. Wilcox' brigade lost only nine personnel including one from the Eighth Alabama. After the battle, the Eighth remained on the Rappahannock, chiefly engaged in picket duty until April 30, 1863.[12]

On January 19, 1863 Burnsides Federal army began moving toward Fredericksburg in a second attempt to cross the Rappahannock. But the winter rains continued and were Burnsides' worst enemy. His advance bogged down in the mud and slime. Ammunition trains and supply wagons were mired; horses and mules were dropping dead; and, the whole army was dispirited, wet and hungry.[13]

By February 3rd, Union General Joseph Hooker had replaced Burnside as commander of the Army of the Potomac. Hooker began to reorganize the army for the upcoming campaign.[14]

Although the Army of Northern Virginia was near Richmond, it was poorly clothed, fed and shod in spite of General Lee's persistent efforts. Since April 28th, 1862, the meat ration had been reduced from twelve to eight ounces per man per day, plus an extra allowance of flour. This was hardly the appropriate food for a fighting army. On January 23rd, 1863, a further reduction was ordered by the Commissary General to four ounces of meat and one fifth a pound of sugar. Lee grew ever more concerned about the health of his army and feared the soldiers would be unable to endure the hardships of the approaching campaign. It was this great need for supplies that motivated the Confederate War Department

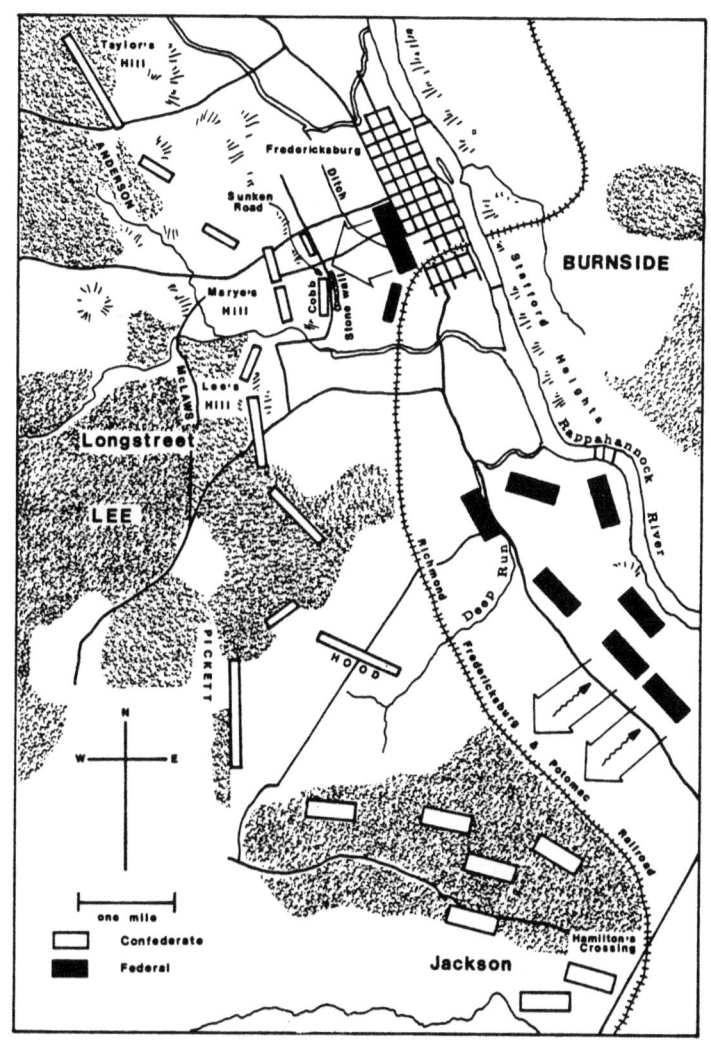

BATTLE OF FREDERICKSBURG, DECEMBER 13, 1862.
Map Taken from The Official Military Atlas of the Civil War

to pressure Lee into sending Longstreet with two divisions for a campaign down toward Suffolk to collect forage and provisions from the counties near the Federal lines.[15]

On February 26th, 1863, Longstreet assumed command of the Confederate Department of Virginia and North Carolina under orders from Richmond to forage for supplies south of the James River in counties near Union lines. By April 1st, Longstreet's command was reorganized by the Confederacy to create the Department of North Carolina under Major General D. H. Hill, the Department of Richmond under Major General Arnold Elzey, and the Department of Southern Virginia under Major General S. G. French. Longstreet still had two divisions with him and was still under orders to forage for supplies for the Army of Northern Virginia. General Longstreet did not rejoin the Army of Northern Virginia until after the Battle of Chancellorsville. Longstreet had left Lee with two of his divisions under McLaws and Anderson when he was ordered to Suffolk.[16]

CHANCELLORSVILLE

Chancellorsville is about a mile within a tract of land known as the Wilderness. The original forest had been cut for charcoal many years before and replaced by a thick and tangled smaller growth. A few clearings were interspersed and a few small creeks drained it. Chancellorsville was merely a brick residence at an important junction of roads. Three roads ran toward Fredericksburg: the Old Turnpike, most directly; the Plank Road, to its right but uniting with the Old Turnpike at Tabernacle Church; and the River Road, by a round about course passing near Banks Ford on the Rappahannock. Above five miles above Fredericksburg via the river, Wilcox' Alabama brigade had been stationed at Banks Ford, an interesting and picturesque crossing since the battle of Fredericksburg.[17]

The Battle of Chancellorsville began on April 30th, 1863 and ended on May 3rd. The battles of Marye's Heights, Salem Church and Chancellorsville, though each a separate conflict and a different times are known collectively as the Battle of Chancellorsville.[18]

On April 29th, 1863, Union General Joseph Hooker began his spring offensive, with units of his Army of the Potomac crossing the Rappahannock River on pontoon bridges south of Fredericksburg, while the bulk of his force moved upstream beyond the Confederate left. Lee became concerned and wired Richmond requesting that Longstreet with his two divisions in Suffolk rejoining the Army of Northern Virginia. Longstreet was to move as soon as possible, but his supply wagons were scattered across the countryside.[19]

On April 30th, Wilcox was still at Banks Ford. By May 1st, Wilcox' Alabama brigade took up a position on the Mine Road to protect the right flank of

Major General Lafayette McLaws. At the same time, Hooker planned a turning movement around the Confederate flank. However, instead of clearing a forbidding stretch of trees and undergrowth in the Wilderness, Federal troops recoiled under Lee's counter attack and fell back into the Wilderness. This negated Hooker's numerical and artillery strength. By the evening of May 1st, Wilcox had been ordered to return to Banks Ford and hold that position at all costs if assailed. If there was no attack, he was to notify Lee, detach a guard to watch the ford, and march via the Plank Road toward the main battle of Chancellorsville. Since his fine performance at Second Manassas, he had been denied a conspicuous part in most operations. He had been sick at Sharpsburg and Colonel Cummings commanded his brigade, and at Fredericksburg he had been on the far left where he was unable to do very much. Late on the afternoon of May 2nd, General Stonewall Jackson rolled up Hooker's right flank. With this movement, Lee had achieved a tactical masterpiece, but it cost his army and the Confederate cause, Stonewall Jackson. Jackson had been accidentally shot by his own troops on the evening of May 2nd. Surgeons amputated his left arm, and he would die on May 10th of pneumonia.[20]

On the morning of May 3rd, Union General John Sedgwick, succeeded in crossing the Rappahannock below Fredericksburg, and attacked General Jubal Early's portion of the Confederate lines, that portion held by Mississippi General William Barksdale, at Marye's Heights. After a stubborn resistance, Barksdale was forced from the Heights. Wilcox received orders to reinforce Barksdale, but arrived too late. The Federals had captured the Heights and five pieces of Confederate artillery. Wilcox ordered his brigade to drop their knapsacks and prepared to drive the enemy from the Heights. His lines were formed and his skirmishers were becoming engaged, when he perceived the enemy moving in force up the Plank Road. It now became necessary to reach the Plank Road before the Federals to secure communications with the man body of the Army of Northern Virginia. He began forming a line of battle every few hundred yards, waited for the enemy to approach, engaged the enemy, and then retired to avoid capture. This maneuver was repeated off and on until the Alabama brigade, in a rapid march and some maneuvering under artillery fire, formed into line of battle at Salem Church on the Plank Road about three o'clock in the afternoon. Salem Church was where Wilcox decided to make his stand to save Lee's Army of Northern Virginia. Salem Church was a small, unpretentious, red brick building which was situated along a ridge covered with thick woods and underbrush. The position selected by Wilcox for the fight was one that commanded an open approach from the east.[21]

The line of battle at Salem Church was the Fourteenth Alabama under Colonel Lucius Pinkard on the left; the Eleventh Alabama under Colonel J. C. C. Sanders extending to the Plank Road; the Tenth Alabama under Colonel William H. Forney to the right of the road; then the Eighth Alabama on the far right and closest to General Joseph B. Kershaw, under Colonel Young L. Royston; and, the

Copyright 1996, Virginia Historical Society, Richmond, Virginia

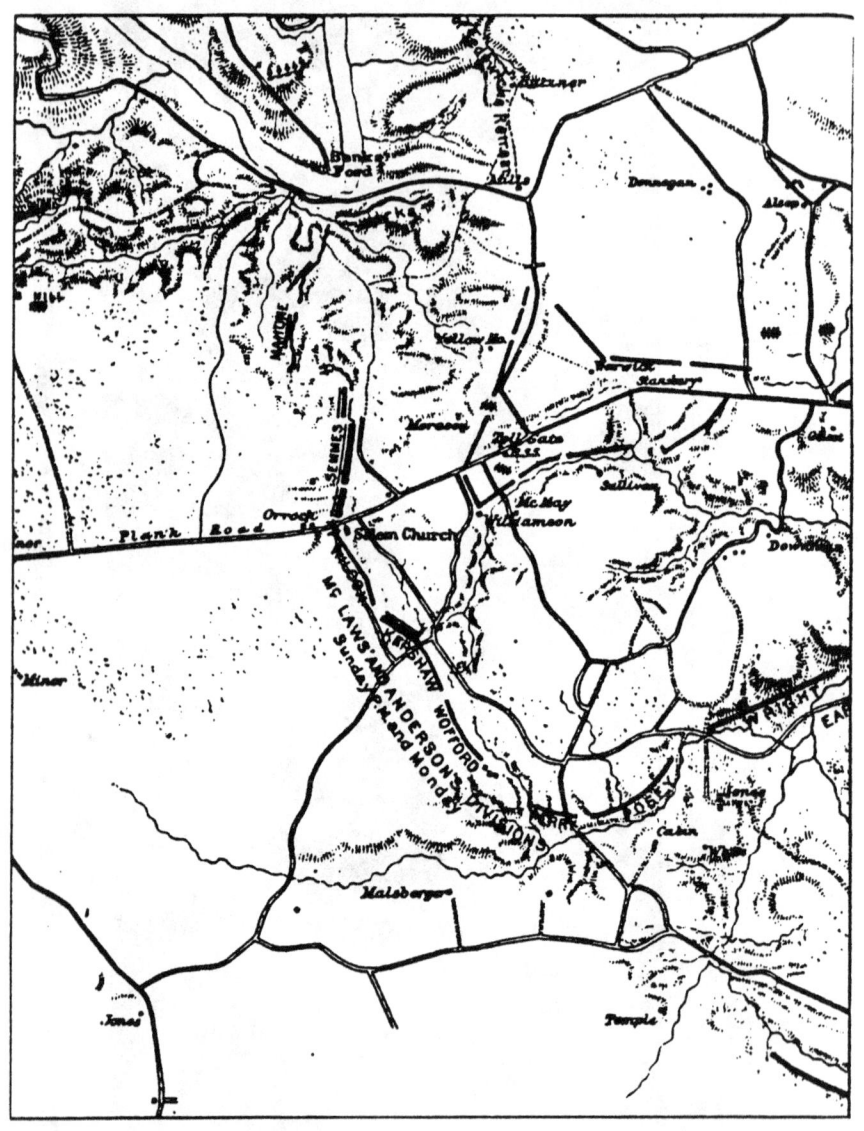

The Battle of Salem Church
Map taken from The Official Military Atlas of the Civil War

Ninth Alabama, which in reserve under Colonel J. H. King. On Wilcox' left was a brigade of General Paul J. Semmes. Kershaw and Semmes had been sent by Lee.[22]

A company from the Eighth Alabama and the Ninth Alabama was placed in the church and a nearby log cabin as sharpshooters. The Alabama boys who occupied the church and the log cabin had a distinct advantage over the Federal troops on the Plank Road for they would catch Federal troops in a crossfire. Wilcox' troops improvised as best they could to form temporary breastworks using anything they could get their hands on. Just a few minutes after the Alabamians had taken up their positions, their skirmishers at the edge of the woods announced the approach of the enemy. After the Federals captured Marye's Heights they gathered up the baggage Wilcox' brigade left behind. The Federals then moved forward rapidly with a force of about twenty five thousand men thinking the Confederates were fleeing. Sedgwick did not know the Confederates had been reinforced.[23]

The Federal troops moved forward in a gallant style, flushed with their success at Marye's Heights and thinking they were assured of victory. The Alabamians were quietly waiting. Not a sound was heard anywhere except the tramp, tramp, tramp of Sedgwick's masses. When the Federal troops came within forty yards of the Alabamians, a wall of flame burst from the Confederate lines. Hundreds of Sedgwick's troops were annihilated. So spirited was the Federal onslaught that the Tenth Alabama gave way on the Plank Road. After the enemy's main line rushed through, a Federal officer was heard to shout, "Show them no quarter!" This command caused the Confederates to redouble their will and increase their fire. It was now apparent that General Sedgwick's whole Sixth Corps was coming up the Plank Road.[24]

As the Federal troops poured through the break in the lines, Colonel Royston of the Eighth Alabama was seriously wounded, and the command devolved to Lieutenant Colonel Hilary A. Herbert. The Ninth Alabama regiment, which had been held in reserve, sprang forward providing needed assistance to repulse Sedgwick's troops. The enemy was now being assaulted simultaneously on its front and left flank by a deadly fire. Sedgwick's troops fled in confusion.[25]

Now the Alabama brigade heard the command "Forward" ring out along its whole line. The Alabamians began advancing rapidly. They followed the enemy nearly a mile with a very deadly fire. The Eighth, Ninth, and Eleventh Alabama regiments charged as the Tenth rallied. The first Federal troops were now pushed back upon the second approaching ranks, which broke and ran into their third line of approaching troops. The Alabamians had advanced nearly a mile when they halted to reform in the presence of the enemy's reserve. The Federals realizing that they were being pursued by only single brigade, reformed, turned and masses artillery upon the pursuing Confederates. The Alabamians held their ground until sundown. At that time, Wilcox deemed it imprudent to push the attack with his small numbers and retired to his original position. The Alabamians had hurled back a force three times their numbers and ended up in charge of the field on that day.[26]

At the battle of Salem Church, the fleeing Federals left a wealth of supplies behind that were eagerly gathered up by Wilcox. The Confederates delighted in casting aside their ragged garments for new underwear and other luxuries proving that a "Yankee's knapsack is the rebel's prize of war."[27]

Wilcox' brigade had captured fifteen hundred prisoners and more field arms and accoutrements than they could use at the time. He made sure his own men got supplies, and then sent two wagon loads of blankets on to Richmond. That night only the rumbling of the ambulances and the cries of the wounded broke the stillness, as the tired Confederates sipped Yankee coffee and waited for the dawn. [28]

After dark, the Federal troops showed no disposition to renew the attack. Sedgwick seemed to have thought Lee was there in force and made no further attempt to advance. He also probably thought General Early had moved to a position which could cause him greater damage on his left flank. Wilcox' brigade slept on the field of Salem Church the night of May 3rd. On the morning of the 4th, the enemy fired occasional shots during the day from a battery about twelve hundred yards away. Three additional brigades arrived on the 4th from Lee, and late that afternoon, a general advance began. General Early was on the right, Anderson with Wilcox' Alabama brigade was in the center, and McLaws held his position on the left. The enemy gave way rapidly. Sedgwick pulled back across the Rappahannock River by pontoon bridge. Wilcox followed the enemy in the direction of Banks Ford with the Eighth and Ninth Alabama regiments until nine thirty in the evening, at which time nearly two hundred thirty six more Federal prisoners had been taken.[29]

General Cadmus Wilcox was "entitled," Lee said, "to especial praise for the judgment and bravery" displayed in impeding Sedgwick on May 3rd, and for the "gallant and successful stand at Salem Church," Wilcox had taken the chance of being destroyed in order to delay the enemy advance. Never before had Wilcox had such an opportunity, nor would he again, but that day he made the most of the situation. He had that day given military history an example far outliving his time, of the manner in which one brigade, courageously led, could change the course of the battle and retrieve a lost day. Lee recommended Wilcox for promotion to Major General. But it was not to be at this time. Wilcox was deeply and bitterly disappointed that he was passed over on May 30th, 1863, especially by officers junior to him in rank.[30]

The Eighth Alabama had lost forty four killed and wounded, including the missing the count came to fifty six. The Roll of Honor of August 10th, 1864 for the Battle of Chancellorsville was published. On it were seven names from the Eighth Alabama. No other Alabamians were recognized on the roll from Wilcox' brigade. Why! Who knows! Sometimes it was just a question of some officer taking the time to process the paperwork.[31]

On the field of deadly conflict, amidst booming cannon and smoke, the battle hardened Eighth Alabama regiment had been stubborn on May 3rd. Wilcox' Alabamians had saved Lee's army from being assaulted in its rear by Sedgwick's Sixth Corps in the Battle of Salem Church. This battle is still regarded as one of the most brilliant engagements of the war. By Wilcox' presence of mind and correct tactical insight, he gained a very important advantage for the Army of Northern Virginia in checking Sedgwick's troops some seven miles from the main battle at Chancellorsville. He had without excessive loss of men or ground frustrated an essential part of the Federal plan to attack Lee's rear.[32]

Longstreet arrived in Richmond on the evening of May 5th for a meeting the following day with the Secretary of War James Seddon. It was May 6th when Longstreet's troops boarded railroad cars for the journey to Petersburg, then on to Richmond. Meanwhile, some fifty miles to the north, the Battle of Chancellorsville was over. Longstreet's failure to reach Lee in time for the battle continued to demonstrate his extreme caution in committing his troops.[33]

On May 30th, 1863, Lee again reorganized the Army of Northern Virginia. This time in to three corps: Lieutenant General James Longstreet commanded the First Corps, Lieutenant General Jubal Early commanded the Second Corps; and, Lieutenant General A. P. Hill commanded the Third Corps. Lee was preparing for the Pennsylvania campaign. On June 4th, 1863, Hill's Corps was the last to leave the Fredericksburg area as Lee began moving north. Wilcox' brigade, still in Anderson's division, was now under General Hill. By June 8th, Lee, with Longstreet and Ewell, arrived in the area of Culpeper Court House, their first stopping pint on their invasion route toward Pennsylvania.[34]

NOTES

[1] Herbert, Grandfather's Talks, 153; Cadmus Wilcox Papers, Library of Congress, Washington, D. C.

[2] Herbert, Short History, 26.

[3] Hoole, Unknown, 5; OR, Series 1, Volume XXI, part 1, 539.

[4] IBID; Longstreet, From Manassas, 267-270, 290-296; Wert, General Longstreet, 214-216; Longstreet, James, "The Battle of Fredericksburg," Battles and Leaders of the Civil War, Vol. 3, New York: Castle Books, 1956, 72, hereinafter cited as Longstreet, Fredericksburg, BLCW.

[5] IBID; Herbert, Short History, 26; Herbert, Grandfathers' Talks, 153; Longstreet, Fredericksburg, BLCW, 73.

[6] Herbert, Grandfather's Talks, 153.

[7] Longstreet, From Manassas, 297; Wert, General Longstreet, 218; Helen Longstreet, Lee and Longstreet, 186-187.

[8] IBID, 298; Wert, General Longstreet, 215, 219.

[9] Herbert, Grandfather's Talks, 153; Cadmus Wilcox Papers, Library of Congress, Washington, D. C.; Wert, General Longstret, 220; Longstreet, Fredericksburg, BLCW, 76.

[10] Hoole, Unknown, 5, 21; Wert, General Longstreet, 221; Helen Longstreet, Lee and Longstreet, 188-190.

[11] Longstreet, From Manassas, 301-309; Wert, General Longstreet, 221; OR, Series 1, Vol. XXI, 556; Hattaway, Herman, Shades of Blue and Gray, Columbia, MO: University of Missouri Press, 1997, 108-110; hereinafter cited as Hattaway, Shades.

[12] Herbert, Short History, 26.

[13] Longstreet, From Manassas, 310-318; Wert, General Longstreet, 222; Hattaway, Shades, 111.

[14] IBID, 323; Hattaway, Shades, 112

[15] IBID, 324-325; Wert, General Longstreet, 231-233.

[16]IBID; Hoole, Unknown, 5; Wert, General Longstreet, 234-235; Freeman, Lee's Dispatches, 84.

[17]Herbert, Grandfather's Talks, 154; Herbert, Short History, 26; Hattaway, Shades, 115; Couch, Darius N., "The Chancellorsville Campaign," Battles and Leaders of the Civil War, Vol. 3, New York: Castle Books, 1956, 159, hereinafter cited as Couch, Chancellorsville, BLCW.

[18]Hoole, Unknown, 21; Couch, Chancellorsville, BLCW, 161.

[19]Longstreet, From Manassas, 322-326; Charles, R. K., "Events in the Battles of Fredericksburg," Confederate Veteran, Vol. XIV, No. 2, Feb 1906, 65-68.

[20]Herbert, Grandfather's Talks, 154-155, 164-166; Longstreet, From Manassas, 332; Sears, Stephen W., Chancellorsville, New York: Houghton Mifflin Company, 1996, 377, hereinafter cited as Sears, Chancellorsville; Hattaway, Shades, 120; McIntosh, David Gregg, "The Campaign of Chancellorsville," Southern Historical Society Papers, Vol. XL, Millwood, New York: Krause Reprint Co., 1977, 44-100.

[21]Hoole, Unknown, 21; Sears, Chancellorsville, 377; Hattaway, Shades, 119; H. A. Herbert to J. O. Bailey April 5, 1918, Herbert Papers.

[22]Herbert, Grandfather's Talks, 166-168; Sears, Chancellorsville, 377; Carmichael, Peter S., Lee's Young Artillerist, William R. J. Pegram, Charlottesville, VA: University of Virginia Press, 1995, 90, hereinafter cited as Carmichael, Pegram.

[23]Herbert, Short History, 27; Sears, Chancellorsville, 378-381; Couch, Chancellorsville, BLCW, 170; H. A. Herbert to J. O. Bailey, April 5, 1918, Herbert Papers.

[24]IBID, 28; Sears, Chancellorsville, 382-383; Stewart, Vaughn, et.al, The McClellan and Allied Families, 1985, 49, hereinafter cited as Stewart, McClellan; H. A. Hebert to J. O. Bailey, April 5, 1918, Herbert Papers.

[25]IBID, 29; Sears, Chancellorsville, 383; H. A. Herbert to J. O. Bailey, April 5, 1918, Herbert Papers.

[26]IBID, 30; Sears, Chancellorsville, 384-385; Papers of Cadmus M. Wilcox, Washington, D. C.: Library of Congress; Clark, George, "Chancellorsville and Salem Church," Confederate Veteran, Vol. XVIII No. 3, March, 1910, 125-126; H.A. Herbert to J. O. Bailey, April 5, 1918, Herbert Papers; OR, Series 1, Vol. XXV, part 1, 811.

[27]IBID; Stewart, McClellan, 52-53.

[28]Hoole, Unknown, 6.

[29]Herbert, Short History, 30-31; OR, Series 1, Vol. XXV, part 1, 849-850.

[30]OR, Series 1, Vol. XXV, part 1, 795-805.

[31]OR, Series 1, Vol. XXV, part 1, 854.

[32]Mosby, John S., Stuart's Cavalry in the Gettysburg Campaign, New York: Moffat, Yard & Co., 1908, xxvii; OR, Series 1, Vol. XXV, part 1, 854-861.

[33]Longstreet, From Manassas, 327.

[34]Herbert, Grandfather's Talks, 169; Longstreet, From Manassas, 334-338.

CHAPTER SIX
GETTYSBURG AND ITS AFTERMATH

At the beginning of the invasion into Pennsylvania, General Lee issued strict orders against foraging and plundering. Necessary food for men and forage for animals was of course taken, but always by officers who, under orders prevented plundering and paid Confederate money or gave receipts specifying the amount and value so the owners could place a claim with the Federal government. General Wilcox directed that none of his men leave camp to forage for fruit or even a pair of chickens that might patriotically wish to give themselves to the Confederate cause. These instructions were prompted both by Lee's own order to respect private property and by Wilcox' believed that if any of his men wandered off, they would fall into the hands of lurking militia.[1]

On the 13th of June, Union General Hooker began moving north, leaving a position in the Federal army he had held for even months. Also General A. P. Hill's Third Corps left Fredericksburg unopposed. From there it moved to the mountains, crossing at Chester Gap, moving north to Front Royal, and on to Shepherdstown, where the Confederates crossed the Potomac River. Passing through Funkstown and Hagerstown in Maryland, the troops reached Chambersburg, Pennsylvania, moving on to Fayetteville where they halted for three days.[2]

On June 27th President Lincoln replaced General Hooker with Major General George G. Meade. Hooker had resigned in a dispute with the administration over the abandonment of Harper's Ferry. On this same date, the main forces of Lee, Longstreet, and Hill arrived at Chambersburg. By June 28th, Lee was planning his drive on Harrisburg when he learned the Federals were north of the Potomac. He changed his plans and ordered Longstreet, Ewell, and Hill to march to Gettysburg and Cashtown.[3]

Around noon on July 1st, Wilcox's Alabama brigade in Richard Anderson's division of A. P. Hill's Third Corps reached the town of Fairfield. Heavy firing could be heard off to the east. The brigade was not only eight miles from Gettysburg. The march was resumed at an even quicker pace. In their approach, the din of battle became more audible, the echoing sounds were well understood. The Federal army was disputing the Confederate advance into their territory and that large number of Confederate troops would never return from Pennsylvania soil. It was late in the evening when the brigade arrived in the Gettysburg vicinity. The men slept on their arms that night. Wilcox' brigade and a battery were placed on picket duty on the night of July 1st about a mile below and south of the Chambersburg Pike, at a mill on Marsh Creek.[4]

DAY TWO

Wilcox' brigade was recalled from picket duty. Leaving its post early on the morning of July 2nd before sunrise, the brigade marched to the front lines passing other regiments and brigades. The Alabama brigade continued marching over small undulating hills and wooded crests nearly in a straight line until it reached its assigned position. Wilcox was ordered to post the right of his brigade against Pitzer's woods three fourths of a mile in front and to the right, with the left connecting with the other brigades of the division. It soon became apparent that Wilcox' brigade had been selected to reconnoiter for the army and open the battle on that day.[5]

On the morning of July 2nd, Anderson's division deployed Wilcox', Perry's, Wright's, Posey's and Mahone's brigades from right to left. Wilcox' brigade moved into position next to General Barksdale of McLaws' division, which was on the extreme left of Longstreet's corps. Thus, McLaws' was to the right of Anderson's troops. About seven o'clock in the morning, Colonel William H. Forney's Tenth Alabama was attacked by the First New York Sharpshooters and the Third Maine. When the firing began the Eighth halted and remained in reserve for the time being. The Tenth Alabama was standing its ground and driving the enemy back.[6]

After four in the afternoon, McLaws' division began moving forward. The Tenth Alabama began moving diagonally across the field to the left. The Eighth Alabama, commanded by Lieutenant Colonel Hilary A. Herbert, was east of the wall that edged the woods and to the left or rear of the Tenth. The Eighth now marched in columns of fours by the left flank east until the regiment crossed over a rise near the Staub farm. Then it broke cover and attracted the fire of a Federal skirmish line. "Never did troops go into action with greater spirit or more determined courage. The ground afforded them but little shelter, and for nearly three quarters of a mile they were compelled to face a storm of shot, shell, and bullets; but there was no faltering." Herbert deployed the Eighth and advanced east toward the Emmitsburg Road. This caused a gap between Herbert's Eighth Alabama and the Tenth Alabama of about two hundred yards.[7]

The Eighth advanced east with Trostle's Lane on its right and the 21st Mississippi two hundred yards further it its right on a converging course. When the Eighth was about one hundred thirty yards west of Trostle's house, at a fence that bordered the west side of Trostle's orchard, it exchanged fire with a line of Federal infantry drawn up on the south side of Trostle's Lane opposite the barn. The Eighth Alabama reformed near Trostle's barn and charged. The enemy retreated toward the left of the regiment and the Eighth changed direction to follow. This action disordered the line of the Eighth. They again halted to reform. Now, about one hundred yards to his front, Herbert saw some guns and prepared to charge them. Suddenly, the guns wheeled about and fired canister into the Eighth Alabama, shots whizzed above the heads of the soldiers, Federal infantry

LIEUTENANT-GENERAL AMBROSE P. HILL, C. S. A. FROM A PHOTOGRAPH.

HILARY ABNER HERBERT
Photo from Scrapbook in Herbert Papers

had regrouped and was now firing on the Confederates. The Eighth, now reformed, charged the Federal position; horses were shot own; and, many of the Federal gunners died at their posts. Amid showers of grape and canister and dense musketry, the first line of the enemy began to give way as the Eighth moved forward. Passing beyond the guns they captured, the Eighth then struck the enemy reserve which also broke, leaving several batteries of artillery and many wounded in Confederate hands. The Eighth Alabama continued to move forward without stopping to reform.[8]

About fifty yards to their front were two dense lines of Federal troops, formed at nearly right angles to each other. Beyond this was another compact line. The Federals here had a couple of pieces of artillery which continued to fire on the Eighth. The Eighth regiment had so far captured all the artillery in their path except these two pieces.[9]

Worn out in the charge, exhausted by the excessive July heat, their ranks thinned by a fearful loss of killed and wounded, the Eighth was unable to follow up on its victory. For twenty minutes the fight continued at short range. The enemy seeing how few were charging and that the Confederates were unsupported by artillery, attempted to attack. One Federal line came within twenty five yards of the Eighth Alabama before it was driven back. The rest of the brigade was off in the distance. Would reinforcements arrive to save the Eighth? "Oh! For a single brigade appearing on the hill behind us, even a shout announcing the arrival of Confederate reinforcements. But no such sound was heard. Federal troops were about to crush the left flank of the Eighth when the order was given to fall back. The enemy did not pursue. But, during the night the Federals removed the cannon they had regained. "It is the opinion of the officers that our regiment never slaughtered more of the enemy than on this day; certainly the men never fought with more spirit."[10]

The rest of Wilcox' brigade stepped along at a lively pace for about a half a mile over open rolling fields cut up by stone and rolling fences, which at first furnished the only serious obstacles to their advance. Wilcox' brigade, apart from the Eighth Alabama, had struck that portion of Union General Humphrey's line between Seely's battery and the Klingle house on its right and the Rogers house on the left. Perry's small brigade swept through a trough between the Rogers house and the Codori barn. After crossing the Emmitsburg Road, Wilcox found that his and Barksdale's lines "impinged." To avoid overlapping, Wilcox veered slightly to the left about four hundred yards to the low ground between Spangler's Woods and the Spangler farm. Then the brigade faced by the right flank to face the enemy and advanced. Wilcox' regiments came under heavy fire from two batteries widely spaced apart on Cemetery Ridge. The hollows between the low ridges afforded some protection from the enemy gunfire which increased in intensity with every step, and gave the men opportunities to stop, catch their breath, and dress the ranks before going on. Most got no further than the bottom of Plum Run Valley or the low ground north of it between the east slope of the

Emmitsburg Road ridge and the west slope of Cemetery Ridge. By the time the small brushy drain at the foot of the enemy's position was reached, the brigades of Barksdale, Wilcox, Perry and Wright were in marked confusion, mixed up indiscriminately, officers apart from their men, men without officers, but all were pushing forward. A deadly stream of fire and canister fell upon the Confederate troops from the Federal batteries on Cemetery Ridge. "The battle rages furiously, but our lines move onward—straight onward. The roaring of artillery, --grape and canister that came plunging through our ranks,--bullets thick as hailstones in winter, men falling on every side as leaves fall when shaken by the rude blasts of autumn, is terrible, yet our men falter not, and we succeed in breaking their first and second lines of battle capturing many prisoners, artillery and colors. At their third and last line we met stern resistance; hell for the third time since the war began we met the famous Irish Brigade and they fought with a bravery worthy of a better cause."[11]

> "Cannon to the right of them,
> Cannon to the left of them,
> Cannon in front of them,
> Volley'd and thunder'd."
>
> The Charge of the Light Brigade by
> Alfred, Lord Tennyson

Wilcox', Perry's and Wright's Confederate brigades pressed up the ridge, outflanking Humphrey's right and left. The air was thick with missiles; the roar of artillery was practically drowning the shrill hiss of the minnies. The weather had been intolerably hot all day and the heat of battle increased its intensity. In spite of every obstacle, the confused and practically disorganized mass of Confederates pushed up the incline. Wilcox' and Wright's brigades advanced with great gallantry, breaking successive lines of the enemy's infantry, and compelling him to abandon much of his artillery. Wilcox was under heavy fire. One courier had been killed and another badly wounded. The General's bridle rein had even been cut by a bullet and his horse was rearing. "Wilcox seeing the valor of his troops moved among them and before them as if courting death by his own daring intrepidity. The fight goes on and the blood flows like water."[12]

Upon striking the third line of the enemy on Cemetery Ridge, couriers were send back to have the two brigades held in reserve by Anderson move forward. Anderson had refused to send the division reserve forward as Wilcox requested. Anderson told him to hold his own, things would change. They did. There was little support from the Third Corps artillery except that given by two or three batteries of Lane's battalion which employed not more than sixteen guns. Wilcox and Wright had advanced too far and became separated from McLaws. General Wright had broken through and seized the guns in his front on the western end of Cemetery Ridge. Wilcox and Wright had driven the enemy from their entrenchments, inflicting very heavy losses. Wilcox' brigade succeeded in capturing eight pieces of artillery, and Wright's about twenty. This stronghold,

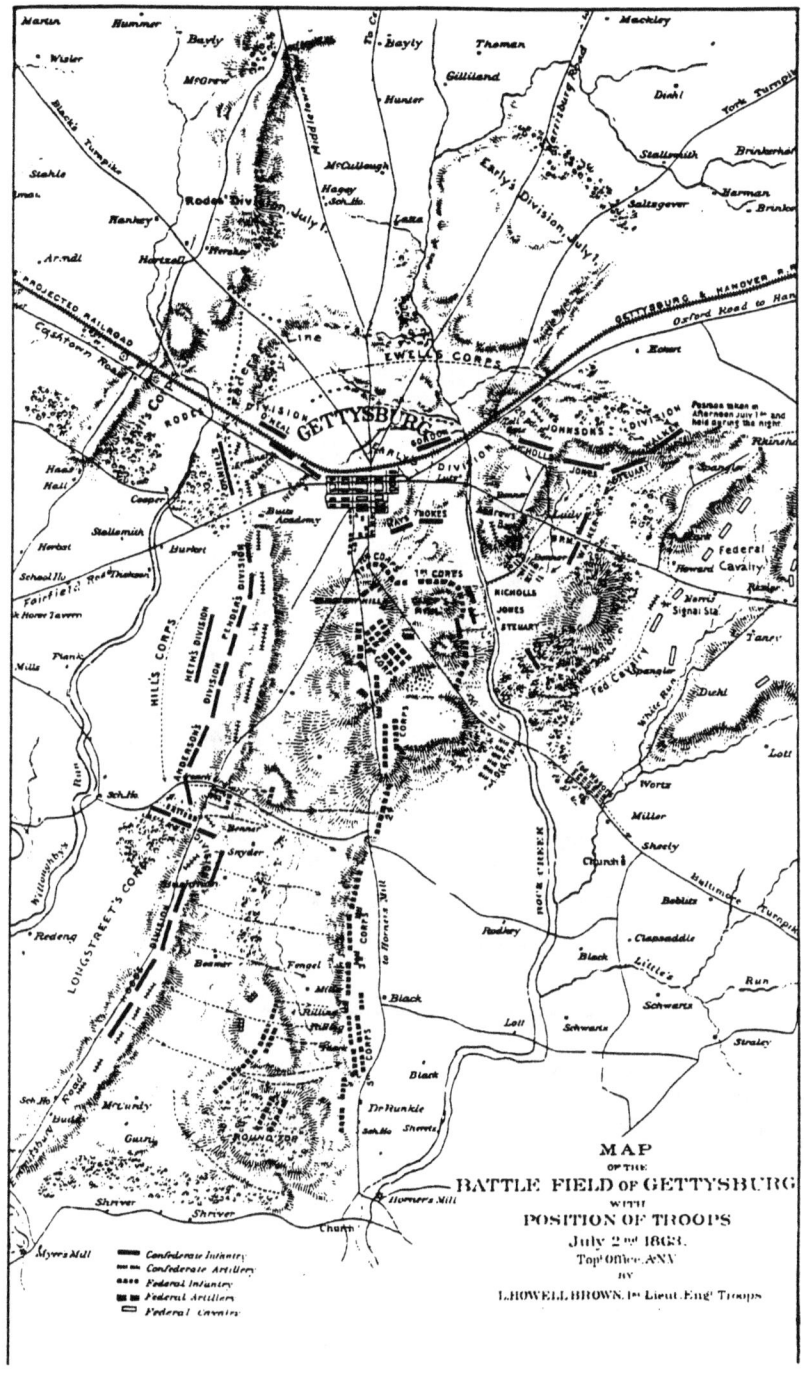

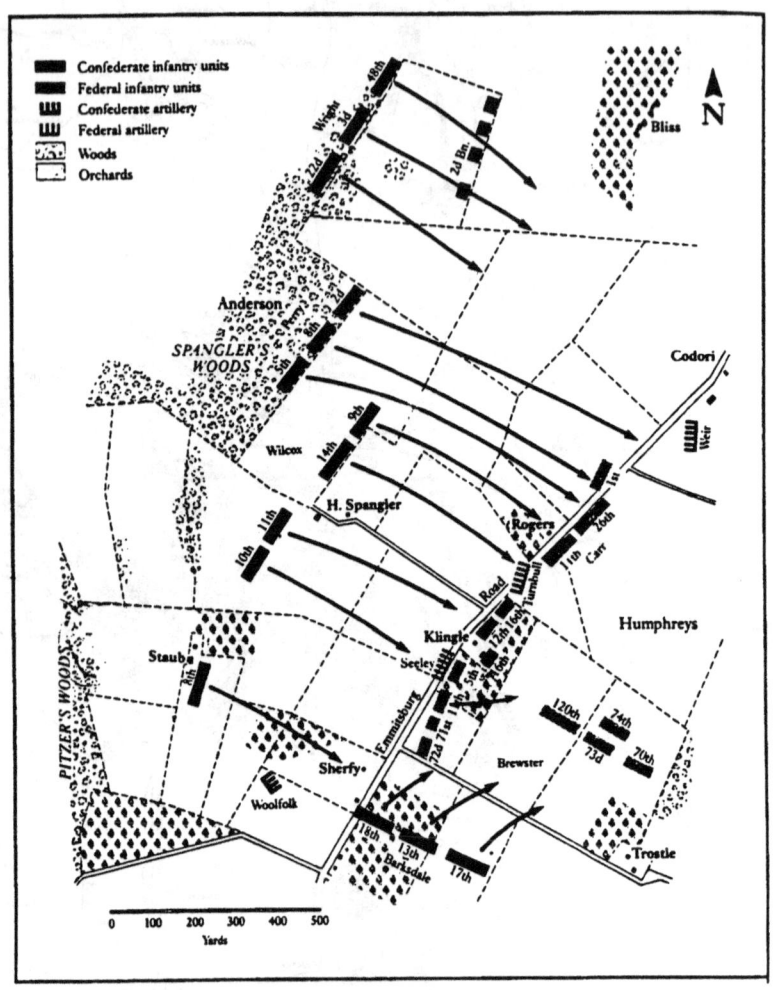

BARKSDALE'S, WILCOX' AND PERRY'S BRIGADES ATTACK HUMPHREYS'S POSITION ALONG THE EMMITSBURG ROAD, JULY 2, 1863. Map Taken from The Official Military Atlas of the Civil War.

with the numerous batteries stationed there, was nearly won, when the Federals then threw in heavy reinforcements descending from the slope in double quick time to support their fleeing comrades and in defense of the batteries. Wilcox and Wright were attacked in the front and on both flanks. The Confederates were compelled to retreat, and were unable to bring off any captured artillery. The Alabama brigade lost about half its strength in casualties and captured on this day.[13]

Anderson could have avoided some of his difficulties if he had stayed closer to the front instead of setting up a command post as he did on the wooded western slope of Seminary Ridge. Here it was easier for couriers carrying messages to find his headquarters, but as the battle line moved forward, communications between him and his brigadiers became precarious and delayed. If he had been nearer to the field, he could personally have coordinated the movements of his brigades and possibly cut down their heavy losses. Wilcox said he came near to preferring charges against Anderson for the lack of support on July 2nd. In their defeat, Anderson's men were outgeneraled, not outfought. Both Wright and Wilcox in explaining their repulse complained of a lack of supporting columns.[14]

DAY THREE

The Alabama brigade had consumed no rations since the morning of July 2nd, and had endured the dangers and fatigues of that day. On July 3rd, the infantry of the Third Corps assigned to support Longstreet's First Corps, in the main attack, were Heth's and Pettigrew's divisions and Wilcox' brigade of Anderson's division.[15]

Wilcox moved his tired troops early on the morning of July 3rd to the far right of Longstreet's lines to support his artillery. General Pickett's troops formed in the rear of Wilcox. Wilcox visited with General Richard Garnett before the attack. Wilcox, whose brigade had charged Cemetery Ridge the day before told Garnett that Cemetery Ridge was twice as strong as Gaines' Mill. Wilcox estimated that he had lost between four and five hundred men in less than twenty minutes "without making the slightest impression."[16]

After hours of waiting, Confederate artillery opened with a fury beyond description. The earth seemed to rise up under the concussion, the air was filled with missiles, and the noise and din were so furious and overwhelming as well as continuous that one had to scream to the solider next to him to be heard at all. The constant roar of nearly four hundred cannon on both sides, with the explosion of shells, and frequently the bursting of a caisson wagon, was terrific beyond description. Men could be seen especially among the artillery, bleeding at both ears from concussion. Wilcox' five regiments lay in position during the cannonading that preceded Pickett's attack. His brigade, which was supporting

Colonel E. Porter Alexander's artillery, suffered the most during the bombardment.[17]

All of the Wilcox' regimental officers had been on foot July 2nd, and it was expected they would be on this terribly hot day. Fearing a return of his sunstroke from the day before, Lieutenant Colonel Herbert of the Eighth Alabama was determined to fight on the 3rd from horseback. Herbert was sure he was riding to his execution.[18]

When the order came to advance, Pickett's troops marched over Wilcox' men, they then changed direction by wheeling to the left; this maneuver placed Wilcox' brigade to the right rear of Pickett's division. Pickett's columns moved forward for at least a half hour before Wilcox, supported by Perry, began moving forward to support Pickett's right. The crumbling of Pettigrew's left precipitated Longstreet's decision to have Pickett order Wilcox to advance. Pickett sent three staff officers seeking Wilcox with orders for him to advance at the rear and beyond Pickett's right. Wilcox had about eleven hundred men.[19]

Every private in the brigade saw the madness of the attempt, but never was their courageous devotion to duty more nobly illustrated by their calm and quiet obedience to orders on that day. The advance was made in a very handsome style, all the troops keeping their lines accurately, and taking the fire of the enemy batteries with great coolness and determination. Wilcox' brigade moved at a double quick step so as to be uncovered by Pickett's men as speedily as possible in order to draw upon his own command a portion of the very heavy and destructive fire then directed at Pickett's troops. The Federals on Cemetery Ridge must have been twenty thousand strong. Their line, almost impregnable by nature, was concave. Wilcox got within a hundred yards of the enemy's lines when Pickett's troops, on Wilcox' left, were repulsed.[20]

Wilcox' line of advance from right to left was the Ninth, Tenth, Eleventh, Eighth, and the Fourteenth regiments. As they advanced, they changed direction, slightly to the left, so as to cover part of the ground over which Pickett's division had moved. Not a single man of the division Wilcox was ordered to support could be seen. But he had his orders to move forward to their support. Now, when all was over, the single Alabama brigade, supported by Perry, was still moving forward, and there was no one there with authority to stop it. It was a wonder that the men did not refuse to budge. Wilcox' brigade proceeded to charge Meade's army. What an absurd and tragic movement! The brigade moved forward rapidly. They advanced several hundred yards beyond the Confederate guns, under sharp fire. Then, they halted and opened fire from some undergrowth and brush along a small ravine. A Federal force was observed bearing down on their left flank. Herbert could hear the grape shot crashing through the bones of his devoted men like "hail stone breaking through glass." The Eighth halted for a moment and it became evident that nothing could save them but a retreat. Wilcox had personally gone to the rear to try to get artillery support, but the artillery had no ammunition

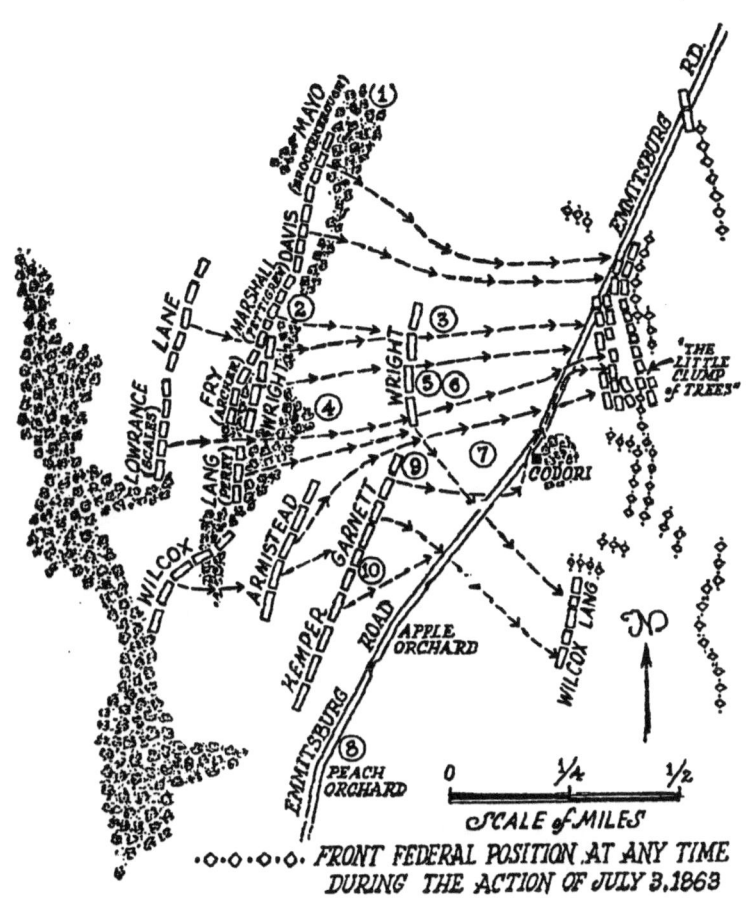

Sketch of the lines of advance of Pickett, Pettigrew and Trimble, at Gettysburg, afternoon of July 3, 1863. The numbers indicate: 1-2, position of the massed artillery of the Third Corps; 3, the advance position of Poague's Artillery Battalion, Third Corps; 4, position of Woolfolk's Battery, First Corps; 5, position of Wright's Brigade which did not participate in the charge but went out to rally the broken assault troops; 6, position of Cabell's Artillery Battalion, First Corps; 7-8, position of the massed artillery of the First Corps from the vicinity of the Codori House to the Peach Orchard; 9-10 intermediate position of Wilcox, directly in front of the position occupied by Garnett before the final stage of the assault.

left. After Perry fell back under heavy Federal artillery fire, Herbert moved by his right flank trying to reach the cover of the Peach Orchard. But Federal artillery found its range and a storm of shot and shell poured into the Alabama boys. Shrapnel shot burst in their front and caused great gaps in their ranks, but the ranks closed and the line moved forward. At last they came within range of the grape and canister, and a hurricane of missiles seemed to burst from a hundred cannon plowing a deadly path through the ranks of the small Alabama line.[21]

Herbert was the senior officer in the brigade at the front of the battle at Colonel William H. Forney had been wounded the day before and left on the field and Wilcox had gone to the rear. After consulting with the other regimental commanders, Herbert ordered the brigade to fall back. Shot and shell shrieked and howled like devils around the Alabamians. As the brigade fell back, the enemy did not pursue. Meeting General Wilcox in the rear, Herbert explained that he took full responsibility for ordering the brigade to fall back. Wilcox indicated he had sent a messenger forward with orders for Herbert to have the brigade fall back, but Herbert never got those orders.[22]

The brigade reformed its lines behind the brow of Seminary Ridge. General Lee was seen riding along our lines in an effort to restore morale. For more than twenty four hours neither army moved. Then on the night of July 4th, Lee ordered a retreat.[23]

On reaching the flooded Potomac, Lee drew up his army in line of battle near Hagerstown where he waited for an assault by the enemy for five days. It never came. The army then began crossing the Potomac to the safety of Virginia.[24]

The losses of the Eighth Alabama at Gettysburg were twenty two killed and one hundred thirty nine wounded of the four hundred twenty in the fight. The Eighth had the greatest losses of all the regiments in the brigade. Of the twenty six officers, seventeen were killed and wounded. Four of Wilcox' colonels had been wounded. In Wilcox' report to Lee, he said "that he did not like to make a disagreeable report, that there was no protection to the great number of batteries on the Emmitsburg Road, but his single brigade." When Wilcox complained about the condition of his brigade, Lee said, "Never mind General; all this has been my fault.: Wilcox' total losses for two days fighting were seven hundred seventy seven and of this number two hundred fifty seven were captured or missing. Most of these casualties occurred on July 2nd. The Roll of Honor published in August 1864 for the battle of Gettysburg had ten soldiers from the Eighth Alabama Regiment, Company K declined to submit any names.[25]

On the return from Pennsylvania, the Eighth had a small skirmish at St. James College near Hagerstown, Maryland, where several were wounded. Wilcox, in a letter to his sister-in-law said, "I sometimes of late think they are not quite so full of ardor as they were the first two years of the war." Hill's Corps moved to cross on the pontoon bridges at Falling Water on the July 13th.

Anderson's division crossed without molestation. On the 15th, the brigade moved to Bunker Hill where it remained until the 21st. Then the march was resumed toward Culpeper Court House. Anderson's division moved two miles to just south of Winchester. On the 22nd Anderson crossed the Shenandoah River and halted for the night at Front Royal. The division spent the night of the 23rd at Flint Hill. By July 25th, the command arrived at Culpeper Court House where it would remain for the winter, except for some minor actions.[26]

Whether Hill had responsibility for preliminary arrangements for those units that were assigned to Longstreet for the assault, or whether Longstreet did was an unanswered question. This had its sharpest point in the tragic and cruel wastage of Wilcox brigade in a futile advance after Pickett had gone forward.

Wilcox was promoted August 9th, 1863 to Major General, and assigned to the division previously commanded by General William D. Pender, still in Hill's Third Corps. Colonel John Caldwell Calhoun Sanders (J.C.C.) was left in charge of Wilcox' old brigade until General Abner Perrin took over. Sanders commanded the Eleventh Alabama Infantry.[27]

Major General Cadmus M. Wilcox, C.S.A.
From a Photograph

NOTES

[1] Cadmus Wilcox Papers, Library of Congress, Washington, D. C.; Herbert, Grandfather's Talks, 169; Wert, General Longstreet, 248; Hassler, William W., A. P. Hill, Lee's Forgotten General, Chapel Hill, NC: University of North Carolina Press, revised, 1962, 150, hereinafter cited as Hassler, A. P. Hill.

[2] Longstreet, From Manassas, 339; Wert, General Longstreet, 249; Hassler, A. P. Hill, 150

[3] Herbert, Grandfather's Talks, 169; Report of Brig. Gen. Cadmus M. Wilcox, July 17, 1863, Cadmus Wilcox Papers, Library of Congress, Washington, D. C.; Wert, General Longstreet, 255; Hattaway, Shades, 142.

[4] Report of Brig. Gen. Cadmus M. Wilcox July, 17, 1863, Cadmus Wilcox Papers, Library of Congress, Washington, D. C; Vaughn, McClellan, 57.

[5] Herbert, Short History, 32; Hassler, A. P. Hill, 160-172.

[6] Herbert, Short History, 31-32; Herbert, Grandfather's Talks, 172; Vaughn, McClellan, 57; Hassler, A. P. Hill, 162.

[7] Hoole, Unknown, 6; Vaughn, McClellan, 58.

[8] Herbert, Short History, 33.

[9] Herbert, Short History, 35; Herbert, Grandfather's Talks, 173; Author Unknown, "University of North Carolina in the Civil War," Southern Historical Society Papers, Millwood, New York: Kraus Reprint Co., 1977, Vol. XXIV, 35.

[10] Herbert, Grandfather's Talks, 174-175; Herbert, Short History, 40.

[11] Report of Brig. Gen. Cadmus M. Wilcox, July 17, 1863, Cadmus Wilcox Papers, Library of Congress, Washington, D. C.; Wilcox, General C. M., "General C. M. Wilcox on the Battle of Gettysburg," Southern Historical Society Papers, Millwood, New York: Krause Reprints, 1977, Vol. VI, 99, hereinafter cites as Wilcox, Southern Historical Society; Clark, George, "Wilcox's Alabama Brigade at Gettysburg," Confederate Veteran, Vol. XVII, No. 5, May, 1909, 229-230; Patterson, Yankee Rebel, 116

[12] Hoole, Unknown, 7; Longstreet, From Manassas, 367; Patterson, Yankee Rebel, 117

[13] Wilcox, Southern Historical Society, 99; Herbert, Short History, 33; Longstreet, James, "Lee's Right Wing at Gettysburg," Battles and Leaders of the Civil War, Vol. 3, New York: Castle Books, 1956, 350.

[14] Herbert, Short History, 44; Herbert, Grandfather's Talks, 177; Codington, Edwin B., The Gettysburg Campaign, A Study in Command, New York: Charles Scribner's Sons, 1968, 352, hereinafter cited as Codington, Gettysburg.

[15] Herbert, Short History, 41; Report of Brig. Gen. Cadmus M. Wilcox, July 17, 1863, Cadmus Wilcox Papers, Library of Congress, Washington, D. C.

[16] Herbert, Grandfather's Talks, 177-178; Purifoy, John, "Assault of Anderson's Division, July 2, 1863," Confederate Veteran, Vol. XXXI, No. 10, Oct. 1923, 377-378.

[17] Report of Brig. Gen. Cadmus M. Wilcox, July 17, 1863, Cadmus Wilcox Papers, Library of Congress, Washington, D. C.; Herbert, Grandfather's Talks, 179-180; Alexander, E. Porter, "The Great Charge and Artillery Fighting at Gettysburg," Battles and Leaders of the Civil War, Vol. 3, New York: Castle Books, 1956, 363-367, hereinafter cited as Alexander, The Great Charge.

[18] Herbert, Grandfather's Talks, 178; Wilcox, Cadmus M., "General C. M. Wilcox on the Battle of Gettysburg," Southern Historical Society Papers, Millwood, New York: Kraus Reprint Co., 1977, Volume IV, 114.

[19] Herbert, Short History, 41; Alexander, The Great Charge, 366; Coddington, Gettysburg, 505.

[20] Herbert, Grandfather's Talks, 181; Coddington, Gettysburg, 519-520; OR, Series 1, Vol. XXVII, part 2, 633.

[21] IBID, 180-182; Hassler, A. P. Hill, 164-165; Hunt, Henry J., "The Third Day at Gettysburg," Battles and Leaders of the Civil War, Vol. 3, New York: Castle Books, 1956, 370, 375; Freeman, Lee's Dispatches, 117.

[22] IBID, 179-180; Talcott, T. M. R., "The Third Day at Gettysburg," Southern Historical Society Papers, Millwood, New York: Kraus Reprint Co., 1977, Vol. XXV, 77-90.

[23] IBID, 181-184.

[24] IBID, 185; Phillips, B. F., "Wilcox' Alabamians in Virginia," Confederate Veteran, Vol. XV, No. 11, Nov., 1907, 490.

[25] Herbert, Short History, p. 42-43; Report of Brig. Gen. Cadmus M. Wilcox, July 17, 1863, Cadmus Wilcox Papers, Library of Congress, Washington, D. C.; OR, Series 1, Vol. XI, part 2, 994.

[26] Report of Brig. Gen. Cadmus M. Wilcox, July 17, 1863, Cadmus Wilcox Papers, Library of Congress, Washington, D. C.; Longstreet, From Manassas, 428; Wilcox, Cadmus M., "General C. M. Wilcox on the Battle of Gettysburg," Southern Historical Society Papers, Millwood, New York: Kraus Reprint Co., 1977, Vol. VII, 208-287.

[27] Freeman, Lee's Dispatches, 116

CHAPTER SEVEN
THE WINTER OF UNCERTAINTY
AND A SPRING OF STRUGGLE

The organization of the Army of Northern Virginia as of July 31, 1863, still had the Eighth Alabama being led by Colonel Young L. Royston, even though he was again on convalescent leave. Lieutenant Colonel Hilary A. Herbert had been in command during the battle of Gettysburg.[1]

On the 8th of August 1863, General Lee offered to resign for his failure at Gettysburg. A few days later, President Davis rejected his resignation.[2]

By the end of August, 1863, Colonel J. C. C. Sanders was in command Wilcox' old brigade of Anderson's division; the other brigades included Mahone's, Wright's, Perry's and Posey's. Returns for the Army of Northern Virginia for August 1863 at Orange Court House show Anderson's division having twelve thousand seven hundred seventy five and the Third Corps with a total of thirty two thousand three hundred thirty three. Returns from the Army of Northern Virginia by September 30th, 1863 now show General Richard Anderson with twelve thousand six hundred fifty eight, and by October 20th he had only seven thousand two hundred seventy one. The officers finally got around to actually counting noses after Gettysburg.[3]

BRISTOW VIRGINIA CAMPAIGN

The Army of the Potomac was on the move by September 13th, 1863 toward Culpeper Court House. Lee had to withdraw. Lee had only Ewell's Second Corps and Hill's Third Corps as Longstreet had been sent to Chattanooga to aid General Braxton Bragg. The Bristow Virginia Campaign began late on October 9th with minor skirmishing, but by October 10th there was extensive skirmishing which broke out in the Rapidan River area of Virginia as the Federals probed to find Lee. On October 11th, heavy skirmishing continued between the Rapidan and Rappahannock Rivers as Lee's army gained momentum in its newest move northward. By October 13th, the Army of Northern Virginia, with Hill's Corps in the lead, moved toward Manassas and Washington.[4]

Hill's Corps struck the retreating rear units of Meade's Army of the Potomac near Bristow, Virginia on October 14th. Hill's Corps rushed forward in an attempt to seize a railroad embankment which was supposed to be unoccupied, and was badly surprised by a full compliment of Federal troops from behind the embankment. The Confederates were compelled to retreat with heavy losses. Before reinforcements could come up, the last of Meade's columns had disappeared.[5]

Brigadier General
John C. C. Sanders
Alabama Brigade
Courtesy Alabama Department of Archives and History

General Anderson had been directed to take his division down the Warrenton and Alexandria Turnpike toward Buckland, and, if possible, to strike the enemy there. Anderson had been sent to look out for the threatened right and no support would be immediately available. Wilcox' division had not yet arrived. The Alabama brigade under Colonel Sanders crossed the river twelve miles above Orange Court House, but Meade had already retreated. Sanders' brigade had arrived just after the fight, but it was put into a line of battle in a pine thicket where it remained until dark without being ordered forward. The artillery covering the rear of Meade's army, having seen the Alabamians go into the thicket, shelled it vigorously for sometime, doing very little damage. The Eighth Alabama regiment, however, had the greatest losses even though the numbers were few. The Eighth lost one killed and six wounded. In this action, the Alabama brigade had a total loss of one enlisted man killed, one officer wounded and eight enlisted men wounded.[6]

Hill's force had not been sufficient to defeat the strongly posted Federals. The Confederates had also failed to strike the center of the long Federal column as it retreated. The rear guard action gave Meade time to repair his lines near Centreville. While there was skirmishing, there was no Third Battle of Manassas. Lee had no chance to disrupt the Federal army, although he succeeded in forcing it back near the Potomac. This was a campaign of maneuver with several lost opportunities on both sides.[7]

MINE RUN OPERATIONS

In November, 1863, General Meade, in an attempt to strike a major blow against the Army of Northern Virginia, crossed the Rapidan River below General Lee's right at Rappahannock Station and Kelly's Ford with severe engagements at both places on November 7th. Lee began withdrawing to a line along the Rapidan River. By November 26th, the Army of the Potomac had completed its crossing and was attempting to turn Lee's right flank. On November 27th, south of the Rapidan, Lee moved quickly eastward to block Meade's new offensive. Meade headed toward the small valley of Mine Run.[8]

Anderson's division was on the Old Turnpike on November 28th. The troops rapidly dug rifle and gun pits for on that day there was considerable skirmishing at Mine Run. Meade found Lee's lines so strong and so improved that he withdrew without much of a battle. Lee had halted the Federal offensive before it really got started. Colonel J. C. C. Sanders commanded Wilcox' old brigade and annotated his report of actions at Mine Run. He noted that he Eighth Alabama had lost one man wounded at Mine Run.[9]

Anderson's and Wilcox' divisions were withdrawn from the trenches at three o'clock in the morning on December 2nd and moved toward the right side of the Confederate lines in preparation for an attack. As soon as it was daylight, it was discovered that the enemy's pickets along the entire Third Corps line had left.

General Stuart found the enemy's whole force had recrossed the Rapidan River. Lee's Army of Northern Virginia was safe for now and it returned to its former lines along the Rapidan River.[10]

WINTER IN VIRGINIA

Following some sporadic skirmishing and marching that fall, the Alabamians settled into comfortable winter quarters that December near Orange Court House. Their log huts were warmed by fireplaces. Lee, during the winter of 1863-1864, occupied a line along and south of the Rapidan River. The Alabama brigade had pickets posted along the Rapidan River. Some of them were across the river opposite the crossing of the Orange and Alexandria Railroad.[11]

The last year of the Confederacy opened with an air of gloom which gave little prospect of ultimate success. The area west of the Mississippi had been lost; the enemy was concentrating of Chattanooga; and, Grant was concentrating heavy masses of Federal troops on the Rapidan to begin his movement of "on to Richmond." The Confederate states already gave indications of exhaustion both as to men and materiel. The Confederate government could have done better if its transportation had been better, but Confederate railroads were preoccupied with carrying troops, rails and rolling stock were wearing out all the time, and there was no sufficient means of replacing them. Every thinking soldier in Lee's army foresaw readily the serious and desperate work ahead of them. But, there was no lack of enthusiasm in the army, and every man acted as if the result rested upon him.

On January 29th, 1864, the Eighth Alabama regiment re-enlisted unconditionally for the war. The re-enlistment was entirely conducted by the non-commissioned officers and privates of the regiment. General Orders No. 14 dated February 3, 1864 announced with gratification the re-enlistments of several regiments of the Army of Northern Virginia including the Eleventh and the Eighth Alabama regiments. Lee hoped this patriotic movement would be followed by every brigade in the Army, until the soldiers of the South determined never to yield.[12]

During the month of January, rations had been even scantier than at any previous period. Full rations of meat consisted of three-fourths of a pound of bacon or one and a quarter pound of beef per one hundred men. The Alabamians were always most content when they got bacon. Sometimes they had half and now and then only a third of a ration. So it was with their hardtack or flour or meal, which ever they got. The usual ration of bacon, a quarter pound was frequently cut down to two ounces and often no meat was issued at all. The discipline of the regiment was good and the men were in excellent health and spirits. They felt that they had never tarnished their honor on any battlefield.[13]

Abner Monroe Perrin

Abner Monroe Perrin of South Carolina
Brigadier General, Commanding
Alabama Brigade formerly commanded by Cadmus M. Wilcox
from a photograph

When Wilcox was promoted to a divisional command in August 1863, Colonel J. C. C. Sanders had been left in charge of the brigade until early in 1864 when Brigadier General Abner Perrin took over. John Caldwell Calhoun Sanders started out as a captain of a company in the Eleventh Alabama and was wounded at Frazier's Farm. He returned to take command of the Eleventh Alabama on August 11th, 1862. At the battle of Sharpsburg, he was wounded in the face by pebbles thrown up by a cannon ball. On his return to Virginia, he was commissioned a Colonel. At Fredericksburg, he was under fire again. During the battle of Chancellorsville, he was conspicuous for his gallantry at Salem Church. At Gettysburg, he was wounded in the knee. During the winter of 1863-1864 he served as President of the Division's Court Martial Board.[14]

Abner Perrin had been promoted to Brigadier General in September 1863. He temporarily commanded a brigade of South Carolinians in Pender's division of Hill's Corps. Then, he was transferred to the Alabama brigade of Anderson's division in early May 1864. He passed through the fiery ordeal of the Wilderness, but at Spotsylvania Court House, he was killed on May 12th 1864. He was leading his brigade through a terribly destructive fire, and fell dead from his horse. The veteran Alabamians had chafed under his leadership and even sought his removal through a petition to General Lee. With his death, there was no further need to pursue his official removal.[15]

On June 7th, 1864, Sanders was promoted to Brigadier General for his gallantry at Spotsylvania at the "Mule Shoe" salient. He was assigned to command the Alabama brigade which included the Eighth, Ninth, Tenth, Eleventh, and Fourteenth Alabama regiments. Lee's army was undergoing another painful reorganization. The desperate battles that spring had taken a dreadful toll, especially on general officers[16]

WILDERNESS

On April 8, 1864 Near Orange Court House Virginia, Colonel Herbert transmitted to the governor of Alabama, Governor Thos. H. Watts, the tattered old battle flag of the Eighth Alabama Regiment. As reported in the Montgomery Weekly Advertiser of April 20, 1864, Herbert indicated that four of Alabama's noblest sons had died with it in their hands and two hundred twenty eight have under it in battle, sealed with their life's blood their devotion to their country's cause. He noted that the regiment was the first from Alabama that volunteered "for three years or the war," and that on January 29th last, it re-enlisted, unconditionally "for the war." He continued with the "proud feeling, that Alabama's name and fame, in our hands, has not been tarnished, in a single combat." Governor Watts' response was dated April 12, 1864 to Lt. Col. H. A. Herbert Commanding the Eighth Alabama Volunteers. Watts indicated he accepted the tattered and torn flag as the emblem of a noble cause and the momento of deathless deeds by Alabama's dauntless sons. The sadness occasioned by the knowledge that so many brave Alabamians have lost their life blood in defense of its honored folds, is turned into admiration for the heroism and its immortal defenders....Alabama "rejoices in the truth, that none have shown more devotion to the calls of freedom and none are entitled to more grateful remembrances and praises, than those of the Eighth Alabama; none will receive a heartier welcome home, when peace shall crown their efforts, in behalf of Liberty and Independence."[16A]

The Eighth Alabama was sent to the front on the afternoon of April 30th, 1864 to reconnoiter. Colonel Herbert found himself with his regiment occupying a hill overlooking the Rapidan just below the railroad bridge. On the afternoon of May 1st, the Eighth was relieved from duty at the front.[17]

By early May 1864, Longstreet had rejoined the Army of Northern Virginia from Tennessee and still commanded the First Corps. He would play a major role in the Wilderness Campaign.[18]

At midnight on May 3rd, the Army of the Potomac began moving across the Rapidan, the Fifth and Sixth Corps at Germanna Ford, the Second Corps at Ely's Ford. General Grant had no fixed plan of campaign beyond the general idea of avoiding the strong defensive line occupied by General Lee behind Mine Run, and find a way to draw him out into open battle.[19]

The Wilderness was a forest of land about fifteen miles square, lying between and equidistant from Orange Court House and Fredericksburg. There were small farms and two roads—the Orange Plank Road and the Old Turnpike. On May 4th, it was discovered that the Army of the Potomac was moving across the Rapidan to march around Lee's right flank heading toward Richmond. As soon as Grant crossed the river, Lee attacked in the Wilderness, where Grant's immense superiority and artillery could not help him. It was to be an infantry fight. Hill advanced with Heth's and Wilcox' divisions along the Orange Plank Road.[20]

On May 5th, Hill continued pushing the divisions along the Orange Plank Road until they reached the Brock Road Crossing where they encountered Union General Gettys' division of the Sixth Corps. Heth's and Wilcox' men, under Lee's eye, maintained themselves well against a heavy enemy assault while greatly outnumbered. On May 6th, Generals Sedgwick and Warren drove westward in the early morning along the Orange Plank Road. Major General Hancock's Second Corps attacked at five o'clock in the morning. Most of Wilcox' men were slightly in advance of Heth's front, and they received the shock of the Federal advance. Scattered as they were, they were soon driven back. They did not run fast or far, but they ran. Heth's troops did not wait for the onslaught. They made for the rear at once to form their lines. The break of the two veteran divisions was a disgrace. So heavy had been the attacks on Heth and Wilcox that other brigades had to he shifted to help out. At one time, the only troops not engaged in the wild fighting

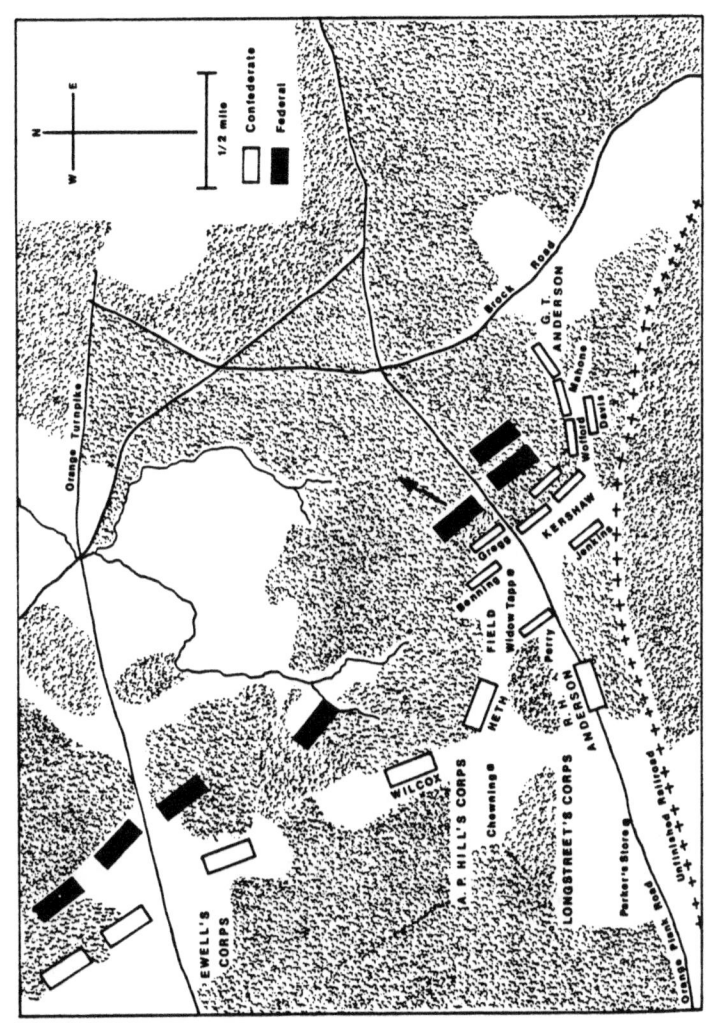

BATTLE OF THE WILDERNESS, MAY 6, 1864
Map Taken from The Official Military Atlas of the Civil War

were one hundred twenty five Alabamians who were acting as a guard over prisoners. Even this detachment had to be called to repulse the assault.[21]

Wilcox hurried to Lee, then down the Plank Road to find Longstreet. The immediate question was whether anything should be done to untangle the front of Heth and Wilcox. Wilcox believed that a skirmish line should be left where the fighting of the day had ended and a new line should be formed in the rear. Lee informed Wilcox that Anderson and Longstreet would arrive soon and the two divisions that had been so actively engaged would be relieved before daybreak. Wilcox had to content himself with this information from General Lee.[22]

By the evening of May 6th, Heth's and Wilcox' men were thoroughly worn out. Their lines were ragged and irregular, with wide intervals, and in some places fronting in different directions. Heth and Wilcox were to have their men to get much sleep as they could hope to get in the presence of the enemy. In the expectation that they would be relieved during the might, no effort was made to strengthen them to meet the storm that was brewing.

Anderson's division of Hill's Corps had been left on the Rapidan Heights with ordes to follow on May 5th. On the afternoon of May 5th, the division took up its line of march toward the scene of action, and marched until late at night, when it bivouacked. All afternoon, the Eighth Alabama marched toward the battle. They knew what was before them but no sound of the battle was reached by the time darkness set in. Anderson's division rested at Verdiersville that night. In front of them was Grant's army, and news of the day's fighting began to filter back to upcoming troops. And now, no doubt, every soldier as he stretched himself upon the ground that night was thinking of loved ones at home, wondering whether he would ever see them again.[23]

Anderson's division was called to the front in the morning of May 6th. He arrived and reported to Longstreet about eight o'clock in the morning. The command was roused and formed and took up its line of march for the scene of the action. The Alabama Brigade (now called Wilcox' old brigade) was still part of Anderson's division with Brigadier General Perrin in command.[24]

Marching rapidly Anderson's division came up. The Alabamians could hear the din of battle, loud and sustained; the pace toward the battle three miles away quickened. The brigade soon reached the immediate vicinity of the conflict and took up a position on the left of the Texas brigade. Heth's and Wilcox divisions were being driven back. The musket fire was dense and hundreds of wounded were passing back through their lines. Soon the order was given to advance, and after moving forward three hundred yards through the dense undergrowth, the brigade line rested and awaited the attack. The woods were very thick as they were about to cross a little swampy piece of lowland and all the regimental officers dismounted. The regiment marched another hundred yards or so and then halted throwing out skirmishers in front, who within a few moments became engaged with the enemy's skirmishers.[25]

The enemy was advancing in heavy lines behind their skirmishers, and the Alabama brigade began to pull back. The Eighth was lying flat on the ground; the enemy was coming up on them through the thick woods. The enemy came in full force, and the firing was intense; but no cannon were used on either side. After continuous infantry fire, a charge was ordered. Yelling and firing, the Confederates slammed into Federal units. Some Federal units were hit by fire on three sides. The enemy broke, and the Alabama brigade began to pursue through the bushes and timber.[26]

Lieutenant Colonel Herbert had been struck in the right arm, shattering the bone. The sound could be heard all up and down the line. Herbert would be out for the remainder of the war recovering from his wounds. The command then passed to Captain Nall. Captain Nall had scarcely taken command in the center of the regiment, when he was shot down. Captain Heard next assumed command and in the charge he was wounded.[27]

For most of the morning, the firing rolled on with no great advantage to either side. Longstreet's men were making ready for the shock. Toward noon, part of Longstreet's Corps struck the Federal line on its flank and rear. Hancock's men reeled back and more Confederates drove in, but Longstreet was severely wounded.[28]

Four commanding officers of the Eighth Alabama had been wounded in that one fight. Yet the losses of the regiment were not heavy. They had obeyed ordered and fought from their position on the ground until they had broken the enemy's line, and then they swept forward and easily drove the enemy a considerable distance.[29]

As soon as Mahone's division arrived, Perrin's and Harris' brigades were sent to General Ewell's assistance and went into action under his command. All day long the battle went on without cessation, and the brigade's lines continued to advance through the brush. Frequently one could not see twenty yards ahead and more than once the brigade was fired upon from the rear and was forced to about face to meet the enemy.[30]

The Alabama brigade's five regiments were sent to join General Law's brigade of Ewell's Second Corps under attack by Federal forces from General Ambrose Burnside's Ninth Corps. Burnside threw twelve regiments of nearly green recruits against the Confederate line, only to have them hurled back. Attack and counter attack raged back and forth, until the Federals could stand it no longer and withdrew. On the next morning about ten o'clock the enemy advanced, but were easily and quickly repulsed, as the movement was evidently made to discover Confederate positions. The Alabamians remained all day on May 7th, in their positions until after dark when they moved about a mile to the right.[31]

Major General Richard H. Anderson now took command of Longstreet's Corps after Longstreet had been critically wounded. He marched by night to Spotsylvania Court House where Grant's army was headed. Spotsylvania Court House was important only because roads through it were to Chancellorsville, Wilderness Tavern, and Fredericksburg.[32]

Two bloodied foes stumbled toward Spotsylvania Court House. On May 8th, Anderson's Corps reached Spotsylvania Court House first. Fighting revealed the new line. The Federals of Sedgwick and Warren assaulted entrenched Confederates. The attack failed and during the night both sides established new lines. Major General Jubal Early took temporary command of Hill's Corps due to Hill's illness. On May 8th a detachment, from the Eighth Alabama, was sent forward to ascertain the whereabouts of the enemy. Failing to discover enemy lines, the march was resumed toward Spotsylvania Court House, arriving on May 9th, and taking up a position on the right.[33]

Lee was now firmly entrenched in the Wilderness in an irregular position somewhat resembling a horseshoe. On May 10th, the Federals hit Anderson's Corps northwest of Spotsylvania Court House. Assaulting the entrenched Confederates twice, the Federals were thrown back. Late in the afternoon, the Alabama brigade was ordered to the extreme left as the enemy's movement indicated an attack on the brigade's left flank.[34]

SPOTSYLVANIA COURT HOUSE

On May 11th, the Alabama brigade occupied the extreme left, skirmishing heavily, but making no active movement until May 12th. At dawn, a massed Federal attack caught the Confederates off guard at "the Mule Shoe salient and swept more than two thousand prisoners and twenty guns before a counter attack could be organized."[35]

Lee ordered General William Mahone now temporarily in charge of Anderson's old division, to move reinforcements to the salient. Perrin's Alabama brigade followed Mississippi troops into the fray. Perrin's troops were assigned the brutal job of going all the way to the apex or toe of the "shoe." The Alabamians stumbled in the misting rain through the cluttered woods until they came within striking distance of the outer parapet, where Federal soldiers crouched on the other side. Finally, an order came directing the brigade to move rapidly to the scene of the action. With hurried march, a small stream was forded, and the brigade soon reached the scene. The field was covered with fugitives, and it looked as if some dreadful catastrophe had happened or was about to happen to the army. The brigade and others were formed into line promptly, and moved forward. Perrin ordered a charge and was shot dead in his saddle. Advancing quickly, the Federals were soon encountered and the rattle of musketry began. The lines of the Federal troops were broken, but in the rush through the woods, the brigade's lines became so mixed that they entered the breastworks of General Edward Johnston's troops, now held by Federal troops, without regard for organization. It was every man for himself. To add to the confusion, the rain poured down in torrents and continued its downpour all day making it tough to keep gun powder dry. The regiments were quickly swallowed up in the sickening debris of the Bloody Angle's carnage. Desperate men confronted each other on opposite sides of the Confederate works at the salient's apex, hurling bayoneted rifles over the top and firing through chinks in the wall.[36]

Upon reaching the breastworks, the Eighth Alabama found itself in a bad predicament. Those works had been constructed without much regard for the essentials of military engineering or proper protection, and that portion occupied by the Eighth was subjected to a direct cross fire from right to left. The fire from the enemy never ceased during the day. The cannon's roar was continuous, and many brave Alabamians were killed. Their ammunition gave our several times. Several men were sent back for fresh supplies and some were killed. No man faltered, but kept steadily at his post, with a resolve to hold that line at all cost.[37]

This was probably the most depressing day of the war to the small command of the Eighth Alabama huddled up in small pens, with the enemy furiously assaulting at intervals during the entire day and with no hope of relief. The contest went on until the darkness brought a cessation to a drenched and famished crowd, absolutely worn out. With complete exhaustion, men fell asleep in the rain drenched pits. The night was extremely dark, but the watch was kept up from hour to hour. At midnight, Lee finally allowed his half dead survivors to fall back to a new line that had been hastily constructed at the base of the salient. Orders came about one o'clock in the morning. The men were directed to creep out quietly in small squads of two or three and take a position beyond the new line, which had been prepared about a quarter mile to the rear. Never before had such intense fighting been witnessed according to Brigadier General Samuel McGowan, whose brigade followed Perrin's into action. He reported that the trenches ran with blood and had to be cleared of dead bodies more than once. The next morning the brigade was retired to a mile in the rear where it was notified that a rest of three days was granted unless some emergency occurred.[38]

COLD HARBOR

By June 1st, near the 1862 Seven Days battlefields, the Confederates again arrived before Grant's forces. During the night both sides entrenched. Grant planned to attack Lee early in the morning, but troop movements, ammunition problems, and fatigue necessitated postponement until late afternoon on June 2nd. The attack was actually delayed until June 3rd. Privates fashioned crude name tags for they knew the impending battle would be a desperate one. Lee had received reinforcements from the Shenandoah and southern Virginia. He made adjustments to his well entrenched lines. The stage was now set for one of the bloodiest battles in history.[39]

On June 3rd a sudden crash of cheers and drumming of musket fire signaled the attack of Grant, Meade and the Army of the Potomac. With Richmond scarcely beyond the horizon, Grant hoped a surprise shift in tactics would split and possibly crush Lee's army. The Army of Northern Virginia was lined up behind strong fortifications from the Chickahominy on the south to the swamps along the Totopotomoy River on the north. Disposition of units was mixed, but basically Hill's Corps including the Eighth Alabama was on the right and Early's Corps was on the left with Anderson in the Center.[40]

At four thirty in the morning the blow came. For the Confederates, holding was crucial for a serious breakthrough by Grant might end the war. They were willing to hold till the last man. Immediately the cost was great. General Perrin's brigade (now commanded by Sanders) barely had time to complete its formation before the expected attack came. The firing was heavy for a short time, especially toward the right; but the enemy was repulsed, and made no further effort at this point during the day. The overall attack failed and Grant later regretted that it was ever made. It was a great victory for Lee and it was his last major triumph in full battle. Around noon, Grant called off the attack. The rest of the day was spent strengthening lines and caring for casualties.[41]

Both armies were still well entrenched on June 4th at Cold Harbor. Things were basically quiet except for an abortive attack by Early toward Burnside on the Federal right on June 6th.[42]

Grant began moving the Army of the Potomac across the James River on June 12th. The initial movement of over one hundred thousand deceived Lee for some days. Then the race began for Petersburg, where the forces would again come into active collision, and the siege which began would culminate nearly a year later in the downfall of the Confederacy.[43]

NOTES

[1] Herbert, Grandfather's Talks, 193.

[2] Longstreet, From Manassas, 432; Freeman, Lee's Dispatches, 108-114; OR, Series 1, Vol. LI, part 2, 752-753.

[3] Hoole, Unknown, 28; Herbert, Grandfather's Talks, 193.

[4] Freeman, Douglas S., Lee's Lieutenants: A Study in Command, Volume 3, New York: Charles Scribner's Sons, 1944, 238-239, hereinafter cited as Freeman, Lee's Lieutenants.

[5] IBID, 240-241; Hattaway, Shades, 186-187.

[6] IBID, 241; OR, Series 1, Vol. XXIX, part, 1, 426; Herbert, Grandfather's Talks, 196.

[7] IBID, 242-247; Hassler, A. P. Hill, 177-180

[8] IBID, 265-269; OR, Series 1, Vol. XXIX, part 1, 614; IBID, 611, 616.

[9] Herbert, Grandfather's Talks, 196; OR, Series 1, Vol. XXIX, part 1, 896.

[10] IBID, 901-906; Freeman, Lee's Lieutenants, 275.

[11] IBID, 279; Tower, R. Lockwood, Lee's Adjutant, the Wartime Letters of Colonel Walter Herron Taylor, 1862-1865, Columbia, S. C.: University of South Carolina Press, 1995, 80, hereinafter cited as Tower, Lee's Adjutant.

[12] General Orders No. 14, February 3, 1864, OR, Series 1, Vol. XXXII, part 1, 1144-1145; Herbert, Short History, 44.

[13] Herbert, Short History, 44; Herbert, Grandfather's Talks, 198-199.

[14] John Caldwell Calhoun Sanders Papers in the Collection of Papers of William Henry Sanders, Montgomery, Alabama: Alabama Department of Archives and History hereinafter cited as Sanders Papers; Thomson, Bailey, "John C. C. Sanders: Lees 'Boy Brigadier'," Alabama Review, Vol. 32, April 1979, 83-107, hereinafter cited as Thomson, Boy Brigadier.

[15] Rhea, Gordon C., The Battle of the Wilderness May 5-6, 1864, Baton Rouge: Louisiana State University Press, 1994, 313, hereinafter Cited as Rhea, Wilderness; Perry, General William F., "Reminiscences of the Campaign of 1864 in Virginia," Southern Historical Society Papers, New York: Kraus Reprint Co.,

1977, Vol. VII, 57, hereinafter cited as Perry "Campaign," SHSP; Freeman, Lee's Lieutenants, 407-410; OR, Series 1, Vol. XXXVI, part 1, 1030, 1073, 1094.

[16]IBID.

[16A]Montgomery Weekly Advertiser April 20, 1864; Papers of Thos. H. Watts, Montgomery, AL: State Department of Archives and History; Herbert Papers.

[17]Herbert, Grandfather's Talks, 200.

[18]Longstreet, From Manassas, 551.

[19]IBID, 555.

[20]Herbert, Grandfather's Talks, 200; Longstreet, From Manassas, 555.

[21]IBID, 202; IBID, 556-559; Hattaway, Shades, 208-210.

[22]Papers of Cadmus M. Wilcox, Washington, D. C.: Library of Congress; Hassler, A. P. Hill, 190-194.

[23]Rhea, Wilderness, 364-365.

[24]IBID.

[25]Herbert, Grandfather's Talks, 206; Rhea, Wilderness, 353-376.

[26]Herbert, Grandfather's Talks, 206.

[27]IBID, p. 207.

[28]Rhea, Wilderness, 371-372; Longstreet, From Manassas, 564; Hassler, A. P. Hill, 196.

[29]Herbert, Grandfather's Talks, 207-208, 214.

[30]Rhea, Wilderness, 360-375.

[31]Longstreet, From Manassas, 561-563; Rhea, Wilderness, 384-404; Hassler, A. P. Hill, 200.

[32]Longstreet, From Manassas, 565; Freeman, Lee's Lieutenants, 379-381.

[33]Freeman, Lee's Lieutenants, 382-385; Hassler, A. P. Hill, 199-200.

[34]Perry, "Campaign," 57-60.

[35] Freeman, Lee's Lieutenants, 384-386; Hattaway, Shades, 212-214.

[36] IBID, 388-389, 548, 581, 594; Freeman, Lee's Dispatches, 181-187.

[37] IBID, 390-391; Law, E. M., "From the Wilderness to Cold Harbor," Battles and Leaders of the Civil War, Volume 3, New York: Castle Books, 1956, 133, hereinafter cited as Law, BLCW.

[38] IBID, 392-410; G. Norton Galloway, "Hand-to-Hand Fighting at Spotsylvania," Battles and Leaders of the Civil War, Volume 3, New York: Castle Books, 1956, 170-174.

[39] Freeman, Lee's Lieutenants, 502-503, 505-506, Law, BLCW, 142-143; Hattaway, Shades, 216-217.

[40] OR, Series 1, Vol. XXVII, part 3, 1061; Martin T. McMahon, "Cold Harbor," Battles and Leaders of the Civil War, New York: Castle Books, 1956, 213-220.

[41] Freeman, Lee's Lieutenants, 594; Thomson, Boy Brigadier, 83-107.

[42] Freeman, Lee's Lieutenants, 515.

[43] Vance, S. W., "Heroes of the Eighth Alabama Infantry," CONFEDERATE VETERAN, Vol, VII, 492-493 (Nov, 1899); Freeman, Lee's Lieutenants, 524-527; Clark, George, "From the Rapidan to Petersburg: Wilcox Alabama Brigade in that Memorable Campaign," Confederate Veteran, Vol. XVII, August, 1909, 381-382.

CHAPTER EIGHT
PETERSBURG:
THE SIEGE OF NO RELIEF

Lee had two Corps, Longstreet's and Hill's, and the Second Corps under General Early was over in the Shenandoah Valley. Early was making a heroic effort to take pressure off Lee by even going so far as to threaten Washington.[1]

By June 13th, 1864, the bulk of the Army of the Potomac had moved rapidly from Cold Harbor toward the James River. Lee had learned the Federals had left Cold Harbor and had reports they were aiming at Richmond from the Long Bridge area of the Chickahominy. So the Army of Northern Virginia shifted southward taking a position from Malvern Hill to White Oak Swamp, blocking the road to Richmond; a road Grant did not intend on taking. Lee was still unaware of the magnitude of Grant's move.[2]

On June 14th, Grant's army began crossing the James. By the morning of the 15th all the infantry and four batteries of artillery of Hancock's Second Corps had crossed to the south bank. The Federal army continued to give Lee false evidence that they planned to attack north of the James.[3]

On June 15th, an unholy mix up of orders, lack of rations, poor maps, missed opportunities, and delays by commanders combined with courageous southern defense, saved Petersburg, and undoubtedly lengthened the war by several months. General P. G. T. Beauregard told Richmond the attack would be at Petersburg. Lee still believed Grant was north of Richmond.[4]

Beauregard stripped his Bermuda Hundred defenses facing General Benjamin Butler to a mere one thousand on June 16th and pulled all troops he could to Petersburg, which then numbered only fourteen thousand. Lee, still not convinced that Grant was south of the James, felt compelled to send reinforcements to reoccupy Bermuda Hundred.[5]

On June 17th, Beauregard's Confederates launched a successful counterattack late in the day. After midnight, the Confederates pulled back to shorter, more defensible prepared positions. Beauregard was still trying to convince Lee that the bulk of the Army of the Potomac was south of the James. Lee finally ordered A. P. Hill's Corps and Richard H. Anderson's Corps to Petersburg.[6]

The Federal assault on Petersburg failed. Grant then decided Petersburg could not be won by assault; it would have to be invested and the railroads cut off. Lee's army had arrived and defenses had stiffened. The siege of Petersburg was underway. The Federals held two of the five railroads into the city and several roads.[7]

The campaign against Petersburg, the longest sustained operation of the war, began in the summer of 1864 and lasted for ten months, until the spring of 1865. The fighting covered an area of more than one hundred seventy square miles, with thirty five miles of trenches and fortifications stretching from Richmond to the southwest of Petersburg.[8]

Mahone's division—including Sanders' brigade of Alabamians—would rank among the most renowned of Lee's army following a summer of fierce fighting which began when A. P. Hill took his Corps across the James River on June 18th, 1864. Hill's men extended the Confederate right south to the Petersburg and Weldon Railroad and under cover of a labyrinth of trenches and bomb proofs endured the war's uncertainties. Sanders' Alabamians occupied a position on the Jerusalem Plank Road. Defending the Petersburg and Weldon Railroad consumed much of Sanders' efforts over the next several months. "Day before yesterday I received the appointment of Brigadier General with a temporary rank in accordance with an act of Congress. The commission may be taken away at anytime or may be given me permanently, the latter is probably."[9]

Grant and Meade began cavalry operations on June 21st against the railroads into Petersburg. Orders were also issued to the Second and Sixth Corps to extend the siege lines to the left toward the Appomattox River west of Petersburg. The goal was to form a semi-circle south of Petersburg from the Appomattox on the East to the Appomattox on the west.[10]

Lee was cognizant of the move planned by Grant to extend the siege lines to the south and west. He had Hill's Corps move out to strike the Federal Second Corps which was heading for its new position (Second Corps was now under General David B. Birney as Hancock's war wound forced him to take sick leave). On June 22nd, Grant ordered a complicated swinging maneuver to outflank Lee's right and extend the Federal lines across the Petersburg and Weldon Railroad. The Confederates discovered a wide gap between the Federal Second and Sixth Corps. By a concealed route, Mahone rushed in Sanders and two other brigades and hit the Federal flank and rear. Surprised and filled with panic, the Federals of the Second Corps fled to the cover of the breastworks and rifle pits they had left earlier in the day or simply threw up their hands and surrendered. The Confederates pressed forward to roll up the Federal line.[11]

On reaching the enemy works, Sanders' men seized a battery of four artillery pieces. During this engagement, Sanders' horse was struck by a Minnie ball. "All of the railroad communications have been cut off. All the roads leading to this place have been recently broken up and the telegraph wires cut. On the evening of June 22nd, three brigades of our division were moved out to attack the enemy left flank. We captured ten stands of colors and one thousand six hundred fifty prisoners. The brigade had six killed and one hundred ten wounded." The Second Corps was driven back in the engagement on the Jerusalem Plank Road. Grant's drive against the Petersburg and Weldon Railroad had been halted. The plan to

General P. G. T. Beauregard,
Fired on Fort Sumter, Co-Commanded at First Manassas,
Fell in disfavor with Jefferson Davis and held many positions as a result,
Commanded at Petersburg before General Lee could arrive.
Photo courtesy of the Beauregard Library.

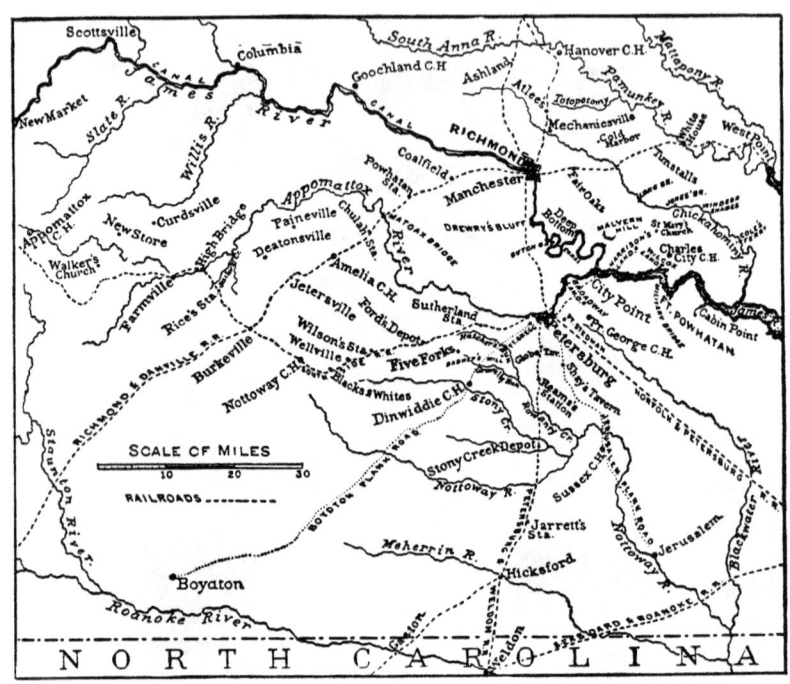

MAP OF THE PETERSBURG AND APPOMATTOX CAMPAIGNS
Map Taken from The Official Military Atlas of the Civil War

extend the lines west was given up for a while. The Confederates had gone two nights without sleep, but the railroad was again safe.[12]

Shortly after midnight on June 29th, Sanders' men were roused and ordered towards Reams' Station. Reams' Station was a few miles south on the Petersburg and Weldon Railroad. Rapid marching got them there by daylight.[13]

The Confederates attacked first, but their assault buckled, giving up prisoners. Sanders' men fell back to the cover of the woods where he formulated a plan to trap the Federal soldiers. As the morning wore on, the Federals struggled to keep awake on the skirmish line. Finally, late in the day, the Federal troops cut their way out of the trap. And, into Confederate hands fell one thousand prisoners, all of the Federal guns, vehicles of all kinds crammed with plunder and a throng of fugitive black slaves. Despite their precipitous retreat, the raiders had managed to destroy sixty miles of the railroad.[14]

As the summer wore on, Sanders' men endured the rigors of trench life under the broiling sun. "All of the railroads leading south are now running as well as the Lynchburg line. Our rations are pretty good, corn-meal and bacon with small quantities of coffee, peas, sugar and rice. We have coffee enough for a cup and breakfast every morning, very little sugar. Negroes from the woods show up peddling pies. Though we buy them, they are not of the best quality. I see no prospect of starving as the pies continue to come."[15]

At Petersburg, the Federal engineers began digging a tunnel on June 25th toward the Confederate lines hoping to blow apart the Southern earthworks. Before dawn on July 30th, Sanders and his staff were lounging on the porch of a little house behind his lines, when they were startled by a loud explosion. Jumping on his horse, Sanders galloped off to his brigade to see what had happened. A Federal mine had blown up Battery No. 5 and part of the 18th and 22nd South Carolina regiments. The enemy had exploded this mine under a fort then known as Elliot's Salient, subsequently named the Crater. Of the many battles the Alabama brigade fought, none equaled or approximated in bloody and stubborn fighting as the battle for the Crater, where the Federal losses were five thousand and Confederate losses were under two thousand out of the number engaged and for all about two acres of land. The explosion left behind a Crater one hundred seventy feet long and eighty feet wide.[16]

Lee ordered Mahone to bring up two of his brigades by a covered way. They would have to plug this gaping hole in the Confederate lines, or else Petersburg and possibly Richmond would be lost. Mahone arrived by eight thirty in the morning, sized up the situation and sent word for Sanders' brigade to come up too. General Lee informed Sanders before the attack that there were no other troops available to capture the Crater. If the brigade did not succeed, they would be reformed to renew the assault and Lee would himself, if necessary, lead the attack. At this time the brigade had in line some six hundred twenty eight muskets. Sanders' brigade arrived about eleven o'clock and formed in a ravine. By a circuitous route, the brigade arrived at Blandford Cemetery and then entered the zigzag covered way, through which the brigade had to file in single order to shield themselves from the enemy. The covered way emptied into a ravine which ran parallel to the Federal lines and also the Confederate lines. Mahone directed the brigade to move up the ravine as far as possible. The men were instructed to crawl still farther and to keep as quiet as possible, not to yell, and wait for Confederate artillery to draw the fire of the Federal artillery. Soon, a tremendous bombardment began which lasted for a couple of hours. The men waited under the hot sun for their chance to assault the captured works.[17]

    The objective of the attack that afternoon was to recapture the rifle pits on the rights as well as the Crater. At one o'clock Sanders attacked. The Alabama brigade was to move out of the ravine. Then the brigade moved forward in a stooping posture at "trail arms" with bayonets fixed. They were not to yell or fire a gun until they drew enemy fire, then the Alabamians were to charge double quick. The Crater was quickly made the bloodiest scene of all the battles of the war.[18]

    The Eighth Alabama was now commanded by Captain M. W. Mordecai; the Ninth, by Colonel J. H. King; the Tenth, by Captain W. L. Brewster; the Eleventh, by Lieutenant Colonel George P. Tayloe; and, the Fourteenth, by Captain Elias Polk. This one brigade of six hundred twenty eight was charging a fort in an open field, filled with the enemy numbering over five thousand supported by fifty pieces of artillery. The brigade saw a flash of sunlight on the enemy's guns as they were leveled above the walls of the wrecked fort; then a stream of fire and the awful roar of battle. This volley seemed to awaken the demons of hell and appeared to spread. Everybody within range of the fort began firing. The heavy guns joined in the din, and the air seemed literally filled with missiles. It was generally known that the situation was a critical one and the Alabamians moved with celerity and enthusiasm. For a moment or two, the enemy overshot the brigade and did no damage. As the brigade moved closer to the Crater, many were struck down and the gaps were apparent, but the alignment remained perfect. It was as handsome a charge as ever made on made on the field.[19]

    The brigade continued to move forward "into the mouth of hell." There were a large number of muskets with bayonets on them lying on the ground around the fort from the dead of the 18th and 22nd South Carolina regiments. The brigade began pitching them in the fort. Bayonets first, trying to harpoon the men inside. On reaching the works, the real battle began. The brigade poured into the Crater, and hand to hand combat began. Men were brained by gun butts, and run through with bayonets. Men fell in heaps and human gore ran in streams that made the very earth mire beneath the tread of Sanders' brigade. Men were falling like leaves under the raking volleys of the enemy, but there was not a break in the

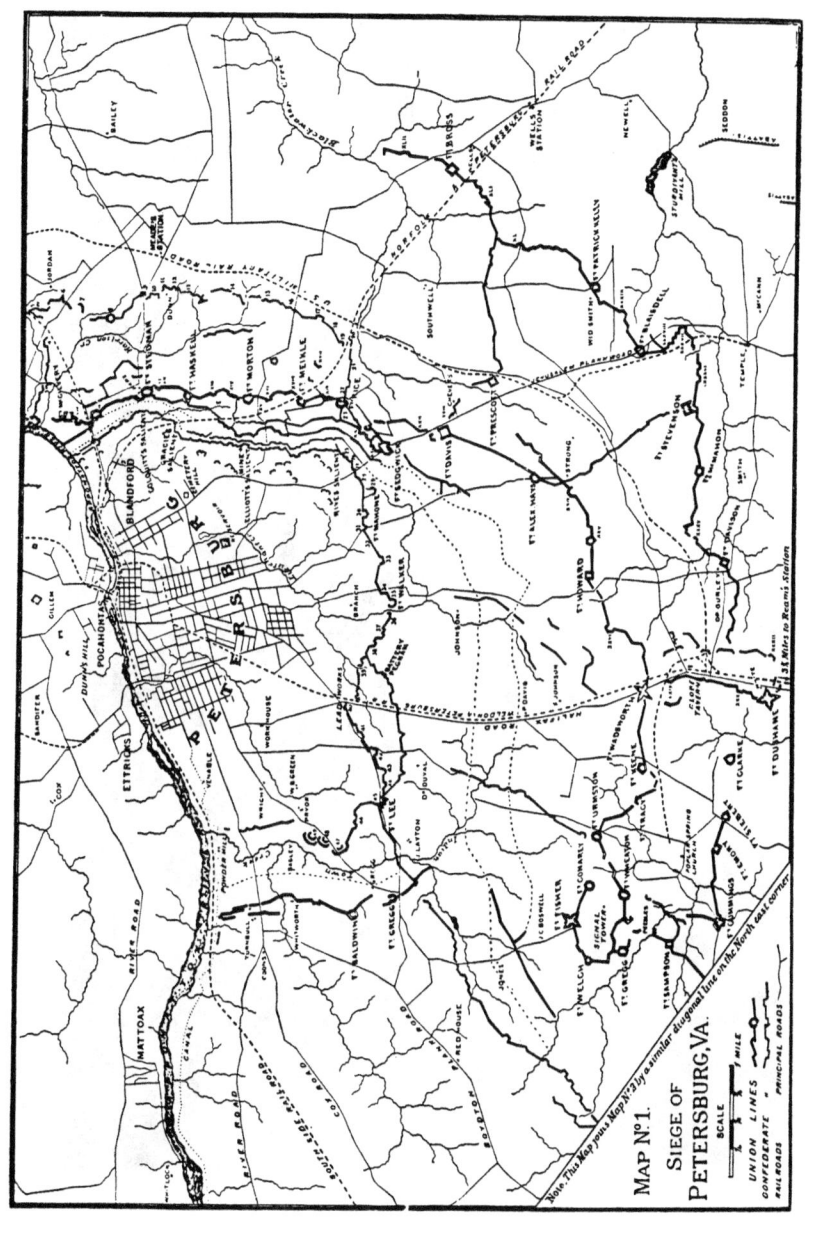

Map Taken from The Official Military Atlas of the Civil War

UNION TROOPS   CONFEDERATE TROOPS
THE BATTLE OF THE CRATER. PHOTOGRAPH OF AN OIL PAINTING

line that was not instantly filled up with calmness and a precision that were sublime[20].

Inside the captured works, bayonets flashed, and rifle butts flew, with skull crushing force. "The men were fighting hand to hand with the Yankees, very soon however, the enemy in the pit numbering about five hundred surrendered to us. We captured three stands of colors. This was the first time were have ever come into contact with Negroes, they fight much better than I expected." Sanders himself dueled at close range with a Negro soldier. Both proved to be poor marksmen.[21]

The Federals shrank back and the death grapple continued until most of the Federal soldiers were killed. This melee was kept up for at least fifteen minutes, the enemy fighting with desperation because they were impressed with the idea that no quarter would be given. As the Confederates bore down on the works, the Federals had no choice but every man to fend for himself. Orders had already been received to withdraw, buy constant Confederate firing kept them from withdrawing.[22]

The credit for capturing the Crater and all its contents belongs to Major Smith Cleveland, then Adjutant of the Eighth Alabama regiment. Standing in the Crater, in the midst of the horrid carnage, with almost bursting heart, he said to a Federal Colonel who was nearby him, "Why in the Hell don't you fellows surrender?" The Federal officer replied, "Why in the Hell don't you let us?" The enemy threw down their arms, marched out as prisoners, some being killed or wounded by their own cannon as they filed past, and the day was saved for the Confederacy.[23]

Many of the Alabama brigade were a gallant band. Many of them slept their last sleep in the soil of old Virginia having given their lives in defense of its firesides. The brigade lost eighty nine in the battle for the Crater, eighteen from the Eighth Alabama. After dark, tools were brought in with which the fort was reconstructed. During the night, in strengthening the wrecked fort, numbers of Confederate soldiers who had been killed in the explosion were unearthed. The dead were buried in the fort covering them with the earth, as enemy fire was too great to carry them out.[24]

The next morning, Mahone called for one hundred volunteers from Sanders' brigade to go into the pit and finish the gruesome job. Mahone walked over the field as did Sanders who had successfully retaken the Crater. The Young Alabamian was superintending the Confederate side of the truce to recover the wounded and bury the dead. On the night of the 31st the brigade was relieved, and it returned to its former position over a mile away from the Crater and remained there until March.[25]

On August 4th, 1864, Anderson's old division commanded by Brigadier General William Mahone so distinguished itself by its success during the current campaign as to merit the special mention of the Corps Commander and "he tenders to the division, its officers and men, his thanks for the gallantry displayed by them whether attacking or attacked. Thirty one stands of colors, fifteen pieces of artillery and four thousand prisoners are the proud mementos which signalize its valor and entitle it to the administration and gratitude of the county," said General A. P. Hill.[26]

The week of August 13th, 1864, was full of serious demonstration by the Federals on the north bank of the James River east of Richmond at Four Mile and Dutch Creeks, Deep Bottom, Fussell's Mill, Gravel Hill, Bailey's Creek, White's Tavern, the Charles City Road, and the New Market Road. The Federals hoped to divert attention from Petersburg and to probe or take Confederate defenses. Lee was attentive but not too concerned. Major General Charles W. Field of Longstreet's Corps was threatened at Deep Bottom on August 16th, 1864 by concentrated Federal forces on the north side of the James River. Sanders took his brigade across the river and reinforce the hard pressed southerners. The brigade lost six killed or wounded in this action.[27]

On the Confederate left Sanders commanded his and Wright's brigades and Lane's North Carolina brigade. His long line was stretched to only a single rank deep. The Alabamians struggled to hold their ground. Sanders rode furiously up and down the line trying to rally the men of Wright's and Lane's brigades. Exhausted from his efforts, Sanders believed he had never seen a more severe battle. On August 18th, Sanders' and Wrights' brigades were brought back from Deep Bottom to rejoin Mahone's division in preparation to dislodge General Warren's Fifth Corps from the Globe Tavern on the Petersburg and Weldon Railroad.[28]

By August 20th, despite some skirmishing along the railroad near Globe Tavern, the Confederates suspended temporarily their efforts to dislodge the Federals. On August 21st, Hill once more assaulted Warren's Federals south of Petersburg to try to recover the Weldon Railroad. The Federal lines held even though there were severe losses. Sanders had formed his brigade early on August 21st. The Confederates discovered the Federals had extended their lines farther toward Poplar Spring Church. As the muggy morning air began to rise, Mahone gave orders for an attack. Going forward, Sanders' men quickly overran the Federal skirmish line taking prisoners. Emerging from some woods into an open field, the Alabamians were raked by Federal guns. As the shells burst around him, Sanders ordered his brigade forward. Suddenly, Sanders was struck, reeling from the impact of the bullet. He died a few minutes later. In the Battle for the Weldon Railroad, the brigade had eleven killed wounded and missing. Captain Mordecai, next in command was also wounded. The Confederates could not dislodge the Federals and at the end of the day had to concede the loss of the northern section of the invaluable Petersburg Weldon Railroad.[29]

Colonel William H. Forney of the Tenth Alabama had been promoted to Brigadier General and assigned to Sanders' Brigade, the one in which he had served. Sanders was eulogized in typical overstatement of the time: "None was more beloved, or will be more regretted, than the gallant commander of the Alabama brigade," said the Richmond Daily Dispatch of August 23, 1864. Sanders was buried later in Hollywood Cemetery in Richmond. After the war, Sanders was removed from Hollywood Cemetery and taken back to Montgomery Alabama and buried in Oakwood Cemetery.[30]

On August 25th, the Second Battle of Reams' Station occurred striking sharply against Federal infantry destroying the Weldon Railroad south of Petersburg. Hill's beefed up Confederate Corps defeated Hancock's Second Corps in a surprise attack. Hancock's men withdrew with heavy losses, and Hill's men returned to the siege lines. The southern victory did not deter the destruction or the build up of the new westward extension of the Federal siege lines around Petersburg. Sanders' brigade had been held in reserve during this second battle. The first had been on June 29th.[31]

In early September 1864, the Richmond-Petersburg front exploded with a two pronged Federal drive—one north of the James against Richmond and one west of Petersburg. The west of Petersburg, Meade pressed to increase the encirclement of Petersburg west of the Weldon Railroad and to the vital Southside Railroad. The two pronged attack strained the Confederates to the utmost and forces a rapid shifting of troops from one threatened front to another. Meade from September 30th to October 2nd, extended the siege lines three miles further west of Petersburg. On the night of October 3rd, the Federal picket line in front of Fort Alexander Hayes broke a portion of the Confederate line. Later that day that portion of the line was recaptured by detachments of the Eighth Alabama and Tenth Florida regiments. It was a brilliant movement on the part of the Confederates.[32]

On October 27th, the Federals now moved once more to the left about twelve miles south and west of Petersburg aiming at the Southside Railroad. During the engagement at Burgess' Mill (or Boydton Plank Road, or Hatcher's Run) the advance was halted by the Confederates of Heth and Mahone. The Confederates won that day. But skirmishing on the Petersburg front had also occurred at Fort Morton and Fort Sedgewick.[33]

The organization of the Army of Northern Virginia by October 31st, showed Hill's Corps still had Heth's, Wilcox', and Mahone's divisions. In Mahone's division was Sanders' brigade with the Eighth now being commanded by Major John P. Emerich(Emrich), the Ninth by Captain Archer H. Hays, the Tenth by Captain Wilson L. Brewton, the Eleventh by Lieutenant Colonel George E. Tayloe, and the Fourteenth by Captain John A. Terrell.[34]

The returns of the Army of Northern Virginia for December 31st, 1864 showed Hill still commanding the Third Corps, with Heth's, Wilcox' and Mahone's divisions. And in Mahone's division, Sanders' brigade was not led by Colonel William H. Forney. The Eighth was still commanded by Major John P. Emerich(Emrich), the Ninth now commanded by Colonel J. H. King, the Tenth now by Captain John F. Smith, the Eleventh still by Colonel George E. Tayloe, and the Fourteenth by Captain Simon G. Perry.[35]

A Confederate Roll of Honor was published on December 10th, 1864. On the list was Sergeant John H. Deaton of the Eighth Alabama, Private John M. Critcher of the Ninth, and Private James N. Kector of the Eleventh. These soldiers were recognized for gallantry during the battle of the Crater.[36]

By February 5th, 1865, the Battle of Hatcher's Run began. Grant was active again after months of siege at Petersburg. The Federal Second and Fifth Corps plus cavalry again headed toward the Boydton Plank Road and Hatcher's Run. Despite inclement weather, they reached Boydton Plank Road with little difficulty. The movement was in line with the overall strategy of Grant to extend the Federal lines south and west of Petersburg to weaken the already strained defensive positions of Lee. The Confederates did move out troops but were unable to do much against the Federal cavalry and infantry.[37]

Until February 1865, the siege of Petersburg and Richmond consisted mainly of building fortifications, occasional sniping, picketing and patrolling. Some thirty five miles of Confederate lines extended from the Williamsburg Road east of Richmond to Hatcher's Run well to the southwest of Petersburg.

On February 6th, 1865, Lee was named General-in-Chief of all Confederate Armies in the field following an act of the Confederate Congress January 23rd, 1865. On February 7th, the fighting at Hatcher's Run ended with the Federals abandoning the Boydton Plank Road, but fortifying their new lines to Hatcher's Run. The Confederate army of forty six thousand now had to defense some thirty seven miles of lines from Richmond around Petersburg. This was the last principal Federal move to extend its lines prior to the final push in late March and early April.[38]

The defense of Fort Gregg was to be the last stand for Petersburg. Units from Wilcox' division defended Fort Gregg. This was necessary to allow Longstreet's Corps to cross the James River. There were about two hundred fourteen men in Fort Gregg and some in Fort Whitworth with some five thousand Federals advancing upon them. Gregg repulsed assault after assault; the two remnants of regiments, which had won glorious, honor on so many fields, fighting this, their last battle, with a most terrible enthusiasm. Fort Gregg raged like the crater of a volcano emitting its flashes of deadly fires, enveloped in flame and cloud, wreathing the Confederate battle flag in honor as in the smoke of death. Most of these young men were Mississippians and Louisianans. Now little

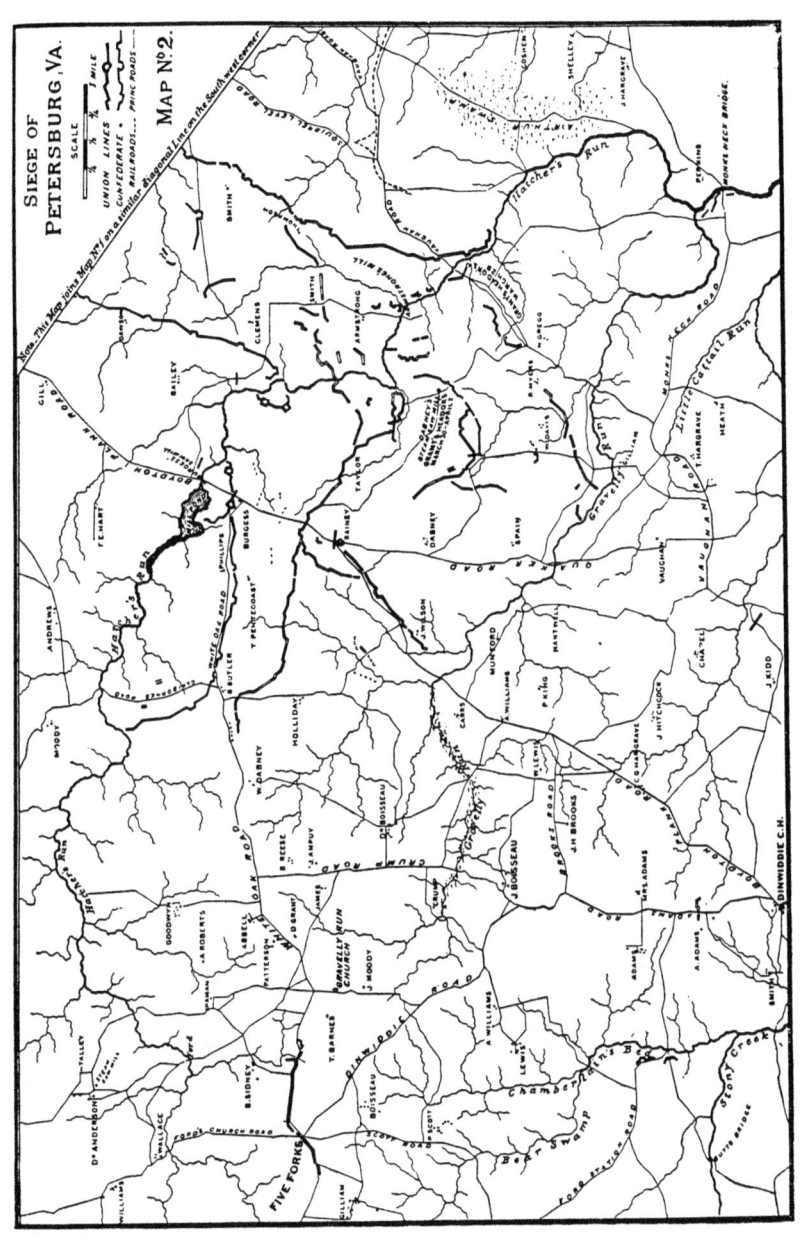

remained except the disheartening withdrawal from Petersburg and Richmond as Lee was intending to move westward where badly needed supplies were to have been stored and then to link up with General Albert Sidney Johnston in North Carolina.[39]

NOTES

[1] Freeman, Lee's Lieutenants, 526; Freeman, Lee's Dispatches, 256

[2] IBID, 528; Hassler, A. P. Hill, 214-215.

[3] IBID; Hassler, A. P. Hill, 216.

[4] IBID, 472, 529; Hassler, A. P. Hill, 214-215.

[5] IBID, 473, 500; Hassler, A. P. Hill, 215fn, Freeman, Lee's Dispatches, 245; Beauregard, G. T. "Notes on the Explosion of the Federal Mine at Petersburg Virginia July 30, 1864," Springfield, IL: Illinois Historical Society, hereinafter cited as Beauregard, Notes.

[6] IBID, 530-533; Hassler, A. P. Hill, 215-216; Freeman, Lee's Dispatches, 249; Beauregard, G. T., "Four Days of Battle at Petersburg," Battles and Leaders of the Civil War, Vol. 4, New York: Castle Books, 1956, 540-544.

[7] IBID, 534-535; Hassler, A. P. Hill, 218-219; Grant, U. S., "General Grant on the Siege of Petersburg," Battle and Leaders of the Civil War, Vol. 4, 574-579, hereinafter cited as Grant, Siege, BLCW.

[8] IBID, 538.

[9] IBID; Letter from J.C.C. Sanders to Fanny Sanders (sister) January 20, 1864, J.C.C. Sanders Papers; Hassler, A. P. Hill, 219.

[10] IBID, 537; Beauregard, Notes.

[11] IBID, 540.

[12] Letter from J. C. C. Sanders to William Henry Sanders (father), June 28, 1864, Sanders Papers.

[13] Letter from J. C. C. Sanders to Fanny Sanders (sister), July 25, 1864, Sanders Papers.

[14] F&S Notes.

[15] Letter from J. C. C. Sanders, July 25, 1864 to Fanny Sanders (sister), Sanders Papers.

[16] F&S Notes; Powell, William H., "The Battle of the Petersburg Crater," Battles and Leaders of the Civil War, Vol. 4, New York: Castle Books, 1956, 545-560,

hereinafter cited as Powell, Crater, BLCW; Hassler, A. P. Hill, 220; Beauregard, Notes.

[17]Powell, Crater, BLCW, 559-560; Houghton, Charles H., "In the Crater," Battles and Leaders of the Civil War, Vol. 4, New York: Castle Books, 1956, 561-562, hereinafter cited as Houghton, BLCW; Hassler, A. P. Hill, 222-223; Carmichael, Pegram, 130-131; Beauregard, Notes.

[18]IBID; Elias Davis to Georgia Davis, August 3, 1864, Elias Davis Papers, Southern Historical Collection, Chapel Hill: University of North Carolina; Hassler, A. P. Hill, 223

[19]IBID; Hassler, A. P. Hill, 222-223; Henry A. Minor to Mrs. M. A. Mosely (his sister), Decatur, AL, August 1, 1864, Mosely Family Papers, Morgan County Archives, Decatur Alabama, hereinafter cited as Minor to Mosely.

[20]IBID; OR, Series 1, Vol. XLII, part 2, 1156.

[21]Thomas, Henry Goddard, "The Colored Troops at Petersburg," Battles and Leaders of the Civil War, Vol. 4, New York: Castle Books, 1956, 563-568; Rogers, George T., "The Crater Battle," Confederate Veteran, Vol. III, 12ff, March, 1895; Beauregard, Notes.

[22]Freeman, Lee's Lieutenants, Vol. 3, 475-477.

[23]IBID; Hoole, Unknown, 9; Draper, Joseph, "Who Fought in the Battle of the Crater," Confederate Veteran, Vol. VII, 502 November, 1900; Todd, Westwood A., "Reminiscences of the War Between the States," Southern Historical Collection, Chapel Hill, NC: University of North Carolina, 236; Beauregard, Notes.

[24]Featherson, Capt. John C., "The Battle of the Crater As I Saw It," Confederate Veteran, Vol. XIV, 23-25, January, 1906; Letter from J. C. C. Sanders to William Henry Sanders, August 3, 1864, Sanders Papers.

[25]Floyd, N. J., "Concerning the Battle of the Crater," Confederate Veteran, Vol. XVI, 159, April, 1908; Stewart, Lt. Col. William H., "The Charge of the Crater," Southern Historical Society Papers, Vol. XXV, 77-90, New York: Kraus Reprint Co., 1977; Elias Davis to Georgia Davis, August 3, 1864, Davis Papers, Southern Historical Collection, Chapel Hill: University of North Carolina; Beauregard, Notes.

[26]Freeman, Lee's Lieutenants, 514, 540, 543-548; OR, Series 1, Vol. XL, part 3, 775.

[27]F&S Notes; Freeman, Lee's Lieutenants, 542-543.

[28] IBID; IBID, 589.

[29] IBID, Hoole, Unknown 10; Willcox, Orlando B., "Actions on the Weldon Railroad," Battles and Leaders of the Civil War, Vol. 3, 568-573, hereinafter cited as Wilcox, Actions, BLCW.

[30] Richmond Daily Dispatch, August 23, 1864; Freeman, Lee's Lieutenants, 634; Thomson, Boy Brigadier, 107.

[31] Willcox, Actions, BLCW, 571; Carmichael, Pegram, 138-139; Hassler, A. P. Hill, 229

[32] IBID, 568-571; F&S Notes.

[33] Grant, Siege, BLCW, 574-579; Freeman, Lee's Lieutenants, 615.

[34] "The Opposing Forces at Petersburg and Richmond," Battles and Leaders of the Civil War, Vol. 4, New York: Castle Books, 1956, 590-594.

[35] IBID

[36] OR, Series 1, Vol. XI, part 2, 994.

[37] Freeman, Lee's Lieutenants, 634-635.

[38] OR, Series 1, Vol. XLVI, part 2, 1205; Tower, Lee's Adjutant, 224-225.

[39] Longstreet, From Manassas, 607-608; Porter, Horace, "Five Forks and the Pursuit of Lee," Battles and Leaders of the Civil War, Vol. 4, New York: Castle Books, 1956, 717 hereinafter cited as Porter, Five Forks.

CHAPTER NINE
THE LONG ROAD TO APPOMATTOX

By the end of February 1865, the Army of Northern Virginia was changing again as it continued to adjust to losses especially among the officer ranks. First Corps was still under Longstreet, Second Corps had no commander but three divisions. Third Corps had no commander with three divisions—Heth's, Wilcox' and Mahone's. Mahone's division now showed Brigadier General William Forney's Brigade which included the Eighth Alabama now commanded by Lieutenant Colonel John P. Emerich. There was still Anderson's Corps with one division and a Cavalry Corps.[1]

On March 29th, 1865, the Army of the Potomac and the Army of the James numbering about 125,000 were on the move against Lee at Petersburg and Richmond. On the lengthy extended line from north of the James River to well west of Petersburg, Lee could muster less than half of the Federal manpower. The time had come to evacuate Richmond and Petersburg and unite with force in North Carolina. Lee had been collecting material and food and waiting for passable roads before pulling out in early April to join General Joseph Johnston in North Carolina.[2]

Pelting rains on March 30th bogged down most of the Federal advance on the Petersburg front. Confederate moves sorely weakened Lee on the other parts of his lines. Reconnaissance near Petersburg by the Federals ascertained that it was practicable for them to continue to press the assault.[3]

On March 31st, General Fitzhugh Lee's Confederate cavalry drove back Sheridan at Dinwiddie Court House—this was a tactical defeat for the Union. But, it was the beginning of the operations that were to end only with the surrender of Lee and the Army of Northern Virginia.[4]

On April 1st, Lee told General George Pickett to hold Five Forks at all cost. If the far right of the Confederate line fell, the entire retreat route of the Army of Northern Virginia from Petersburg and Richmond would be threatened. As it was, Lee had necessarily attenuated his defenses to the ultimate danger point to send over ten thousand troops to the right. Pickett's men dug in. The Battle of Five Forks split the remnant of Pickett from the main Confederate army. The Federals not only crumpled Lee's right and seized Five Forks, but they almost encircled Petersburg south of the Appomattox River. Now Grant was close to the vital Southside Railroad, an important Confederate supply and retreat route.[5]

By nine o'clock in the morning on April 2nd, the details of the catastrophe at the Battle of Five Forks began to take form. The Union Sixth Corps had delivered an overpowering attack earlier on Hill's front, had shattered the line held by Heth's and Wilcox' divisions and had driven the Confederates to right and left. West of the Boydton Plank Road while attempting to rally his men, General A. P. Hill was killed. Those men of Heth's and Wilcox' troops who had been driven west in the Federal breakthrough at Petersburg reunited with the main army the afternoon of the 3rd of April 1865[6].

After the death of A. P. Hill, his staff and corps were assigned back to Longstreet's command. Now Heth's, Wilcox', and Mahone's divisions were in the First Corps of the Army of Northern Virginia. Mahone's division was in good order and spirits except the regiments of Harris' brigade that were in Ft. Gregg. The rest of the troops at Petersburg were to cross the Appomattox River Bridge there. Mahone's division including Forney's Alabama brigade was to march to Chesterfield Court House and cover the march of the troops from the North side. The retreat began toward Amelia Court House, some forty miles to the west, where Lee hoped to concentrate his forces.[7]

April 3rd, 1865, Lee's army struggled westward by various roads in the general direction of Amelia Court House. Grant pursued, not in the rear, but on a somewhat parallel course heading toward Burkeville to intercept Lee and keep him from joining up with Johnston in North Carolina. In the forenoon of the 4th of April, Mahone's division crossed the Appomattox River, also part of Heth's division that had been cut off, and had marched up on the south side. The march was continued to Amelia Court House, the enemy's cavalry constantly threatening the left flank.[8]

April 4th, 1865, the retreating Army of Northern Virginia skirmished with Federals at Tabernacle Church on Beaver Pond Creek, and at Amelia Court House. The expected supplies were not at Amelia Court House, and Lee's army had to scrounge the neighborhood for sustenance.[9]

The last major engagement occurred between the Army of Northern Virginia and the Army of the Potomac on April 6th, 1865. Lee's army was nearing Farmville and High Bridge crossings of the Appomattox River. At Saylor's Creek the road forked, one to High Bridge crossing the Appomattox River, and the other by Rice's Station to Farmville. Crossing the stream was imperative for safety. The army attempted to keep together, but it was impossible. In the bottom land of Saylor's Creek, the retreating column split and the Federals moved in. Wilcox' division was so small that it needed Heth's division in immediate support. The fight began toward the middle of the afternoon and in some areas lasted till sundown. The battle which took place on Little Saylor's Creek, on the evening of April 6th, 1865 on the boundary lines of Amelia, Nottoway, and Prince Edward counties, is important because it was the last major battle on a large scale in which Lee's army engaged ere it passed from action into history. In the haste and confusion of defeat and retreat, in which most Confederate commanders had become captives, the Confederates had not time nor opportunity to record and report their operations.[10]

Lee, and Longstreet, with Mahone continued on unaware of the gap between then and the forces of Generals Richard S. Ewell and Richard H. Anderson. Lee never permitted the heads of his columns to stop because of any fighting in the rear. In this way he came very near succeeding in getting to his provision trains and eluding the Federals with at least part of his army. Anderson and Ewell were quickly pressed back but mounted a counter charge which failed in the face of strong artillery fire.[11]

Federal flanks closed in toward the middle and Ewell was forced to surrender. Only a few of his men cut their way out. Some eight thousand Confederates surrendered. The supply wagons had been ordered on a detour to cross the river. General John B. Gordon's troops followed the wagons by mistake. Gordon's southerners became heavily engaged further down Saylor's Creek.[12]

Longstreet headed for Farmville pausing briefly at Rice's Station. Longstreet was to counter the moves of Union General E. O. C. Ord. At Rice's Station, the command prepared for action. Field's placed his division across Ord's road of march; Wilcox on Field's right; and, Heth's division in support of Wilcox. Mahone was to support Field. Hearing troops engaged Lee rode to the sound of the battle at Rice's Station. He waited near Mahone's troops. Mahone's division of Longstreet's corps was in the rear of the corps. Hearing of the disaster as Saylor's Creek, Lee pulled Mahone's division from reserve at Rice's Station to move toward Saylor's Creek. That night Mahone withdrew near midnight through the woods, found the High Bridge (railroad bridge), and had the fragments of commands over before daylight. The Eighth Alabama began pulling back because the parties called to fire the bridge failed to appear. Mahone withdrew his division to the Cumberland Church and deployed for battle. Near the Cumberland Church, General Mahone received the attack of part of the enemy's Second Corps. The Federals eventually crossed in force at High Bridge, and engaged the Confederates north of the Appomattox River before being repulsed. Nevertheless, Lee's retreat had been delayed for several irreplaceable hours scouring the countryside for food. Sheridan with infantry behind him was able to move west and then north to block Lee at Appomattox Station and Court House. Thus, Lee was about to be squeezed between overwhelming Federal forces on the east and west.[13]

Longstreet crossed the Appomattox River at Farmville. Some rations were available there, but hardly enough for the whole Army of Northern Virginia.[14]

A little after night fall on April 7th, a flag of truce appeared under torchlight in front of Mahone's lines bearing a note to General Lee. Generals Mahone, Longstreet, Gordon, met with General Lee and all recommended that General Lee meet with General Grant. Grant received Lee's note of April 7th asking for terms. He offered to meet with Lee to receive a surrender. Lee was not quite ready to surrender.[15]

April 8th, 1865, the road to Lynchburg, the next goal of Lee's harried army, passed through hamlets and villages and Appomattox Station and Court House. Throughout the series of engagements preceding the surrender of the Confederate army, the conduct of the officers and men was admirable. When at times forced back and overwhelmed by largely superior numbers, the command retired in good order, and a line could be reformed at any moment.[16]

The men were trench weary and unused to long marching and had eaten little for months. Lee believed food would restore morale and then the army would be hard to stop. The trudging ranks were numb and dazed; but, the men kept marching because of Lee. Those veteran corps had now shrunken to brigades. Those special men were tired and gaunt and drawn out beyond mortality. Hunger became tangible. Hope now centered on food and reaching Lynchburg's stores.[17]

The fatigue riddled ragtag Alabamians under Forney had their feet rapped in rags as they had no shoes. Many had received no uniforms or clothing for over two years. Shoes were taken from the dead if they were available. Pay had been non-existent for quite sometime. These men fought for Lee, and not the cause.[18]

Behind what was left of the Army of Northern Virginia was General Meade with the Second and Sixth Corps. Lee was blocked in front by Warren's Old Fifth Corps and some of General Ord's men of the Army of the James. Sheridan's cavalry had seized Confederate supply trains at Appomattox Station.[19]

Lee now decided to meet with General Grant. There was a bit of reminiscing, and tales of old wars. Grant laid out the terms, and, Lee thought them generous. Lee suggested his men owned their own horses. Grant agreed that they should keep their animals. On April 9th, 1865, Lee surrendered the Army of Northern Virginia. Veterans of this army now saw Lee with his lowered shoulders, a tragic face, and they knew; they touched Lee; they mumbled things and cried. During the afternoon, Grant sent rations to Lee's troops[20].

Lee's men were still proud and they showed it as they fell in for that last and unhappy parade. "They would have liked to look better, but the tattered clothes and rag-soled shoes, and riddled flags would do. The conduct of the Federals on this occasion was soothing and comforting beyond anything that words could express. As the formal surrender of each of the units took place, the soldiers dropped their route step and fell into parade step, threw back their shoulders, raised their droopy heads and looked at the brave array of blue on both sides and in front of them. We stacked arms on the color line, and then we hung the colors on the center rack, and fell back into line. We looked at our guns, then with eyes blinded by tears we looked for the last time at the colors. Every Federal officer's sword was drawn and held in salute and every man who carried a gun brought and held it at salute as long as we remained there."[21] "The army we had been fighting so long, that we are now surrendering to, had suddenly overwhelmed us with kindly courtesy and high appreciation of our soldierly qualities." [22]

Cadmus Wilcox' own famous brigade of Alabamians was behind him, in Mahone's division, but everyone of Wilcox' brigades that now laid down its arms was renowned. The Army of Northern Virginia would live in infamy; the Alabama brigade had brought honor to the State of Alabama.[23]

Forney's brigade, Mahone's division had from February 28th, 1865 to March 1st an aggregate present of officers and men of 1239. At the surrender an aggregate of 952 officers and men were present. The Eighth Alabama had once numbered over thirteen hundred men, and had been reinforced several times with more men from the Alabama camps, but now numbered only one hundred fifty three plus sixteen officers. Many had been killed, or died of wounds, or captured and died in prisoner of war camps.[24]

The Confederates remained in a "bull pen" four days. The Federals indulged in no boasts nor firing of guns, no cheers could be hears. Never in all history was a captured army treated with so much respect. The Confederates were half starved; too faint and weary. The Confederates were ragged, dirty, unkempt, many were barefooted, many coatless, some hatless, and eyes were swollen.[25]

Those that survived had little to look forward to when they got home. They would face nearly a dozen years of Reconstruction with scalawags and carpetbaggers; no jobs; no farms or farms with taxes due; no money; and some with families to take care of made the situation very bleak in Alabama, the once proud capitol of the Confederacy. The South would suffer generations of poverty and the humility of being beaten. Confederates would suffer the wound of losing, and would nurse the wound in anger until anger became pride. At last a legend would arise, a legend of honor and duty, of sacrifice against great odds, a legend that would pit gallantry against impersonal force. The Eighth Alabama had served with distinction throughout the war. Many were gone, having died in distant states. Now the renowned Eighth Alabama would go home and help rebuilt their proud state.

NOTES

[1] Freeman, Lee's Dispatches, 117; OR, Series 1, Vol. XLVI, Part 2, 1170-1178.

[2] Freeman, Lee's Lieutenants, 655-656; Freeman, Lee's Dispatches, 359.

[3] Freeman, Lee's Lieutenants, 657; Freeman, Lee's Dispatches, 352; Porter, Five Forks, 709.

[4] Freeman, Lee's Dispatches, 352-353; Freeman, Lee's Lieutenants, 656-670, 675.

[5] Freeman, Lee's Dispatches, 353-356; OR, Series 1, Vol. XKVI, part 1, 1263-1264, 1298ff.

[6] Freman, Lee's Dispatches, 359; Porter, Five Forks, BLCW, 721.

[7] Longstreet, From Manassas, 608; Author Unknown, "The Defense of Fort Gregg," Southern Historical Society Papers, Millwood, New York: Kraus Reprint Co., 1977, Vol. III, 82-86.

[8] IBID.

[9] IBID, 609.

[10] IBID, 610-611; Porter, Five Forks, 721; Watson, Walter E., "Sailor's Creek," Southern Historical Society Papers, Millwood, New York: Kraus Reprint Co., 1977, Vol. XLII, 136-151.

[11] IBID, 614.

[12] IBID.

[13] IBID, 615; Freeman, Lee's Lieutenants, 698-699.

[14] IBID.

[15] Papers of James Longstreet, 1821-1904, Special Collections Library, Durham NC: Duke University, hereinafter cited as Longstreet Papers.

[16] Freeman, Lee's Lieutenants, 684, 686-687, 695-696.

[17] IBID, 688-689, 718; Hoole, Unknown, 11; Minor, Henry A., Account of General Lee's Surrender at Appomattox, Macon Beacon(Miss) April 1876, hereinafter cited as Minor's Account. (Minor was a surgeon in Mahone's division)

[18] IBID, 690-691.

[19] IBID, 724-733.

[20] IBID, 738-741; Longstreet, From Manassas, 618-629; Hoole, Unknown, 11.

[21] Minor's Account.

[22] IBID.

[23] Freeman, Lee's Lieutenants, 742-752; Longstreet, From Manassas, 630-631.

[24] OR, Series 1, Vol. XLVI, part 1, 1278-1279; Hoole, Unknown, 11; Paroles of the Army of Northern Virginia from the Duplicate Originals in the Archives of the Southern Historical Society edited with an Introduction by R. A. Brock, published by the Society in Richmond, Virginia, 1887, Southern Historical Society Papers, Vol. XV, 313-316, hereinafter cited as Paroles, SHSP.

[25] Minor's Account.

EPILOGUE

Colonel Young L. Royston, after the Battle of Salem Church, was never with the regiment again. Recovering at home in Alabama, he sought a generalship, which he failed to obtain in order to return to the Army of Northern Virginia. When turned down, he stayed in Alabama and commanded a State Reserve Unit.[1]

Colonel Hilary A. Herbert commanded the Eighth Alabama from early May 1863 to May 1864 when he was disabled at the Battle of the Wilderness and sent home to recover. While recovering, he was promoted to Colonel, after Royston was, through paperwork, removed. Herbert was not present at the surrender in April, 1865, but the Eighth Alabama was under the temporary command of Lieutenant Colonel John P. Emerich.[2]

General Cadmus M. Wilcox wrote General Lee in the fall of 1865 asking for a recommendation for employment. He was considering offering his services to Mexico. General Lee wrote a general recommendation and indicated that he was impelled to remain with the Southern people and share their fate. General Lee feared the South had yet to suffer many evils; and it would require time, patience, and fortitude to heal her afflictions.[3]

After the war, General E. Porter Alexander, who had been in charge of the artillery during Pickett's charge, explained to Colonel Herbert that Confederate ammunition was so defective that he could not count on the explosion of shells at a particular distance. If he had undertaken to fire over the heads of the advancing Confederate infantry, there was a danger that premature shell explosions would do damage to and demoralize the Confederate troops. Alexander also indicated that it was the intension of General Lee that Wilcox should go forward with Pickett, but that somehow or another the orders had miscarried. He noted that this is an important part of the general history of the battle.[4]

It should also be noted that on the mound at Cemetery Heights a monument was erected that marked "The High Water Mark of the Confederacy. It was designed to mark the farthest point reached by the Confederates during Picketts charge. Part of the inscription on the monument reads "Wilcox's Alabama Brigade—Esto Perpetua" or "Wilcox's Alabama Brigade in perpetuity."

During the winter of 1863-1864 Colonel Herbert had met a Miss Nina Cave, who lived with her father near Orange Court House, where the Eighth Alabama was encamped. Miss Cave presented two pennants, one of white and one red ribbon bearing the names of the principal battles in which the regiment had up to that time been engaged. She attached them to the battle flag of the regiment. In April, 1896, while Colonel Herbert was serving in President Cleveland's second administration as Secretary of the Navy, he received a telegram from a John

Colonel Hilary Abner Herbert
Last Commander
Eighth Alabama Infantry
Also, U.S. Congressman, and later
Secretary of the Navy
In President Grover Cleveland's Second Administration
Courtesy of the U. S. Naval Historical Center

Brown of Suffolk, Virginia, expressing a desire to see him. Herbert sent a reply and Brown showed up the next day. Brown had been a gallant member of the Eighth Alabama. He had a box with him which held the two pennants. He had torn them from the staff of the battle flag before the surrender. He offered them to Herbert, who was deeply moved and was anxious to have the pennants, but he decided against it. He told Brown that since he had saved the pennants from capture, the pennants belonged to him. In March, 1897, when Herbert left office, he practiced law in Washington D. C.[5]

As already mentioned, Herbert served as Secretary of the Navy under President Cleveland. He was the last cabinet member approved by the Senate because he had been a Rebel. But Herbert's qualifications for the office were good. He had represented the Montgomery district of Alabama in Congress for sixteen years, and was on the Naval Committee during his last eight years and chairman of that committee for six years. Herbert had much to do with putting the Navy of the United States in a condition to win its victories during the Spanish American War. Many of the ships that fought the Battles of Manila Bay and Santiago had been authorized while he was a member of the Naval Committee and finished while he was serving as Secretary of the Navy. He also served on the committee of the Peace Memorial at Gettysburg and the Committee for the Confederate Monument at Arlington National Cemetery. Thus, the ex-Rebel Colonel made major contributions to the United States and yet he still remembered his heritage, the war and how the war solidified this nation.[6]

NOTES

[1] Herbert, Grandfather's Talks, 219-220.

[2] Paroles, SHSP, 313-316.

[3] Wilcox to Lee, undated, and R. E. Lee to Cadmus Wilcox, 23 December 1865, R. E. Lee Papers, Richmond, VA: The Virginia Historical Society.

[4] E. Porter Alexander, to Hilary A. Herbert, (undated—post war), Herbert Papers. .

[5] Herbert, Grandfather's Talks, 208-211-214.

[6] Scrapbooks full of newspapers articles from the work on the peace memorial and the Confederate Monument at Arlington National Cemetery, Herbert Papers.

INDEX

Appendices are not indexed.

Alabama Rangers, 1
Alexander, 36, 61, 100
Anderson, 10-12, 19-20, 34, 36-37, 40-42, 46-47, 49, 52-53, 57-58, 60-61, 63, 68-69, 73, 75, 77, 81, 86, 93, 95
Antietam Creek, 38, 40
Appomattox Station and Court House, 95-96
Appomattox Station, 96
Armistead, 36
Banks Ford, 46, 49-50, 52
Banks, 15
Barksdale, 50, 58-60
Batteries—Macon, 9, Second Mississippi, 36, Stanard
Battles—Big Bethel, 7-8
Battles—Boydton Plank Road, 87
Battles—Bristow, 68
Battles—Burgess' Mill, 87
Battles—Chancellorsville, 46, 49-50, 53, 71
Battles—Cold Harbor, 76, 81
Battles—Crampton's Gap, 37
Battles—Crater, 83, 85, 88
Battles—Deep Bottom, 86
Battles—Fair Oaks, 15-16
Battles—Five Forks, 93
Battles—Frazier's Farm, 4, 23, 25-26, 71
Battles—Fredericksburg, 48, 71
Battles—Gaines' Mill, 4, 15, 18, 22-23, 26, 61
Battles—Gettysburg, 68, 71
Battles—Globe Tavern, 86
Battles—Hatcher's Run, 87-88
Battles—Malvern Hill, 25
Battles—Manassas, 50
Battles—Manila Bay, 101
Battles—Marye's Heights, 49-51
Battles—Mine Run Operations, 69
Battles—Reams' Station, 83
Battles—Rice's Station, 95
Battles—Salem Church, 4, 49-50, 52-53, 71, 100
Battles—Santiago, 101
Battles—Saylor's Creek, 94-95
Battles—Second Manassas, 25, 30, 32, 34-36
Battles—Second Reams' Station, 87
Battles—Seven Pines, 4, 15-17, 25

Battles—Sharpsburg, 30, 39, 41-42, 50, 71
Battles—South Mountain, 38
Battles—Spotsylvania Court House, 71
Battles—Weldon Railroad, 86
Battles—Wilderness, 71-72, 100
Battles—Williamsburg, 4, 11-12, 25
Beauregard, iii, 81
Beaver Dam Creek, 18
Birney, 82
Blandford Cemetery, 84
Bolger, 41
Bragg, 68
Brewster, 84
Brewton, 87
Bristoe Station, 31
Brown, 41, 101
Buch, 26
Bull Run Creek, 34-35
Burnside, 46-47, 74, 77
Butler, 7, 81
Caldwell, 35
Callahan, 41
Caney, 26
Casey, 16
Cave, 100
Chinn Ridge, 34
Cities—Amelia Court House, 94
Cities—Appomattox Court House, 93
Cities—Ashland, 19
Cities—Baltimore, 37
Cities—Boonsboro, 37
Cities—Buckland, 69
Cities—Burkeville, 94
Cities—Cashtown, 57
Cities—Centreville, 35, 69
Cities—Chambersburg, 57
Cities—Chancellorsville, 46, 49, 75
Cities—Chantilly, 30
Cities—Chattanooga, 68, 70
Cities—Chesterfield Court House, 94
Cities—Covington, 2
Cities—Culpeper Court House, 42, 46, 53, 63
Cities—Dinwiddie Court House, 93
Cities—Fairfield, 57
Cities—Falmouth, 47
Cities—Farmville, 94-95

Cities—Flint Hill, 63
Cities—Frederick, 36, 38
Cities—Fredericksburg, 15, 42, 46-47, 49, 53, 57, 72, 75
Cities—Front Royal, 57, 63
Cities—Funkstown, 57
Cities—Gettysburg, 57, 63, 101
Cities—Gloucester Point, 7
Cities—Gloucester, 1
Cities—Gordonsville, 30
Cities—Greenville, 1-2
Cities—Groveton, 31, 33
Cities—Hagerstown, 37-39, 57, 63
Cities—Hampton, 7-8
Cities—Harper's Ferry, 36-39, 41, 57
Cities—Harrisburg, 57
Cities—Leesburg, 37
Cities—Lynchburg, 96
Cities—Malvern Hill, 81
Cities—Manassas, 30, 36, 68-69
Cities—Martinsburg, 37, 42
Cities—Mechanicsville, 12, 16, 18, 21
Cities—Mobile, 2
Cities—Montgomery, iii, 1-3, 87
Cities—Newport News, 7-8
Cities—Orange Court House, 68-70, 72, 100
Cities—Pensacola, 1
Cities—Petersburg, 15, 53, 77, 81-83, 86-89, 93
Cities—Radfordsville, 3
Cities—Rice's Station, 94-95
Cities—Richmond, 1-3, 11-12, 15, 17-18, 24-25, 30, 46, 49, 52-53, 72, 77, 81-83, 86-89, 93
Cities—Selma, 3
Cities—Sharpsburg, 38-39
Cities—Shepherdstown, 39, 57
Cities—Spotsylvania Court House, 75
Cities—Stevensburg, 30
Cities—Suffolk, 49, 101
Cities—Verdiersville, 73
Cities—Warrenton, 31, 69
Cities—Washington, 15, 36-37, 68
Cities—West Point, 2, 15
Cities—White House, 15
Cities—Williamsburg, 10-11, 15
Cities—Winchester, 15, 42, 63
Cities—Yorktown, 2-3, 7-8, 10, 15
Cleveland, 9, 24, 85, 100

Cochran, 26
College of William and Mary, 11
Colston, 12, 16
Cook, 36, 41
Corse, 36
Costello, 40-41
Couch, 16
Crampton's Gap, 38
Critcher, 88
Cumberland Gap, 4
Cummings, 39
Curry, 41
Davis, iii, 12, 18, 35, 39, 68
Deaton, 26, 88
Deep Run, 46-47
Donoho, 26
Duke, 25
Early, 11, 50, 52-53, 75, 77, 81
Ely's Ford, 72
Elzey, 49
Emancipation Proclamation, 42
Emerich, 42, 87-88, 93, 100
Emrich, 42, 87-88
Ewell, 21, 31, 68, 74, 95
Fairfax, 40
Fairfield Race Course, 1
Featherston, 19-21, 30-32, 34, 36, 46
Field, 86, 95
Forney, 50, 58, 62, 87-88, 93-94, 96-97
Fort Gregg, 88, 94
Fort Magruder, 10
Fort Pickens, 1
Fort Sumter, iii
Fort Whitworth, 88
Fortress Monroe, 7
Franklin, 38
Frazier, 3-4, 9
Fraziers' Farm, 15
French, 49
Gaines, 20
Ganavan, 25
Garnett, 36, 61
Garrison, 26
Geddes, 26
Germanna Ford, 72
Gettys, 72

Gordon, 95
Gould, 41
Grant, 70, 72-73, 75-77, 81-82, 88, 93-96
Griffin, 26
Hall, 26
Hamilton's Crossing, 46
Hancock, 47, 72, 74, 81, 87
Hannon, 23
Harris, 24, 39, 41, 74, 94
Harwood's Mills, 7-8
Hatch, 33
Hays, 87
Heard, 74
Henry Hill, 34
Herbert, 1, 9-10, 17, 25, 32, 35, 40-42, 46, 51, 58, 61-63, 68, 71-72, 74, 100-101
Heth, 61, 72-72, 87-88, 93-95
Hill, 10-12, 15-16, 18-20, 23, 25, 38, 41, 49, 53, 57, 63-64, 68-69, 71-73, 75, 77, 81-82, 86-88, 93-94
Hinson's Mill, 31
Hippler, 26
Hollywood Cemetery, 87
Hood, 31, 33-34, 36, 39-40, 46-47
Hooker, 10-11, 39, 47-50, 57
Hopewell Gap, 31
Howard, 26
Huger, 15, 18
Humphrey, 47, 59-60
Hundley's Corners, 19
Irby, 3-4, 9-11
Jackson, 15, 18-19, 21, 25-26, 30-32, 34-35, 37-39, 46-47, 50
Jansen, 23
Jenkins, 36
Jennings, 35
Johnston, 9-12, 15-17, 76, 89, 93
Jones, 33-34, 40-41
Kector, 88
Kelly's Ford, 30, 69
Kemper, 19, 30, 36,
Kempter, 34
Kennedy, 18
Kershaw, 50
King, 51, 84, 88
Lane, 23, 60, 86
Law, 36
Laws, 74

Lee, 12, 17, 25-26, 30-31, 33-39, 42, 46-53, 57, 63, 68-69, 70-73, 75-77, 81-83, 88-89, 93-96, 100
Lee's Mill, 7
Lincoln, 15, 42, 57
Longstreet, 9-12, 15-16, 18-19, 22-23, 25, 30-38, 40, 42, 46-47, 49, 53, 57-58, 61-73, 68, 72-75, 81, 86, 88, 93-95
Loughry, 11, 18
Lynch, 26
Magruder, 7-10, 12, 16, 36, 46, 58, 68, 74-75, 82-88, 93-95, 97
Marye's Heights, 47-48
Maynard, 23
McClellan, 8-10, 15-17, 23, 25, 34, 36-38, 42
McCloskie, 41
McDowell, 15, 33
McGowan, 76
McGrath, 23
McGraw, 26
McHugh, 23
McKewn, 26
McLaughlin, 23
McLaws, 36-37, 41, 46-47, 49-50, 52, 58, 60
McWilliams, 40
Meade, 57, 62, 68-69, 77, 82, 87, 96
Milner, 26
Mine Run, 72
Mordecai, 84, 86
Murphy, 35
Nall, 10, 74
Oakwood Cemetery, 87
Ord, 95-96
Ordinance of Secession, iii
Pender, 64, 71
Pendleton, 12
Perrin, 64, 71, 73-77
Perry, 36, 46, 58-60, 62, 68, 99
Pettigrew, 61-62
Pettus, 3-4
Phelan, 4, 9, 23
Philips, 25
Pickett, 10-12, 18-19, 36, 46-48, 61-62, 64, 93, 100
Plum Run Valley, 59
Pole Green Church, 18-19
Polk, 84
Pope, 30-31, 33-35
Poplar Spring Church, 86
Posey, 58, 68

Powell, 25
Powhite Creek, 20
Pryor, 9-12, 16-22, 30-32, 34
Racoon Ford, 30
Ransom, 36, 46-47
Regan, 41
Regiments—18th South Carolina, 83
Regiments—18th South Carolina, 84
Regiments—22nd South Carolina, 83
Regiments—22nd South Carolina, 84
Regiments—Eighth Alabama, 1-5, 7-12, 17, 19-25, 30, 32-42, 46-48, 50-53, 58-59, 61-63, 68-77, 84-85, 87-88, 93, 95, 97, 100-101
Regiments—Eleventh Alabama, 10, 21, 35-36, 51, 62, 64, 70-71, 84, 87-88
Regiments—First New York Sharpshooters, 58
Regiments—Forty-first Virginia, 36
Regiments—Fourteenth Alabama, 9, 17, 36, 50, 62, 71, 84, 8-88
Regiments—Fourteenth Louisiana, 9
Regiments—Nineteenth Mississippi, 10, 36
Regiments—Ninth Alabama, 10, 12, 17, 21-22, 35-36, 40, 51-52, 62, 71, 84, 87-88
Regiments—Second Florida, 21
Regiments—Sixteenth Mississippi, 36
Regiments—Sixteenth Virginia, 36
Regiments—Sixth Virginia, 36
Regiments—Sixty-first Virginia, 36
Regiments—Tenth Alabama, 10, 20-21, 35, 50-51, 58, 62, 71, 84, 87-88
Regiments—Third Maine, 58
Regiments—Thirteenth Alabama, 7
Regiments—Twelfth Mississippi, 36
Regiments—Twelfth Virginia, 36
Regiments—Twenty-eighth Alabama, 4
Regiments—Twenty-first Mississippi, 58
Rivers—Appomattox, 82, 93, 95
Rivers—Chattahooche, 2
Rivers—Chickahominy, 12, 15-16, 18, 20-22, 23, 77, 81
Rivers—James, 8, 11, 23, 49, 77, 81-82, 86-88, 93
Rivers—Pamunkey, 15
Rivers—Potomac, 36-39, 57, 63
Rivers—Rapidan, 30, 68-70, 72
Rivers—Rappahannock, 30-31, 35, 48-49, 52, 68
Rivers—Shenandoah, 63
Rivers—Totopotomoy, 77
Rivers—Warwick, 7-8
Rivers—York, 8, 11
Robbins, 3
Robertson, 36

Robinson, 41
Roh, 41
Royston, 1, 4, 9-12, 18, 23-24, 42, 51, 68, 100
Ryan, 39, 41
Sanders, 35, 50, 64, 68-69, 71, 77, 82-84, 86-88
Search, 41
Secretary of the Navy, 100-101
Seddon, 53
Sedgwick, 50-53, 72, 75
Seely, 59
Semmes, 51
Sheridan, 93, 95-96
Shields, 26
Shortridge, 26
Sickles, 11
Siege of Petersburg, 81, 88
Smith, 12, 16-17, 26, 41, 88
Stafford's Heights, 47
Stephens, iii
Stuart, 11-12, 15, 38, 47, 70
Summer, 17
Tallen, 26
Tayloe, 84, 88
Taylor, 87
Terrell, 87
Thoroughfare Gap, 30-31, 35
Toombs, 36
Trimble, 31
Tucker, 41
Walker, 26, 37
Walton, 30, 36
Warren, 72, 75, 86, 96
Watts, 71
Whiting, 16, 19
Wilcox, 9-10, 12, 16, 18-25, 30-31, 33-36, 38-42, 46-53, 57-64, 68-69, 71-73, 87-88, 93-95, 97, 100
Williams, 25, 35, 40
Winston, 3-4, 7-10, 12, 17-18
Wright, 36, 46, 58, 60-61, 68, 86
Wynn's Mill, 8
Wynn's Mill, 9

APPENDIX A

ALPHABETIC ROSTER
EIGHTH ALABAMA INFANTRY REGIMENT
Compiled from National Archives Microfilm (11 Reels)

Aarens, A. H.	Co. E	Private
Abbott, John E.	Co. I	Private
Abbott, John H.	Co. I	Private
Abbott, John N.	Co. I	Private
Adams, Robert	Co. E	Private
Adams, Thomas	Co. E	Private
Adier, Jos. M.	Co. A	Private
Ahern, Patrick	Co. I	Sergeant
Ahern, Patrick	Co. G	Private
Aldridge, Joseph	Co. G	Private
Albert, J.	Co. I	Private
Allen, Alijah	Co. E	Private
Allen, Benjamin S.	Co. E	Private
Allen, James	Co. H	Private
Anderson, David L.	Co. D	Private
Anderson, Alexander	Co. G	Private
Anderson, Ezekeal	Co. F	Private
Anderson, George	Co. H	Private
Anderson, J. M.	Co. D	Private
Andrews, G. D.	Co. F	Private
Andrews, James C.	Co. C	Private-Cpl.
Andrews, J. F.	Co. F	Private
Ard, James	Co. E	Private
Armfield, Thomas	Co. G	Private
Armspaugh, John H.	Co. B	Private
Armstrong, Charles	Co. C	Private
Armstrong, W. C.	Co. E	Private
Armstrong, William B.	Co. A	Private
Arnold, B.R.	Co. B	Private
Arnold, David C.	Co. B	Private
Arnold, Isaac	Co. D	Private
Arnold, J.	Co. B	Private
Arnold, R. P.	Co. B	Private
Arons, Henry	Co. E	Private
Ashley, W. N.	Co. A	Private
Ashlock, Henry	Co. C	Private-SGT.
Aubrey, James	Co. A	Private
Aunspaugh, John H.	Co. D	Private-QM SGT.
Austill, J. W.	Co. H	Private
Baber, J. M.	Co. A	Private

Baggett, John	Co. C	Private
Bailey, A. V.	Co. B	Corporal
Baker, C.L.	Co. H	Private
Baker, John	Co. D	Private
Baker, J.W.	Co. B	Private
Baldwin, J.A.	Co. F	Private
Baldwin, James W.	Co. E	Sergeant
Baldwin, William J.	Co. E	Private
Bamburg, Lysander P.	Co. A	Private
Barrick, C. K.	Co. H	Private
Barefield, C.	Co. F	Private
Barefield, John	Co. A	Private
Barkloo, Henry P.	Co. H	Private
Barkman, John	Co. G	Private
Barnett, D. W.	Co. A	Private
Barnett, W.	Co. A	Private
Barnett, W. F.	Co. F	Private
Barrett, James	Co. A	Private
Barrier, Jacob	Co. G	Private
Barron, G.J. [T.J.]	Co. B	Private
Barron, J.B.	Co. B	Private
Barron, R. H.	Co. K	Private
Bartlett, E. H.	Co. E	Private
Barton, M. C.	Co. C	Private
Barwick, James G.	Co. B	Private
Basinean, J. S.	Co. B	Sergeant
Batchelor, George	Co. C	Private
Bates, J. R.	Co. C	Private
Batton, T. H.	Co. H	Private
Bauer, Charles	Co. G	Sergeant
Bauman, F.	Co. G	Corporal
Bayzer, T. W.	Co. F	Corporal
Beale [Bell], John	Co. D	Private
Beck, W. E.	Co. B	Private
Becker, Winslow P.	Co. D	Private
Beer, Joseph	Co. H	Private
Bell, John G.	Co. D	Private
Bell, W. Randolph	Co. D	Private
Benbow, Adam J.	Co. F	Private
Benefield, J.	Co. D/G	Private
Bennett, Columbus L.	Co. K	1 Lieutenant
Bennett, Jno. S.	Co. K	Private
Bennett, James W.	Co. K	Private
Bennett, Newton	Co. K	Private
Bennett, R. E.	Co. K	Private
Bentley, William W.	———	Private

Benton, B. P.	Co. B	Private
Berger, Jacob	Co. G	Private
Bern, L. H.	———	Private
Berry, Thomas	Co. G	Private
Berryfield, C.	Co. A	Private
Berwick, Wm.	Co. H	Private
Betts, William L.	Co. B	Private
Bice, James M.	Co. E	Private
Bice, John T.	Co. E	Private
Bice, William J.	Co. E	Private
Biggs, William	Co. B	Private
Bill, James A.	Co. D	Private
Black, J. T.		Private
Black, W. E.	———	Private
Blackall, Simon	Co. I	Private
Blackburn, John	Co. K	
Blackman, Jonah	Co. E	Private
Blackman, J. W.	Co. H	Private
Blackwood, Cranford	Co. E	1 Lieu-Captain
Blair, James H.	Co. A	Private
Blake, William	Co. B	Private
Blakely, J. T.	Co. A	Corporal
Bledsoe, A, M.	Co. K	Private
Bledsoe, Thomas J.	Co. K	Private
Bledsoe, W. E.	Co. K	Sergeant-Pvt.
Blount, B. B.	Co. H	Private
Blount, W. H.		Conscript
Blumenfeld, John	Co. G	Private
Blunt, W. H.	———	Private
Boggs, Benjamin F.	Co. A	Private
Bogle, Andrew	Co. D	1 Lieutenant
Bogston, L. P.	Co. B	Private
Bohlia, George W.	Co. D	Private
Boley, Marion A.	Co. D	Private-Cpl.
Bolls, John	Co. D	Private
Bolling, Allen	Co. A	Private
Bolling, Daniel	Co. C	Private
Bolling, J. S.	Co. K	Private
Bolling, S. A.	Co. K	Private-Cpl.
Bonham, Simeon	Co. C	Private
Bonneau, H. S.	Co. C	Private
Boone, L. H.	Co. I	Private
Boring, D. W.	Co. B	Corporal
Bosworth, J. Larry	Co. D	Private
Bosworth, M. F.	Co. E	Private
Bouchelle, Jo. A. G.	Co. E	Private

Bourke, P.	Co. I	Sergeant
Bousson, David	Co. E	Private
Bowden, John W.	Co. E	Private
Bowdoin, John W.	Co. B	Private
Bowley, G. W.	Co. B	Private
Bowley, W. H.	Co. B	Private
Bowline, W. R.	Co. A	Private
Bowling, H.	_____	Private
Bowring, D. W.	Co. B	Corporal
Bowring, Thompson	Co. B	Musician
Boyd, Jno. A. J.	Co. K	Private
Boyd, W. L.	Co. K	Private
Boykin, George M.	Co. K	Private
Boykin, Moscow B.	Co. A	Private
Boyle, Maurice J.	Co. B	Private
Bracken, James	Co. E	Private
Bradberry, George W.	Co. A	Private
Bradley, A. J.	Co. K	Private
Bradley, James W.	Co. A	Private
Branagan, C P.B.	Co. I	1 Lieu-Captain
Brannan, James E.	Co. H	Private
Brannan, J. W.	Co. H	Private
Brannan, W. J.	Co. H	Private
Braswell, B. B.	Co. D	Private
Brewer, George	Co. I	Private
Brewer, J. S.	_____	Private
Brice, Wm. J.		
Briggs, W. Ben	Co. C	2 Lieu-Captain
Brinson, Hiram H.	Co. E	Private
Brogan, Patrick	Co. F	Private
Brooks, Anderson B.	Co. E	Private
Brooks, Dow P.	Co. F	Private
Brooks, Eugene	Co. F	Bvt 2 Lieu-1 Lieu.
Brosell, A. B.	Co. C	Private
Brosneau, C.	Co. F	Private
Brown, Andrew	Co. G	Private
Brown, Charles F.	Co. D	Private-1 Lieu.
Brown, David	Co. A	Private
Brown, David	Co. E	Private
Brown, F. W.	Co. B	Corporal
Brown, Henry C.	Co. E	Private
Brown, H. H.	_____	Ord. Sergeant
Brown, H. S.	Co. C	Private
Brown, John	Co. C	Private
Brown, John	Co. D	Private
Brown, John A.	Co. D	Private

Brown, John H.	Co. B	Private
Brown, Jonathan	_____	Private
Brown, J.S.	_____	Private
Brown, N. L.	Co. B	Private
Brown, Oliver C.	Co. A	Private
Brown, Peter	Co. G	Private
Brown, Stephen	Co. E	Private
Brown, Thomas	Co. A	Private
Brown, Tom	Co. I	Private
Brown, William	Co. A	Private
Brown, William	Co. G	Sergeant-Pvt.
Browning, B.	Co. A	Private
Browning, F. W.	Co. F	Private
Broyles, B. F.	_____	Private
Broyles, George	_____	Private
Brum, David	_____	_____
Bryan, James	Co. E	Private
Bryant, Henry	Co. C	Private
Buch, Henry W.	Co. H	Private
Buckner, Charles G	Co. I	Private
Buckner, M. W.	Co. B	Private
Buell, David	Co. F	Private-Ord.Sgt
Bulger, L. P.	Co. B	Private-Sergeant
Bundy, John	Co. D	Private
Burk, Henry W. C.	Co. B	Private
Burke, John	Co. I	Corporal-Pvt.
Burmaster, C. F.	Co. I	Private
Burnett, William A.	Co. E	Private
Burns, James	Co. H	Private
Burr, Charles H.	Co. D	Corporal
Burroughs, Bryan	Co. A	Private
Burt John F.	Co. A	Private
Burton, B. F.	Co. B	Private
Bush, C. G.	Co. G	Private
Bush, John H.	Co. B	Private
Bush, R. T.	Co. B	Private
Bushard, James Duke	Co. A	Private
Bussey, D. J.	Co. F	Sergeant
Butler, D.	Co. B	Musician
Butler, D. W.	Co. K	Private
Butler, James	_____	Private
Butler, Sumner E.	Co. D	Private
Butler, W. J.	Co. I	Private
Butler, W. L.	Co. K	1 Lieutenant
Bynum, Robert	Co. E	Private
Byrd, William M. Jr.	Co. D	Pvt.-Sgt.Maj.

Caddell, William J.	Co. A	Private
Cady, David B.	Co. A	Private-2 Lieu.
Cady, George M.	Co. A	Private
Caesar, William	Co. A	Musician
Cain, J. Berry	Co. E	Private
Cain, G. W.	Co. H	Private
Cain, Wm. P.	Co. B	Private
Cakhela, J.	Co. B	Private
Callahan, John C.	Co. C	Private
Callahan, Thomas	Co. K	Private
Callaway, B.C.	Co. G	Private
Callen, James C.	Co. D	Private
Cameron, James	Co. E	Private
Cameron, William	Co. E	Private
Campbell, G. W.	Co. B	Private
Campbell, John	Co. B	Private
Campbell, O.H.	Co. C	Private
Campbell, Samuel	Co. C	Private
Canavan, James	Co. I	Private
Canavan, Patrick	Co. E	Private
Candle, John A.	Co. A	Private
Canney, John	Co. I	Private
Cannon, James	Co. I	Private
Cannon, R. J.	Co. G	Private
Cannon, William	Co. E	Corporal
Canterbury, J. W.	Co. B	Sgt.-2 Lieu.
Carden, John B.	Co. B	Private
Carey, John	Co. C	Private
Cariker, George H.	Co. B	Private
Cariker, Henry	Co. A	Private
Cariker, William W.	Co. B	Private
Carlen, M. Jr.	Co. H	Private
Carleton, Reuben J.	Co. A	Private-Sgt.
Carleton, Wm. E.	Co. K	Private
Carleton, Seaborn	Co. B	Private
Carney, George	Co. I	Private
Carney, W. S.	Co. C	Private
Carpenter, E. E.	Co. H	Private
Carr, H. G.	Co. F	Private
Carr, William	Co. I	Private-Cpl.
Carral, J. P.	Co. I	Private
Carter, John	Co. I	Private
Carvile, J. C.	Co. I	Private
Case, John	Co. I	Private
Casar, William	Co. A	Musician
Cashin, John	Co. H	Private

Cashin, John	Co. I	Private
Caskell, J. B. McCoy	Co. G	Private
Cassaday, John	Co. I	Private
Cassady, John	Co. A	Private
Cassady, John	Co. I	Private
Cassey, John D.	Co. C	Private
Cassidy, S.	Co. I	Private
Castello, James	Co. G	Private
Cathran, James	Co. K	Private
Catleton, William	Co. E	Private
Caughlin, J. A.	Co. C	Private
Cavanagh, B	Co. H	Private
Cavanaugh, William	Co. E	Private
Cenen, P. C.	Co. E	Private
Chaffin, Moses	Co. I	Private
Chandler, C. J.	Co. K	Private
Chaney, J. P.	Co. B	Private
Chapman, Wm. S.	Co. G	Private
Chappell, James L.	Co. B	Private
Chason, Reuben	Co. A	Private
Chastang, Harrison	Co. H	Private
Chavers, G. W.	Co. F	Private
Cherry, Charles	Co. I	Private-Cpl.
Chism, J. W.	Co. H	Private
Church, W. S.	Co. K	Private
Churchill, D.	_____	Private
Clark, C. A.	Co. G	Private
Clark, Edmond	Co. A	Private-Sgt.
Clark, H.	Co. G	Private
Clark, John	Co. H	Private
Clark, Richard	Co. C	Private
Clark, S. W.	Co. H	Private-Sgt.
Clark, William	Co. A	Private
Clement, Joseph	Co. E	Private
Cleveland, Joseph C.	Co. C	Private
Cleveland, Morgan S.	Co. D/F&S	Private-1 Lieu
Cleveland, William F. Jr.	Co. H	Captain
Clousett, John	Co. C	Private-Sgt.
Cobini, Eugene A.	Co. H	Private
Cochran, Jacob H.	Co. I	Private
Cochran, John W.	Co. A	Private
Cochran, Samuel L.	Co. A	Private
Coffee, James	Co. E	Private
Coffield, C. W. J.	Co. C	Private
Coggins, David C.	Co. D	Private
Coker, W. S.	Co. B	Private

Colburn, John W.	Co. A	Private
Coleburn, George W.	Co. E	Private
Coleman, J. F.		Private
Coleman, J. R.	Co. F	Private
Coleman, Robt. C.	Co. B	Private
Coleman, William J.	Co. E	Private
Coley, Robert F.	Co. A	Private-Cpl.
Collier, John D.	Co. H	2 Lieutenant
Collins, Benjamin	Co. G	Private
Collins, Charles	Co. H	Private
Collins, Rice		Private
Colton, Edward G.	Co. D	Private
Commerce, William	Co. H	Private
Conaly, Louis Alexander	Co. D	Private
Conklin, J		Sergeant
Connelly, Patrick	Co. D	Private
Connelly, Randolph	Co. D	Private
Conner, B. F.	Co. B	Private
Connors, Thomas	Co. I	Private
Convy, William	Co. I	Corporal-Pvt.
Conway, P.	Co. I	Private
Cook, B. F.	Co. H	Private
Cook, Enoch		Currier
Cook, F. M.	Co. B	Private
Cook, John J.	Co. A	Private
Cook, Thos. M.	Co. B	Private
Cook, William C.	Co. A	Private
Cook, W.J.	Co. F	Private
Cook, William R.	Co. C	Private
Coon, John	Co. H	Private
Cooper, Henry	Co. C	Private
Cooper, Jackson M.	Co. C	Private
Cooper, John H.	Co. E	Sergeant
Cooper, R.G.D.	Co. B	Private
Cortright, A. W.	Co. C	Sergeant-Pvt.
Cosby, Joseph W.	Co. K	Private
Cosby, J. R.	Co. K	Private
Costello, Joseph	Co. E	Private
Couch, Henry V.	Co. H	Private
Couch, William	Co. A	
Coville, David A.	Co. D	Private
Cox, Francis	Co. C	Private
Cox, Robert	Co. F	Private
Cox, T.	Co. E	Private
Coyne, James	Co. I	Private
Cranford, J. J.	Co. F	Private

Crassin, Fernando A.	Co. H	Private
Creech, A. C.	Co. H	Private
Crevallair, Thomas	Co. I	Private
Crittenden, Elijah T.	Co. B	Private
Crocker, John M.	Co. K	Private
Croft, E. D.	Co. F	Private
Crooks, Samuel B.	Co. B	Private
Croswell, Robert H. Jr.	Co. D	Private
Croughan, Patrick	Co. A	Private
Crow, W. T.	Co. B	Private
Crowly, Patrick	Co. I	Private
Crumpler, L. H.	Co. B	2 Lieutenant
Crutch, E. C.	Co. H	Private
Cumby, A. B.		Private
Cummings, C. C.	Co. K	Private
Cummings, F. P.	Co. K	Private
Cummings, J. W.	Co. C	Private
Cunningham, G. W.	Co. D	Private
Curt, H. C.	Co. F	Private
Curley, W. J.	Co. D	Private
Curmeitter, C. F.	Co. C	Private
Curry, John	Co. C	Private
Curtin, John	Co. I	Private
Curtis, H. K.	Co. C	Private
Cutchins, J.	Co. H	Private
Cutts, James M.	Co. E	Private
Dade, Jerry	Co. C	Musician
Dailey, John	Co. A	Private
Daisy, John	Co. I	Private
Daley, Robert T.	Co. E	Private-1st SGT.
Dallinger, J. G.	Co. B	Private
Dalton, A. W.	Co. D	Private
Danavan, J. T.	Co. F	Private
Dargan, Pat	Co. I	Private
Darrah, H. F.	Co. B	Private
Daubach, John H.	Co. G	Private-Sgt.
Daughdrill, John L.	Co. H	Private
Daughtry, William T.	Co. D	Private
David, L. J.	Co. C	Private
Davies, T. W. W.	Co. B	Captain
Davis, James H.	Co. A	Private
Davis, John F.	Co. H	Private
Davis, Milton	Co. I	Private
Davis, Uriah	Co. K	Private
Davis, W. C.	Co. I	Private
Davis, William J.	Co. H	Private

Davis, W. J. R.	Co. H	Private
Davis, W. S.	Co. F	Private
Day, Marshall	Co. D	Private
Deacent, A. J.	Co. B	Private
Deal, Lewis	Co. H	Private
Dean, Thomas R.	Co. A	Private
Dearman, Thomas L.	Co. C	Private
Deason, Andrew John	Co. B	Private
Deaton, John H.	Co. E	Corporal-Sergeant
Debardeleben, A. M.	Co. B	Sgt.-2 Lieu.
DeBarleder, A. H.	Co. A	Private
Deboise, G. W.	Co. I	Private
Dee, G. W.	Co. F	————
Deelay, John H.	Co. G	Private
Dees, J.	Co. D	Private
DeHaven, Robert	Co. E	Corporal
Deith, William	Co. H	Private
Delannon, Eugene	————	Private
Demins, M.	Co. F	Private
Denman, Robert	Co. C	Private
Denmark, W. B.	Co. C	Private
Denny, Joseph W.	Co. C	Cpl.-Pvt.
Densberry, Joseph C.	Co. D	Private
Densmore, Samuel	Co. I	Private
Derden, W. D.	————	Private
Devaney, William	Co. E	Private
Devine, Peter	Co. I	Private
Diamond, Edw.	Co. E	Private
Diamond, James	Co. E	Private
Dix, Frisby D.	Co. C	Private-Sgt.
Dixon, Abram	Co. F	Private
Doherty, John C.	Co. I	Private
Dolan, Thomas	Co. I	Private
Donald, T. J.	Co. H	Private
Donegan, Thomas	Co. I	Private
Doneley, John	Co. E	Private
Donivan, Henry	Co. A	Private
Donivan, Moses E.	Co. A	Private-Sgt.
Donivan, Thomas	Co. A	Private
Donnavan, W. G.	Co. H	Pvt.-Cpl.
Donnavan, William	Co. C	Private
Donnell, Edward O.	Co. I	Musician
Donnell, J. M.	————	Private
Donoho, William E.	Co. D	Private
Doremas, T. J.	Co. A	Private
Doswell, F.	Co. F	Private

Doty, Joseph W.	Co. E	Private
Dougherty, James A.	Co. D	Private
Dovely, John	Co. D	Private
Dowling, Dennis	Co. I	Private
Dowling, James	Co. I	Private
Dowling, John	Co. I	Private
Downs, W. W.	Co. B	Private
Drake, Norman B.	Co. D	Private
Draper, W.	Co. A	Private
Drayman, J.	Co. E	Private
Driver, F. A.	Co. K	1st Sergeant
Duff, Michael	Co. I	Private
Duke, Perry M.	Co. A	Private
Duke, William H.	Co. A	Private
Dukes, William	Co. B	Private
Duncan, John	Co. A	Private
Dunklin, J. B.	Co. K	Private
Dunlap, G. R.	Co. D	Private
Dunn, D. W.	Co. H	Private
Dunn, H.	Co. F	Private
Dunn, J. W.	Co. F	Pvt.-Cpl.
Dunn, Martin	Co. F	Private
Dunn, William H.	Co. H	Cpl.-2Lieu.AQM
Dupes, C. W.	Co. C	Private
Durden, John W.	Co. E	Private
Dwyre, Walter	Co. I	Private
Dwyre, William	Co. I	Private
Dye, Thomas	Co. E	Private
Dyer, S.	Co. C	Private
Eagan, M.	Co. I	Private
Earnest, J. S.	Co. F	Private
Eastburn, C. R.	Co. C	Private
Echols, Lewis B.	Co. C	Private
Eddins, Joseph	Co. E	Private
Edmonds, J. H.	Co. D	Private
Edmondson, William B.	Co. D	Private
Edwards, A.	Co. B	Private
Edwards, F. M.	Co. K	Private
Edwards, James	Co. K	Private
Edwards, James Jr.	Co. K	Private
Edwards, James Sr.	Co. K	Private
Edwards, John R.	Co. B	Private
Edwards, R. H.	Co. D	Private
Edwards, S. A.	Co. K	Private
Edwards, S. W.	Co. D	Private
Edwards, W. J.	Co. K	Private

Egger, Francis	Co. G	Private
Eldre, Daniel	Co. I	Private
Elliott, Toler	Co. K	Private
Ellis, Edward	Co. D	Private
Ellis, J. S.	Co. E	Private
Elmore, R. G.	Co. D	Private
Embry, David	Co. E	Private
Emrich, John P.	Co. G/F&S	Capt., LT. Col
Engar, Charles	Co. D	Private
Engle, Charles	Co. E/G	Pvt.-Cpl.
England, W. S.	Co. K	Private
Ennis, William	Co. C	Private
Enslen, J. H.	Co. B	Private
Estes, W.	Co. E	Private
Evans, Bronson R.	Co. B	Private
Evans, Jas.	_____	Private
Evans, J. H.	_____	Corporal
Evans, W. H.	Co. G	Private
Evans, Wade Hampton	Co. D	Private
Evans, W. R.	Co. G	Private
Ezell, Joseph W.	Co. D	Private
Faelar, Jerome	Co. G	Private
Fagan, William	Co. E	Private
Fagan, William L.	Co. K	2 Lieu.-Captain
Fahy, John	Co. E	Private
Fain, J. W.	Co. K	Private
Fallon, Thomas	Co. I	Private
Farnon, James	Co. C	Private
Faxon, Henry	Co. D	Private
Feeney, Bernard	Co. I	Private
Ferguson, George W.	Co. H	Private
Ferguson, W. A.	_____	Lieutenant
Fibry, S. H.	Co. A	_____
Fike, C. E.	Co. K	Private
Fike, James H.	Co. K	Private
Filbert, W. S.	Co. K	Private
Finch, James A.	Co. C	2 Lieutenant
Finigan, Timothy	Co. I	Private
Finley, Edgar S.	Co. E	Private
Finley, T. J.	Co. G	Private
Finn, J.	Co. B	Private
Finton, John	Co. H	Private
Fisher, John	Co. G	Corporal
Fiske, Charles E.	Co. H	Corporal
Fitzgerald, James	Co. D	Private
Fitzgerald, James	Co. I	Private

Fitzgerald, Michael	Co. E	Private
Fitzpatrick, Bernard	Co. E	Private
Flager, P.	Co. G	Private
Flanagan, James	Co. I	2 Lieutenant
Flannery, Phil	Co. I	Private
Fleming, R. H.	Co. A	Private
Flemming, G. R.	Co. B	Private
Flemming, J. I.	Co. A	Private
Floyd, M. C.	Co. B	Pvt.-Cpl.
Flynn, E. E.	Co. I	Private
Fogg, W. R.		Private
Folter, E.	Co. A	Private
Forbus, Geo. F.	Co. B	Private
Forbus, Josiah S.	Co. B	Private
Ford, Homer M.	Co. K	Private
Forman, Arthur	Co. I	Private
Foster, J. A.	Co. D	Private
Foster, R. M.	Co. A	Private
Foster, Samuel N.	Co. D	Private
Foster, William M.	Co. G	Private
Fowler, G. W.	Co. K	Private
Folwer, Lawson	Co. K	Private
Fowler, O. C.	Co. K	Private
Foy, James	Co. I	Private
Foy, Thomas	Co. C	Private
Franklin, O.	Co. H	Private
Franz, Peter C.	Co. G	Private
Frasier, William	Co. G	Private
Frazer, J. F.	Co. E	Private
Frazer, John W.	F&S	Lt. Col
Frische, William	Co. G	Private
Frith, Henry H.	Co. K	Private
Frith, Jos. M.	Co. K	Private
Fuller, B. J.	Co. K	Mus.-2 Lieu.
Fuller, George W.	Co. K	Private
Fuller, Jesse S.	Co. K	Private
Fuller, John T.	Co. A	Private
Fuller, Jas. M	Co. K	Private
Fuller, Richard P. T.	Co. K	Private
Fullmer, C. G.	Co. E	Private
Furgerson, John T.	Co. B	Private
Gaddes, Robert	Co. C	Private-2 Lieu.
Gaines, H. F.	Co. E	Private
Gallagher, Charles	Co. E	Private
Gallagher, W. C.	Co. C	Private
Galloway, B. C.	Co. G	

Galloway, G. W.	Co. F	Private
Gambell, S.	Co. F	Private
Gamble, M. J.		Private
Gambrel, W. T.	Co. K	Private
Gandey, A. E.		Private
Gantt, David	Co. B	Private
Gardner, G. P.	Co. C	Corporal
Gardner, G. Thomas	Co. D	Private
Gardner, M.	Co. H	Private
Garner, W. L.	Co. F	Pvt.-Cpl.
Garrett, B. L.		Private
Garrett, William A.	Co. D	Private
Garrison, Benjamin F.	Co. K	Private
Garrison, John P.	Co. K	Private
Garrison, S. D.	Co. K	Private
Garrison, S. F.	Co. K	Private
Garrod, J. D.		Private
Gates, Joseph C.	Co. E	Private
Gay, J. H.	Co. B	Private
Gay, Joshua N.	Co. B	Private
Gay, Thomas B.	Co. E	Private
Gayle, George B.	Co. C	Private
Geary, Cornelius	Co. I	Private
Gedling, Fred	Co. C	Private
Gengenbach, Gottlieb	Co. G	Private
Gensler, Samuel	Co. G	Private
Gentry, Jasper M.	Co. A	Private
Gentry, John M.	Co. A	Private
Gentry, Manly	Co. A	Private
Gentry, Reason J.	Co. A	Private
Gentry, R. H.	Co. F	Private
George, M. D.	Co. K	Private
Gilchrist, John	Co. G	Private
Gilday, Patrick	Co. F	Private
Gill, G. W.	Co. H	Private
Gill, Joseph K.	Co. C	Private
Gill, N. H.	Co. H	Private
Gilland, B. F.	Co. B	Private
Gilliland, A. J.	Co. A	Private
Gilpin, R. G.	Co. A	Private
Ginn, A. V.	Co. B	Private-Sgt.
Ginn, W. J.	Co. B	Private
Glancy, J. R.	Co. F	Sergeant
Glaye[Glaze], William	Co. I	Private
Godwin, James P.	Co. G	Private
Goggins, D. C.	Co. D	Private

Golden, G. W.	Co. A	Private
Golding, John	Co. I	Private
Golding, Patrick	Co. I	Private
Goldsby, Jackson	Co. E	Private
Goldsmith, Robert	Co. G	Pvt.-1st SGT
Golson, W. H.	_____	Conscript
Goocher, W. J.	Co. K	Private
Goodman, J.	Co. H	Private
Goodson, C.	_____	Private
Goodson, David	Co. H	Private
Goodson, J.	_____	Private
Goodwin, Ferderick H.	Co. C	Private
Goodwin, J. R.	Co. D	Private
Goodwin, Thomas J.	Co. B	Private
Gordon, Thomas	Co. I	Private
Gore, C. A.	Co. F	Private
Gore, J. M.	Co. H	Private
Gore, William J.	Co. F	Private
Gottmanshausen, Gustave	Co. G	Private
Gould, B. E.	Co. G	Private-2 Lieu.
Gould, H. L.	Co. C	Private
Gould, M. B.	Co. C	Private
Govini, E. A.	Co. H	Private
Graham, J. A.	Co. H	Private
Graham, Jesse H.	Co. C	Private
Graham, J. L.	Co. G	Private
Graham, W.	Co. G	Private
Grandberry, C. F.	Co. G	Private
Grangentes, G.	Co. G	Private
Granger, Luther B.	Co. D	Private
Granger, William H.	Co. D	Private
Gratrix, Joseph	Co. G	Private
Gray, B. B.	Co. E	Private
Gray, M. M.	Co. H	Private
Green, J. P.	Co. K	Private
Green, W. P.	Co. K	Private
Gregery, S.	Co. A	Private
Griffin, F. M.	Co. H	Private
Griffin, Jas. H.	Co. D	Private
Griffin, John W.	Co. K	Private
Griffin, Richard C.	Co. A	Sergeant
Griffin, R. F.	_____	Private
Griffin, Sam'l F.	Co. K	_____
Griffin, Samuel T.	Co. D	Private
Griggs, D. M.	Co. C	Corporal
Groce, G. L.	Co. C	Private

Grove, D. J.	Co. G	Private
Guilford, E.	Co. A	Private
Guinn, G. A	Co. D	Private
Guntry, S. C.	Co. D	Private
Haas, Augustus A.	Co. E	Pvt.-Cpl.
Hachmeyer, Heinrich	Co. G	Private
Hadeler, Adolphus T.	Co. D	Private
Haden, James	Co. B	Private
Haden, Joel W.	Co. D	Private
Hain, T. N.	Co. K	Private
Haley, Timothy	Co. E	Private
Hall, B. F.	Co. D	Private
Hall, Dennis	Co. I	Private
Hall, George W.	Co. F	Private
Hall, J.	Co. B	Private
Hall, Joseph	Co. B	Private
Hall, William A.	Co. B	Private
Halpin, John T.	Co. I	2 Lieutenant
Ham, Philip	Co. A	Private
Hamilton, E. C.		Private
Hamilton, J. L.	Co. G	Cpl.-Pvt.
Hamilton, John	Co. I	Private
Hamilton, William	Co. I	Private
Hammock, J. H.	Co. C	Private
Hamrick, James	Co. A	Private
Hancock, N.	Co. G	Private
Handley, H. H.	Co. D	Private
Handley, J. E.	Co. D	Private
Hanlein, Frank	Co. G	Cpl.-Sergeant
Hanlon, William	Co. I	Private
Hanney, T.	Co. A	Private
Hannon, Charles	Co. I	Sergeant
Hannon, G. W.	Co. B	1 Lieu.-Captain
Hannon, J. B.	Co. B	2 Lieu.-1 Lieu.
Hanse, Philip	Co. H	Private
Hanson, John W.	Co. K	Private
Harbour, C. C.	Co. K	Private
Harbour, E. T.	Co. K	Private
Harbour, John R.	Co. K	Private
Hark, A. A.	Co. E	Private
Harley, Michael	Co. K	Private
Harman, A. E.	Co. A	Private
Harman, T. W.		Private
Harold, D.	Co. B	Private
Harp, Angus	Co. D	Private
Harp, Joseph	Co. D	Private

Name	Company	Rank
Harrel, C. R.	Co. H	Sergeant
Harrington, S.	Co. D	Private
Harris, A. C.	Co. B	Private
Harris, B. F.	Co. B	Private
Harris, George C.	Co. K	Pvt.-Cpl.
Harris, J. P.	Co. K/F&S	Pvt.-SGT.Major
Harris, O. M.	Co. K	Private
Harris, R. C.	Co. E	Private
Harris, Robt. T.	Co. D	Pvt.-Sergeant
Harris, W. J.	Co. B	Private
Harrison, Benjamin C.	Co. D	Private
Harrison, John	Co. G	Private
Harry, _____	Co. H	Musician
Hart, John	Co. E	Private
Hart, Joseph	Co. I	Private-1st SGT
Hartley, Daniel	Co. C	Private
Hartley, F. E.	Co. C	Pvt.-Cpl.
Hartley, H. C.	Co. C	Private
Hartley, James	Co. C	Private
Harvill, Augustus	Co. I	Private
Harwell, C. R.	Co. H	Cpl.-Sgt.
Harwell, William	Co. H	Pvt.-Cpl.
Harwood, C. F.	Co. A	Private
Hastings, B. W.	Co. I	Private
Hatch, F.	Co. F	Sergeant
Hatch, George	Co. F	Private-1 Lieu.
Hattery, T. J.	Co. D	Private
Hauck, Nicholas	Co. G	Music.-Sergeant
Hauersberger, Jacob	Co. G	Private
Hawking, Thomas	Co. F	Private
Hayes, Albert	Co. C	Private
Hayes, Dennis	Co. D	Private
Hayes, Timothy	Co. E	Pvt.-Sergeant
Haynes, John	Co. B	Private
Haynes, W. J.	Co. F	Private
Haynes, Zachariah	Co. B	Private
Haynie, Henry	Co. D	Private
Hays, W. H.	Co. C	Private
Hays, William R.	_____	Private
Headley, J. N.	Co. F	Private
Heard, R. J.	Co. K	Private
Heard, Thomas Richard	Co. A	2 Lieu.-Captain
Heming, R. H.	Co. A	_____
Hencher, William	Co. E	Private
Henden, J.	Co. B	Private
Henderson, O.S.	Co. F	Private

Name	Company	Rank
Henderson, P.A.	Co. C	Private
Hendrix, A. W.	Co. B	Private
Henessy, Dennis	Co. I	Private
Henly, Edward	Co. K	Private
Heinrich, Sebastian	Co. G	Private
Henre, P.		Private
Henry, S.	Co. G	Private
Herbert, Hilary Abner	Co. F/F&S	Captain-Colonel
Herbert, John	Co. H	Private
Hern, Joseph		Private
Hern, P. A.	Co. G	Private
Herring, Isaac	Co. I	Private
Hester, Samuel B.	Co. F	Private
Hickman, J. H.	Co. D	Private
Hicks, J. L.	Co. K	Private
Hicks, J. N.	Co. A	Private
Hicks, Joseph	Co. E	Private
Higgins, F.	Co. I	Private
Higgins, P. W.	Co. K	
Higglotten, A. A.	Co. C	Private
Hilf, Samuel	Co. H	Sergeant
Hill, H. J.	Co. C	Private
Hill, James	Co. H	Private
Hilston, J.	Co. A	Private
Hilton, William	Co. H	Private
Hingston, S. W.	Co. H	Private
Hippler, A.	Co. G	Private
Hippler, Adam	Co. G	2 Lieutenant
Hippler, Charles	Co. G	Private
Hobart, H. J.	Co. C	Corporal
Hodge, John W.	Co. K	Private
Hodge, W. L.	Co. K	Private
Hoey, Michael	Co. E	Private
Hoffle, A.	Co. B	Private
Hogan, Patrick	Co. C	Private
Hogg, J. F.		Conscript
Hokes, J. D.	Co. A	Corporal
Holland, J. F.	Co. I	Private
Holly, Wm. B.	Co. F	Private
Holstead, John	Co. A	Private
Holton, Horace W.	Co. D	1stSGT.-Sgt.
Holiday, D. G.	Co. I	Private
Hood, James	Co. E	Cpl.-Pvt.
Hopkins, Solaman	Co. K	Private
Hopper, J.	Co. B	Private
Hopper, W. W.	Co. B	Pvt.-Cpl.

Name	Company	Rank
Horton, James L.	Co. B	Private
Horton, W. H.	Co. B	Private
Horsley, G.		Private
Houghs, J. H.	Co. D	Private
Howard, Claiborne	Co. K	Private
Howard, Claudius F.	Co. A	Private
Howard, H. C.	Co. K	Private
Howard, J. N.	Co. B	Pvt.-Cpl.
Howard, John	Co. E	Private
Howard, William H.	Co. F	Private
Howard, Wiley M.	Co. B	Cpl.-Pvt.
Howell, Abel	Co. H	Private
Hubbard, Andrew J.	Co. A	Pvt.-Sergeant
Huff, Ira H.	Co. A	Private
Huff, James M.	Co. K	Private
Huffman, James K.	Co. D	Pvt.-Sergeant
Hugh, H. W.	Co. C	Lieutenant
Hughes, Patrick	Co. E	Private
Hull, Benjamin F.	Co. D	Private
Humes, H. C.	Co. H	Private
Hunt, Felix M.	Co. H	Pvt.-Commissary Sergeant
Hurd, John	Co. A	Corporal
Hursey, G. A.	Co. H	Pvt.-Cpl.
Hurst, Thomas J.	Co. E	Private
Hurt, H. H.	Co. K	Private
Hutchins, Michael	Co. A	Private
Ingram, J. L.	Co. F	Private
Irby, Thomas E.	F&S	Major-Lt.Col
Ireland, W. W.	Co. D	Private
Iron, T. P.		Private
Isley, S. T.	Co. B	Private
Ivey, Hinton C. G.	Co. A	Pvt.-Sergeant
Ivey, William D	Co. A	Private
Izell, J. W.	Co. D	Private
Izell, W. H.	Co. K	Private
Jackson, Charles	Co. H	Private
Jackson, David	Co. C	Private
Jackson, George	Co. K	Private
Jackson, Henry	Co. C	Private
Jackson, J. A.	Co. H	Private
Jackson, John W.	Co. C	Private
Jackson, Joseph	Co. A	Sergeant
Jackson, L. F.	Co. A	Private
Jackson, Thomas	Co. K	Private
Jackson, William O.	Co. H	Private
Jackson, William S.	Co. A	Private

Name	Company	Rank
Jackson, William T.	Co. A	Private
James, Edward D.	Co. A	Corporal
James, Henry	Co. C	Private
Jansen, August	—	Private-2 Lieu.
Jarvis, John W.	Co. C	Private
Jeffreys, James	Co. A	Private
Jenkins, B. H.		Private
Jennings, Henry W.	Co. A	Private
Jennings, Samuel K.	Co. A	Corporal
Jennings, James	Co. I	Private
Jerden, F. M.	Co. C	Private
Jester, Nelson	Co. B	Private
Johnson, Arthur	Co. G	Pvt.-Cpl.
Johnson, B.	Co. B	Private
Johnson, C. C.	Co. A	Private
Johnson, D. E.	Co. A	Private
Johnson, Henry S.	Co. A	Private
Johnson, H. V.	Co. F	Private
Johnson, J.	Co. B	Private
Johnson, James M.	Co. A	Private
Johnson, John J.	Co. E	Private
Johnson, Scott	Co. A	Musician
Johnson, Wm. J.	Co. B	—
Jones, Amos	Co. F	Private
Jones, B. B.	Co. K	Private
Jones, B. M.	Co. F	Private
Jones, Daniel	Co. D/F&S	Private-AQM
Jones, Francis J.	Co. E	Private-2 Lieu.
Jones, Harrison	Co. A	Private
Jones, J. C.	Co. K	Private
Jones, J. J. Jr.	Co. H	Private
Jones, John A.	Co. K	Private
Jones, T. C.	Co. D	Private
Jordan. F. M.	Co. C	Private
Jordan, J.	Co. B	Private
Jordan, J. D. M.	Co. K	Private
Jordan, William	Co. B	Private
Jordan, W. D.		Private
Jordan, W. T.	Co. C	Private
Jowers, J.A.D.M.	Co. B	Private
Joy, W. H.	Co. A	—
Judah, Henry C.	Co. E	Private
Juzand, Pierre	Co. E	Pvt.-Sergeant
Kain, Durham	Co. I	Private
Kane, Michael	Co. I	Private
Kappell, M. G.	Co. B	Private

Kay, Anthony	Co. I	Private
Keane, M.	Co. I	Private
Kearney, Patrick	Co. I	Private
Keefe, Thomas	Co. G	Private
Keinle, John	Co. G	Private
Kelley, C. H.	Co. B	Private
Kelley, J. S.	Co. D	Private
Kelley, S. A.	Co. H	Private
Kelley, Surrey	Co. A	Private
Kelley, Thomas	Co. F	Private-2 Lieu.
Kelly, Daniel H.	Co. B	Private
Kelly, Henry H.	Co. F	Private
Kelly, John	Co. H	Private
Kelly, M. J.	Co. B	Private
Kelly, N. G.	Co. F	Private
Kelly, Richard	Co. E	Private
Kelly, T. A.	Co. F	Pvt.-Sergeant
Kendrick, D.	Co. A	Private
Kennedy, Isaac	Co. H	Private
Kennedy, Joshua	Co. H	1 Lieutenant
Kennedy, T.	Co. G	Private
Kennedy, Thomas W.	Co. C	Pvt.-Sergeant
Kennedy, William	Co. E	Private
Kent, James	Co. D	Captain
Kent, Pierce	Co. I	Pvt.-Sergeant
Keone, H.	Co. I	Private
Ketchum, Charles T.	Co. C	Captain
Kidd, William	Co. G	Private
Kiefer, Peter	Co. G	Corporal
Kieley, Richard	Co. I	Private
Killion, James	Co. I	Pvt.-Lieu.
King, Anthony	Co. I	Private
King, Frank	Co. E	Private
King, J.	Co. F	Private
King, S. J.	Co. G	Private
Kirkland, Abram	Co. E	Private
Kirkland, Benjamin J.	Co. C	Private
Kirkland, John S.	Co. E	Private
Kirkland, M.	Co. A	Private
Kirkland, W. R.	Co. D	Private
Kirkland, William V.	Co. I	Private
Kirkpatrick, James M.	Co. D	Private
Kitchen, R. A.	Co. D	Private
Kline, Ferdinand	Co. G	Musician
Knott, R. F.	Co. C	Private
Knox, Asa W.	Co. C	Private

Name	Company	Rank
Knox, William R.	Co. F/D	Sgt.-Captain
Kohler, Anthony	Co. G	1 Lieu.-Captain
Kohn, Frederick M.	Co. D	Private
Krane, A.	Co. I	Private
Krassin, F. H.	Co. H	Private
Krause, August	Co. F	Pvt.-Cpl.
Kriebel, F.	Co. G	Private
Krueger, Charles	Co. H	1st Sergeant
Kruse, Henry	Co. G	Pvt.-Cpl.
Lacoste, A.	Co. C	Private
Lacunteguey, Victor	Co. E	Private
Lampson, E.	Co. E	Private
Lanahan, John	Co. I	Private
Land, John D.	Co. F	Private
Lander, B. M.	_____	Corporal
Landrum, L. B.	Co. I	Private
Lane, John	Co. C	Private
Lane, R. W.	Co. F	Private
Lane, W. H. A.	Co. F	1st Sgt-2 Lieu.
Lang, T. G.	Co. F	Private
Langan, Thomas	Co. I	Private
Langdon, John	Co. C	Private
Langford, C. M.	Co. K	Private
Langford, J. B.	Co. K	Private
Langford, Neil	Co. K	Private
Langston, L. C.	Co. K	Pvt.-Cpl.
Lappington, Albert P.	Co. C	Private
Lapsley, Robert	Co. D	Private
Lassitter, Joel	Co. C/A/E	Private
Latnor, John V.	Co. A	Private
Lauder, George	Co. G	Private
Lawler, William	Co. E	Private
Lawly, R. P.	Co. K	Private
Lea, Henry C.	Co. A	Private
Lea, Henry C.	Co. C	1st Sgt-Captain
Leak, T. F.	Co. B	Pvt.-Sgt.
Leary, J.	Co. D	Private
Leary, Patrick	Co. I	Private
Leathers, A.	Co. H	Private
Lee, George	Co. F	Corporal
Lee, Geo. W.	Co. F	Corporal
Lee, J. M.	Co. F	Private
Lee, John H.	Co. G	Private
Lee, W. A.	Co. F	Private
Legett, Samuel	Co. C	Private
Leigh, H. B.	_____	Chief Musician

Name	Company	Rank
Lemblom, A. William	Co. E	Private
Leroy, Joseph	Co. D	Private
Lesenbo, J. L.	Co. B	Private
Lester, J. R.	Co. D	Private
Lewis, F.		Private
Lewis, Isaac	Co. H	Private
Lewis, W. D.	Co. B	Private
Linebaugh, William	Co. D	Private
Linn, W. J.	Co. A	Private
Lipscomb, D. W.	Co. H	Private
Livingston, A.	Co. F	Private
Livingston, A. J.		Private
Livingston, Lewis A.	Co. F	Private
Locke, D. W. L.	Co. D	Private
Lockridge, R. G.	Co. D	Private
Loftis, James M.	Co. F	Private
Lofton, A.		Private
Lofton, Van	Co. H	Private
Logan, George W.	Co. A	Private
Logan, Henderson B.	Co. A	Pvt.-Cpl.
Logan, William L.	Co. A	Private
Lohide, John C.	Co. G	Private
Long, E.		Private
Long, J.		Private
Long, J. C.	Co. F	
Loughry, Oliver	Co. I	Private
Loughry, Patrick	Co. I	Captain
Love, William	Co. E	Private
Lovelass, Andrew M.	Co. C	Private
Lowenfield, Hammond	Co. G	Private
Lowery, Thomas	Co. K	Private
Loyall, John M.	Co. B	Sgt.-2 Lieu.
Lundie, Benjamin M.	Co. D	Private
Lybrain, W. J.	Co. C	Private
Lyle, M. P.	Co. B	Private
Lynch, John	Co. I	Private
Lyons, Cornelius	Co. C	Private
Mack, Otto	Co. D	Private
Madden, William	Co. H	Private
Maddox, S. J.	Co. B	Private
Magnier, M.	Co. H	Private
Mahan, John S.	Co. K	Private
Mahir, Dan	Co. I	Private
Maily, John	Co. I	Private
Mallon, John	Co. I	Private
Malone, A. C.	Co. D	Private

Name	Company	Rank
Malone, G. F.	Co. H	Private
Malone, Henry R.	Co. H/G	Sgt.-1st SGT.
Malone, J. C.	Co. D	Private
Malone, J. G.	Co. H	Private
Malone, M. A.	Co. H	Pvt.-Sergeant
Malone, William	Co. K/H	Private
Man, E. L.	Co. I	Private
Mangan, M. E.	Co. H	Private
Manning, W. J.	Co. G	Private
Maples, William S.	Co. D	Private
Marcus, James	Co. K	Private
Markel, P.	Co. H	Private
Marnell, James	Co. E	Private
Marston, P.	Co. I	————
Martin, B.	Co. I	Private
Martin, B.F.	Co. K	Pvt.-Sergeant
Martin, John	Co. B	Private
Martin, Joshua L.	Co. D	Private
Martin, Partrick	Co. E	Private
Martin, Robert P.	Co. G	Private
Martin, William D.	Co. E	Private
Martin, William E.	Co. A	Private
Marx, Henry	Co. H	Private
Mason, Charles	Co. H	Private
Massey, Martin V.	Co. A	Private-2 Lieu.
Massey, William E.	Co. A/F&S	Pvt.-Chaplain
Mathers, William	Co. I	Cpl.-Pvt.
Mathis, S. E.	Co. B	Private
Mattellac, W. E.	Co. G	————
Matthews, B. B.	Co. B	Private
Matthews, H.	Co. B	Private
Maynard, Cornelius M.	Co. B	Cpl.-2 Lieu.
Mays, Patrick H.	Co. D	Pvt.-Jr.2 Lieu.
McAffee, George	Co. I	Private
McAffee, William	Co. I	Private
McAuly, Rody	Co. I	Private
McCabe, Thomas W.	Co. C	Music.-Pvt.
McCarly, James A.	Co. B	Private
McCarney, J.	Co. I	Private
McCarron, John	Co. I	Pvt.-Sergeant
McCaskill, Allen	Co. G	Private
McCaskill, W. C.	Co. F	Sergeant-Pvt.
McCaskill, W. E.	Co. G/I	Private
McClintock, Horace G.	Co. H	Private
McClintock, James A.	Co. C	Private
McClure, J. W.	Co. I	Private

Name	Company	Rank
McCluskey, Peter	Co. E	Private
McCollum, John H.	Co. K	Pvt.-Sergeant
McCool, John	Co. F	Private
McCormick, Neil	Co. H	Private
McCormick, R. P.		AQM
McCosker, Matheas J.	Co. G	Pvt.-Sergeant
McCoy, Stephen		Private (See also 1st LA Cav)
McCrary, Robert A.	Co. D	2 Lieu.-Captain
McCready, William	Co. I	Private
McCudden, James	Co. E	Private
McCullough, Rufus G.	Co. A	Private
McCurdy, Lucius L.	Co. D	Pvt.-Sergeant
McDaniel, James A.		Private
McDaniel, James W.	Co. F	Private
McDevitt, William	Co. I	Private
McDonald, J. A.	Co. G	Private
McDonald, Mike D.	Co. G	Pvt.-Jr.2 Lieu.
McDonnell, Charles	Co. C	Private
McDonnell, William	Co. A	Private
McElroy, Abram J.	Co. C	Private
McEntyre, E. A.	Co. G	Private
McFarland, John	Co. F	Private
McFea, J.	Co. F	Private
McFeely, James	Co. I	Private
McGavin, Frank	Co. F	Private
McGlynn, Thomas	Co. I	Private
McGrath, John	Co. I	Pvt.-Captain
McGraw, William H.	Co. H	Private
McGregor, John J.	Co. G	Private
McHugh, Henry	Co. C	Sgt.-1 Lieu.
McIliver, Andrew	Co. I	Private
McInnerney, Patrick W.	Co. C	Private
McKee, David	Co. F	2 Lieutenant
McKeone, Hugh	Co. I	Pvt.-Cpl.
McKeown, John	Co. I	Sergeant
McKinzie, H.	Co. C/I	Pvt.-Cpl.
McKnight, James	Co. E	Private
McLaine, T. L.	Co. C	Private
McLaughlin, John D.	Co. A	Jr.2 Lieu.-1 Lieutenant
McLendon, J. J.	Co. F	Private
McLeoud, Alex.	Co. H	Private
McManus, Francis	Co. I	Private
McMeehan, James	Co. E	Musician
McMurray, Andrew	Co. K	Private
McNiff, Patrick	Co. I	Private

Name	Company	Rank
McNulty, James	——	Private
McVay, G. W.	——	Private
McWilliams, Mortimer G.	Co. B	2 Lieu.-Captain
Meadows, W.	——	Private
Melton, J. J.	Co. C	Private
Melton, John W.	Co. B	Private
Melton, Thomas M.	Co. K	Private
Mercer, Joseph	Co. E	Private
Merideth, J.T.(Thomas J.)	Co. K	Private
Merideth, W. S.	Co. K	Private
Merriam, James	Co. E	Private
Merrill, M. J.	Co. H	Private
Merritt, G. B	Co. I	Private
Merritt, J. G.	Co. D	Private
Merritt, J. W.	Co. B	Private
Meyers, Charles	Co. G	Private
Meyers, John	Co. G	Private
Michaud, P.	Co. B	Private
Middlebrook, W. E.	Co. C	Private
Mighen, M.	Co. F	Private
Miller, C.	Co. F	Private
Miller, Charles P.	Co. D	Private
Miller, Frank B.	Co. C	Private-2 Lieu.
Miller, Frederick	Co. G	Private
Miller, Jacob	Co. G	Cpl.-Pvt.
Miller, John	Co. B	Private
Millhouse, Clarence A.	Co. A	Private
Mills, L. W.	Co. F	Private
Milner, Erastus L.	Co. F	Private
Milner, J. B.	Co. F	Cpl.-Sergeant
Mimms, W. W.	Co. F	Private
Miner, Peter	——	Private
Mitchel, R. S.	Co. K	Private
Moant, G. B.	Co. I	Private
Mock, George F.	Co. K	Private
Moffat, H. D.	Co. H	Private
Molash, P. A.	Co. K	Private
Monroe, Thomas C.	Co. K	2Music.-1 Lieu.
Mooney, James P. Jr.	Co. E	Private
Mooney, John	Co. E	Private
Moore, Edward	Co. E	Pvt.-Sergeant
Moore, Isaac	Co. D	Private
Moore, James N.	Co. E	Private
Moore, J. F.	Co. F	Private
Moore, O. G.	Co. D	Private
Moore, W. D.	Co. C	Private

Name	Company	Rank
Moorenan, J. L.	Co. K	Private
Moosback, A.	Co. I	Private
Moran, F.	Co. I	Private
Mordecai, William W.	Co. H	2 Lieu.-Captain
Morgan, E. C.	Co. C	Private
Morgan, John	Co. C	Private
Morgan, M. V.	Co. C	Private
Morman, George	Co. C	Private
Morris, F. R.	Co. D	Private
Morris, J.	Co. E	Private
Morris, J.A.J.	Co. D	Private
Morris, James R.	Co. K	Private
Morris, James S.	Co. K	Private
Morris, L. A.	Co. F	Private
Morris, M. W.	Co. D/E	Private
Morris, Richard	Co. F	Private
Morris, Wm. L.	Co. B	Private
Morris, Zachariah S.	Co. D	Private
Morrison, Everell	Co. C	Private
Morrison, L. S.		
Morrison, William	Co. A	Private
Mortin, F.		Private
Morton, N. G.	Co. F	Private
Moss, J. J.	Co. G	Private
Moss, John L.	Co. G	Private
Mulligan, P.	Co. I	Private
Mullins, G. T.	Co. F	Private
Mullins, T. J.	Co. F	Private
Mulner, P. A.	Co. K	Private
Murphy, E. S.	Co. F	Private
Murphy, J.	Co. I	Private
Murphy, Richard	Co. A	Pvt.-Cpl.
Murphy, Patrick	Co. I	Private
Murphy, S. W.	Co. I	Private
Murray, J.	Co. F	Private
Murray, W. E.	Co. A	Private
Myerberg, Louis	Co. I	Music.-Pvt.
Myers, James	Co. H	Private
Naile, W. B.	Co. G	Private
Nall, Duke	Co. K/F&S	Captain-Major
Nall, James C.	Co. K	Cpl.-2 Lieu.
Nall, Robert W.	Co. K	Private
Nall, W. A.	Co. B	Private
Nalley, J. J.	Co. K	Private
Neagle, John	Co. F	Private
Neil, C.	Co. D	Private

Name	Company	Rank
Nelson, John	Co. G	Private
Nere, James		Private
Nesmith, O. W.	Co. C	Private
Newell, N. J.	Co. H	Private
Newman, L.		Private
Newman, Thomas D.	Co. C	Private
Newman, William	Co. H	Private
Newson, W. T.	Co. B	Private
Nicholson, H. G.	Co. H	Private
Nixon, J. T.	Co. K	Private
Noonan, J.	Co. I	Private
Norman, G. W.	Co. C	Private
Norman, James F.	Co. F	Private
Norris, M.	Co. C	Private
Norris, James A.	Co. F/C	Private
Norris, Thomas P.	Co. D	Private
Norton, James	Co. C	Private
Nugent, M.	Co. I	1 Lieutenant
Oakes, George W.	Co. K	Private
Oakes, John D.	Co. A	Pvt.-Cpl.
Oakes, James M.	Co. K	Private
Oakes, John L.	Co. A	Private
Oakes, Marcus D. L.	Co. A	Private
Oakes, W. Thomas	Co. K	Pvt.-Sergeant
Oaks, J. F.	Co. A	Private
Oaks, William T.	Co. A	Pvt.-Sergeant
Oats, W. S.	Co. A	Private
Obering, E. F.	Co. G	Private
O'Brien, James	Co. C	Private-1st SGT
O'Bring, J. L.	Co. G	Private
O'Connor, Thomas	Co. C	Private
Ogly, W. T.	Co. A	Sergeant
O'Neal, Jesse	Co. E	Private
O'Neal, John	Co. E	Private
O'Neal, Thomas	Co. E	Private
O'Neill, Cornelius	Co. C	Private
O'Neill, George	Co. I	Private
Orr, James	Co. A	Private
Orr, Sample	Co. A	Private
Osborn, James Wilson	Co. K	Private
Ovey, F.		Private
Owens, Lewis G.	Co. A	Private
Padgett, Lucas	Co. E	Private
Padgett, W.		Private
Page, James W.	Co. E	Private
Page, Norborne	Co. D	Cpl.-1st SGT

Name	Company	Rank
Pagles, John F.	Co. C	Sergeant
Palmer, P.	———	Private
Palmer, W. W.	Co. H	Private
Palmer, W. W.	Co. F	Private
Parker, Daniel	Co. A/F&S	Cpl-Asst.Surg.
Parker, W. C. Y.	Co. K	Private
Parramore, W. R.	———	Private
Parsons, J. G.	Co. F	Private-2 Lieu.
Partridge, H. H.	Co. G	Private
Pate, T. W.	Co. C	Private
Pate, W. A.	Co. C	Private
Paterson, George	Co. B	Private
Paterson, M. A.	Co. I	Private
Patillo, W. H.	Co. K	Private
Patten, T. H.	Co. H	Private
Patter, John	Co. B	Private
Patterson, George	Co. B	Private
Patterson, Geo. W.	Co. H	Private
Pearce, William	Co. H	Private
Pearl, Thomas	Co. H	Private
Pearson, H. M.	Co. C	Private
Pearson, W. H. A.	Co. G	Private
Pedigo, Thomas J.	Co. A	Private
Pendergast, James	Co. I	Private
Pendergast, L.	Co. H	Private
Pendergast, W.	Co. I	Private
Penn, E. L.	Co. D	Private
Pennington, John	Co. B	Private
Perkins, John	Co. E	Private
Perle, William	Co. C	Private
Perrin, Jasper	Co. A	Private
Perry, Breeden P.	Co. K	Private
Perry, Calvin	Co. A	Private
Perry, E.	Co. F	Private
Perryman, William D.	Co. H	Private
Peters, A. C.	Co. K	Private
Peterson, E. A.	Co. C	Private
Peterson, Jacob	Co. C	Private
Pettus, Wm. T.	Co. C	Private
Pfleger, Philip	Co. G	Private
Phealen, A.	Co. C	Private
Phelan, Thomas	Co. A	1st SGT-Captain
Phillibert, Oscar	Co. C	Private
Phillips, Benjamin H.	Co. E	Private
Phillips, John R.	Co. C	Private
Philpot, John C.	Co. A	Private

Name	Company	Rank
Pickett, W.	Co. I	Private
Pike, J. K.	Co. K	
Pinckard, Emory F.		Private
Pittman, G. P.		Private
Pitts, N.	Co. I	Private
Poland, William	Co. G	Private
Porter, Thomas W. D.	Co. D	Private
Posel, M.		Private
Powell, Charles	Co. C	Corporal
Powell, James F.	Co. C	Private
Powell, J. M.	Co. H	Private
Powell, William H.	Co. D	Private
Powers, John	Co. I	Cpl.-Sergeant
Powers, Michael	Co. C	Pvt.-Sergeant
Powers, W.	Co. C	Private
Prayton, John		Private
Price, F. M.	Co. A	Private
Prim, J. H.	Co. E	Private
Prinz, Charles	Co. G	Private
Privett, G. W.	F&S	ACS
Privett, William G.	Co. D	Private
Proctor, C. W.	Co. K	Private
Province, Levi M.		
Pumphrey, Roland		
Purifoy, M. C.	Co. F	Private
Quill, Patrick	Co. I	Private
Quin, Michael	Co. I	Private
Quinn, Andrew	Co. I	Private-Captain
Radford, A. J.	Co. K	Private
Ragsdale, L. P.	Co. F/F&S	Private-1 Lieu.
Rainey, W. F.	Co. B	Private
Ralls, M. D.	Co. B	Private
Ransey, A.	Co. G	Private
Raphael, H. T.		AQM
Ravises, A. H.	Co. E	2 Lieu.-Captain
Rawls, M. D.	Co. B	Private
Rawson, E.	Co. C	Private
Ray, W. W.		Private
Ready, John L.	Co. K	Private
Reagan, Patrick C.	Co. H	Private
Redlick, J.	Co. G	Private
Reed, H. J.	Co. E	Private
Reed, J. F.	Co. B	Sergeant
Reeves, George	Co. F	Private
Reeves, W. L.	Co. D	Private

Name	Company	Rank
Regan, John	Co. I	Private
Regan, Michael L.	Co. I	Private
Reid, James	Co. E	Private
Reid, John C.	Co. A	1 Lieutenant
Reid, W. J.	Co. D	Private
Reipschlager, Fred. C. F.	Co. H	Pvt.-Sergeant
Remus, Peter	Co. G	Private
Renean, John H.	Co. B	Private
Reneau, J. W.	Co. B	Private
Reves, A. J.	Co. H	Private
Reves, J. H.	Co. B	Private
Reyal, Eugene S.	Co. A	Private
Reynolds, Alonzo	Co. K	Private
Reynolds, James	Co. K	Private
Reynolds, James M.	Co. D	Private
Reynolds, J. R.	Co. D/G	Private
Rice, Charles R.	Co. H	Sgt.-1 Lieu.
Rice, W. J.	Co. E	Private
Rich, James	Co. H	Private
Richards, Peter	Co. E	Private
Richardson, James Madison	Co. K	Private
Richardson, John	Co. F	Private
Richardson, R. R.	Co. K	Private
Richardson, T. J.	Co. K	Private
Ricketson, Oliver	Co. D	Private
Rickland, W. R.	Co. D	Private
Riddle, D. G.	Co. B	Private
Riley, Joseph	Co. I	Private
Riley, M. S.	Co. F	Private
Roach, C. L.	Co. G	Private
Roach, Milton A.	Co. D	Private
Robbins, Julius A.	Co. D/F&S	Private-AQM
Roberson, G. P.	_____	_____
Roberson, J. L.	Co. A	Private
Robert, William	Co. G	Private
Roberts, A.	Co. I	Private
Roberts, John	Co. G	Private
Robertson, Hubert	Co. H	Private
Robertson, J. R.	Co. K	Private
Robertson, Lewis	Co. G	Private
Robeson, John H.	Co. D	Sgt.-Bvt.2 Lieu
Robinson, A. M.	Co. D	Private
Robinson, A. P.	Co. B	Private
Robinson, Charles	Co. C	Pvt.-Sergeant
Robinson, G. S.	Co. B	Pvt.-Sergeant
Robinson, Joseph S.	Co. B	Private

Name	Company	Rank
Robinson, L. D.	Co. B	Private
Robison, G. T. L.	Co. B	1st SGT-Captain
Rodgers, Edward J.	Co. C/I	Private
Rodgers, William W.	Co. H	Private
Rodrigues, Philip	Co. E	Pvt.-Cpl.
Rogers, J. E.	Co. C	Private
Roh, Charles	Co. G	Pvt.-Sergeant
Rollo, J. J.	Co. F	Private
Rooney, James	Co. H	Private
Ross, Asa	Co. F	Sergeant
Rosson, George L.	Co. E	Private
Rosson, Middleton D.	Co. H	Pvt.-Cpl.
Rothschild, A.	Co. G	Pvt-Cpl.
Rowe, James Fletcher	Co. A	Private
Rowe, George T.	Co. D	_____
Rowland, Robert	Co. C	Private
Royston, Robert T.	Co. A/F&S	Private-Surgeon
Royston, Young L.	Co. A/F&S	Captain-Colonel
Rudd, Charles	Co. E	Private
Russel, J. N.	Co. K	Private
Russell, J. R.	Co. K	Private
Russell, Sylvester	Co. I	Private
Rutherford, Thomas J.	Co. A	Private
Rutherford, William C.	Co. A	Private
Rutland, William	_____	Private
Rutledge, Benjamin W.	Co. A	Private
Rutledge, J.	_____	Private
Ryales, J.	Co. G	Private
Ryals, Perry	Co. H	Private
Ryan, James	Co. I	Pvt.-Cpl.
Ryan, John	Co. C	Private
Ryan, John	Co. H	Private
Ryan, M. L.	Co. I	Private
Ryan, Thomas S.	Co. E	Private
Ryan, Timothy	Co. E	Private
Ryan, William A.	Co. E	Private-2 Lieu.
Saek, Richard	Co. A	Private
Salmonds, B. B.	Co. D	_____
Saltonstall, W. C.	Co. H	Private
Sanders, Robert W.	Co. A	Cpl.-Capt.-LTC
Sandford, Thad. Jr.	Co. C	Private
Sansom, Thomas	Co. F	Private
Sanson, Thomas H.	Co. H	Private
Sapp, F. M.	Co. F	Private
Sartin, E. B.	_____	Private
Sassnett, S.	Co. B	Private

Name	Company	Rank
Satterfield, Jas. R.	Co. D	Private
Savage, R.	Co. F	Private
Saxon, A. H.	Co. H	Private
Sayre, C.	Co. H	Private
Scannell, Fred	Co. C	Private
Schaaf, Philip	Co. G	Private
Scharf, Henry	Co. G	Private
Schermerhorn, J. Crane	Co. D	Jr.2 Lieu.- 1Lieu.
Schneider, August	Co. G	Private
Schneider, George	Co. G	Private
Schneider, John	Co. G	Private
Schoolhoffer, Philip	Co. K	Private
Schultz, August	Co. G	Private
Schwartz, George	Co. G	Sgt.-2 Lieu.
Scott, Frank	Co. C	Private
Scott, Robert R.	Co. H	1stSGT-1 Lieu.
Searcy, J. R.	Co. F	Cpl.-Sergeant
Seawell, C. H.	Co. A	2 Lieu.-1 Lieu.
Seawell, William A.	Co. H	Sergeant
Seligsberg, Abraham	Co. D	Private
Sellers, H.	Co. H	Corporal
Senebaugh, W. H.	Co. D	Private
Sessions, J. J.	Co. F	Private
Sexton, M.	Co. I	Private
Shackelford, F.	Co. B	Pvt.-Sergeant
Shadix, Benjamin H.	Co. E	Private
Sharp, Peter W.	Co. E	Private
Sharpe, Samuel H.	Co. C	Private
Shaw, B. H.	Co. F	Corporal
Shaw, E. J.	Co. F	Musician
Shaw, William	Co. C	Private
Shaw, W. J.	Co. H	Corporal
Shedden, Alexander	Co. G	1stSgt.-1 Lieu
Shephard, Alexander	Co. I	Private
Sherry, S. B.	Co. B	————
Shields, John G.	Co. C	Private
Shirley, W.		Private
Shivers, J. B.	Co. K	Pvt.-Cpl.
Shoemake, J.	Co. F	Private
Shorter, George H.	F&S	Captain& Comisary
Shorths, S. P.	Co. K	Private
Shortridge, Eli	Co. D	Private
Shrides, A.	Co. G	Private
Shulse, Frederick	Co. H	Corporal
Sides, W. F.	Co. D	Private
Sidners, J. H.	Co. F	Private

Silenger, C. D.	Co. G	Private
Simmons, A.	Co. D	Private
Simmons, J.	Co. C	Private
Simmons, L. L.	Co. D	Private
Skehan, Edward	Co. E/I	Private
Skipper, Angus	Co. E	Private
Smelley, Stephen	Co. I	Private
Smelley, Thomas J.	Co. A	Private
Smellie, S.	Co. A	Private
Smith, A.	Co. E	Private
Smith, A.	Co. H	Pvt.-Cpl.
Smith, Aaron	Co. A	Private
Smith, Andrew J.	Co. D	Private
Smith C. O.	Co. F	Private
Smith, Frederick	Co. G	Private
Smith, George	Co. C	Private
Smith, George M.	Co. K	Cpl.-Sergeant
Smith, George W.	Co. K	Private
Smith, Henry	Co. F	Private
Smith, H. W.	Co. G	Private
Smith, J.	Co. K	Private
Smith, James	Co. G	Private
Smith, J. E.	Co. A	Private
Smith, J. I.	Co. I	Private
Smith, J. J.	Co. F	Private
Smith, J. L.	Co. A	Private
Smith, J. M.	Co. D	Private
Smith, John	Co. C	Private
Smith, John	Co. G	Private
Smith, John	Co. H	Private
Smith, John T.	Co. B	Private
Smith, J. Y.	Co. B	Private
Smith, N.	Co. A	Private
Smith, Peter	Co. E	Private
Smith, Peter	Co. G	Pvt.-Cpl.
Smith, S. A.	Co. H	Private
Smith, Seaborn	Co. F	Private
Smith, S. H.	Co. F	Private
Smith, Samuel T.	Co. G	Private
Smith, Thomas	Co. I	Private
Smith, Thomas J.	Co. K	Private
Smith, T. R.	Co. C	Private
Smith, Wm.	Co. H	Private
Smith, William T.	Co. E	Captain
Smitherman, J.	Co. F	Private
Snodley, Samuel	Co. A	Private

Name	Company	Rank
Snow, John A.	Co. E	Corporal
Soloman, A. L.	_____	Private
Sommerville, Walter	Co. D	Private
Sommill, John	Co. H	Private
Spears, A. B.	Co. C	_____
Spears, Daniel W.	Co. B	_____
Spears, J. C.	Co. C/F	Private
Spears, J. G.	Co. F	Private
Speir, John P.	Co. A	Private
Spence, P. A.	Co. D	Private
Spence, T. A.	Co. A	Private
Spencer, H. O.	Co. D	Private
Spencer, J. R.	Co. I	Private
Spigner, George M.	Co. D	Pvt.-Sergeant
Spikes, James S.	Co. G	Private
Sponsoby, Warren W.	Co. K	Private
Spradlin, Frank M.	Co. E	Private
Spratt, Samuel	Co. K	Private
Sprowl, John	Co. H	Private
Stack, Richard	Co. A	Private
Stafford, M.	Co. I	Private
Staggers, J. A.	_____	Private
Stanley, Peter	Co. K	Private
Stanton, Jacob	Co. E	Private
Steel, Henry	Co. C	Private
Steel, Jayson	Co. C	Private
Steele, J.	Co. A	Private
Steidel, Ferdinand	Co. G	Sergeant
Stephens, John P.	_____	Private
Stephenson, Steven	Co. H	Private
Sterling, William, R.	Co. E	Sgt.-Captain
Sterne, Joseph	Co. D	Private
Stevens, John H.	Co. F	Private
Stevens, John M.	Co. A	Private
Stewart, C. E.	_____	1 Lieutenant
Sticks, J. D.	Co. K	Private
Stillman, J. F.	Co. C	Pvt.-Sergeant
Stockwell, James A.	Co. A	Private
Stone, W. D.	Co. C	Private
Stone, W. R.	Co. C	Private
Stott, Ira W.	Co. F	Jr.2 Lieu.-Capt
Stott, Stephen W.	Co. F	Private
Straid, William W.	Co. H	_____
Strange, D. B.	Co. K	Private
Strange, R. M.	Co. D	Private
Strickland, James R.	Co. E	Private

Name	Company	Rank
Strickland, J. S.	Co. E	Private
Strickland, S.	Co. F	Private
Stridel,	Co. G	Sergeant
Stringfellow, Frank	Co. G	Private
Stringfellow, James	Co. G	Pvt.-Cpl.
Strock, Jacob S.	Co. B	Private
Stroud, E. D.	Co. H	Private
Stround, William	Co. H	Private
Stryne, Richard	Co. H/K	Private
Stubbs, James A.	Co. D	_____
Stumm, Gustave A.	Co. G	Private
Stusom, Thomas	Co. F	Private
Sudden, Alexander	Co. G	1 Lieutenant
Sullivan, Daniel	Co. I	Private
Sullivan, David B.	Co. D	2 Lieu.-1 Lieu.
Sullivan, Dennis	Co. D	Private
Sullivan, Dennis	Co. I	Private
Sullivan, J.	Co. K	Private
Sullivan, J. A.	Co. I	Private
Sullivan, John	Co. I	Private
Summers, Leonard F.	Co. C	1 Lieu.-Captain
Summers, William	Co. F	Private
Summersell, John W.	Co. E	Private
Sutten, J. E.	Co. C	Private
Suttles, John W.	Co. K	Corporal
Suttles, M. B.	Co. K	Private
Suttles, William M.	Co. K	Private
Swain, Isaac	Co. I	Private
Swartz, H.	Co. G	Private
Sweeny, William H.	Co. D	Private
Swindal, D. W.	Co. B	Private
Swindal, John G.	Co. B	Pvt.-Sergeant
Swindle, E. D.	Co. D	Private
Swint, Joseph	Co. F	Private
Syphret, John T.	Co. H	Private
Taggart, W. A.	Co. D	Private
Talbott, W. T.	Co. E	Private
Tallen, J. B.	Co. C	Private
Tatum, William A.	Co. H	Pvt.-Cpl.
Taylor, A.	_____	Private
Taylor, F. G.	Co. D	Private
Taylor, J. A.	Co. D	Private
Taylor, James A.	Co. G	Private
Taylor, J. J.	Co. B	Private
Taylor, John	Co. G	Private-1st SGT
Taylor, N.	Co. I	Private

Name	Company	Rank
Taylor, Neal	Co. G	Private
Taylor, Samuel	Co. A	Private
Taylor, S. P.	Co. D	Private
Taylor, Thomas G.	Co. D	Private
Taylor, Wm. F.	Co. K	Corporal
Taylor, Wm. S.	Co. E	1st SGT-Pvt.
Tefepaugh, H. P.	Co. F	Private
Teller, J. G.	Co. E	Private
Terrill, G. P.	Co. H	Private
Therath, Hiram	Co. C	Private
Thomas, Bruce P.	Co. D	Private
Thomas, Leroy	Co. F	Private
Thomas, William	Co. G	Private
Thomasson, M. D.	Co. C	Private
Thompkins, J. L.		Private
Thompson, J. H.	Co. H	Private
Thompson, Drury	Co. G	2 Lieutenant
Thompson, George W.	Co. K	Private
Thompson, G. W.		Private
Thompson, John E.	Co. D	Private
Thompson, Samuel	Co. A	Private
Thornton, D. B.	Co. F	Private-2 Lieu.
Thornton, J. A.	Co. F	Private
Till, James	Co. G	Private
Tilman, Berry	Co. H	Private
Tilton, Joshua A.	Co. D	Private
Tinnin, P. P.	Co. C	Private
Tisdale, C. C.	Co. F	Private
Titus, Benj.	Co. H	Private
Tobin, Edward S.	Co. I	Cpl.-Pvt.
Todd, John	Co. E	Pvt.-Sergeant
Tomberlinson, Ulysses	Co. A	Private
Tomblinson, James	Co. A	Private
Tompkins, Charles C.	Co. E	Private
Tompkins, J. A.	Co. I	Private
Towler, H. S.	Co. B	Private
Townsend, C. C.	Co. K	Private
Townsend, W. S.	Co. K	Private
Toxon, Henry Jr.	Co. D	Corporal
Traywick, William H.	Co. A	Private
Tremmell, Arnold	Co. I	Private
Trice, F. M.	Co. B	Private
Trice, L. S.	Co. F	Private
Trice, T. F.	Co. B	
Trimmell, D. W.	Co. H	Private
Troutman, W. A.	Co. E	Private

Name	Company	Rank
Truehart, Charles	F&S	Asst. Surgeon
Truelove, Elijah	Co. C	Private
Tubb, F. T.	Co. A	Private
Tubb, George W.	Co. A	Sgt.-Pvt.
Tuchen, G. A.	Co. H	Private
Tucker, A. W.	Co. C	Private
Tucker, David	Co. A	Pvt.-Cpl.
Tucker, John	Co. A	Private
Tulbird, W. F.	Co. E	
Tumberlinson, James	Co. A	Private
Turner, A. J.		Private
Turner, B.	Co. F	Private
Turner, H. R.	Co. G	Private
Turner, R.	Co. G	Private
Turner, R. M.	Co. G	Private
Tyson, A. J.	Co. C	Private
Underwood, Sylvanus G.	Co. D	Private
Unger, Solomon	Co. E	Private
Van Meeter, Isaac	Co. E	Private
Varner, George W.	Co. H	Private
Vaughn, W. B.		Private
Venable, Joseph	Co. F	Private
Vice, J. R. Jr.	Co. E	Private
Vincent, W. H.	Co. C	Private
Vinson, James A.	Co. C	Private
Vines, J. V.	Co. A	Private
Wacher, George	Co. A	Private
Waddle, Beverly	Co. A	Private
Waddle, Richard J.	Co. A	Pvt.-Sergeant
Wadkins, Robt. O.	Co. E	Private
Wakefield, Wm. R.	Co. C	Private
Walker, Charles F.	Co. G	Cpl.-2 Lieu.
Walker, D. W.	Co. A	Private
Walker, George J.	Co. A	Private
Walker, J. E.	Co. A	Private
Walker, Jenk R.	Co. D	Private
Walker, Richard	Co. I	Private
Walker, S.	Co. G	Private
Walkley, E. A.	Co. B	Private
Wallace, F. D.	Co. B	Private
Wallace, W. F.	Co. F	Private
Wallace, W. H.	Co. F	Private
Wallis, J W.	Co. D	Private
Wallis, William	Co. K	Private
Walsh, John	Co. I	Private
Walstead, J.	Co. A	Private

Name	Company	Rank
Walters, B. F.		Private
Walters, John	Co. F	Private
Wamble, George	Co. A	Private
Ward, Clinton L.	Co. F	Private
Ward, J. J.	Co. E	Private
Ward, Robert J.	Co. E	Private
Ward, William H.	Co. A	Private
Ware, James	Co. F	Private
Warnicker, William	Co. E	Music.-Pvt.
Warren, J. N.	Co. E	Private
Watkins, Robert O.	Co. B/K	Private
Watters, John O.	Co. K	Private
Watters, Samuel B.F.	Co. K	Private
Webster, H. L.	Co. C	Private
Webster, Robert E.	Co. D	Private
Weekes, John W.	Co. E/A	Private
Weeks, Henry J.	Co. A	Private
Weis, John	Co. B	Private
Weiser, Lewis	Co. G	Private
Welch, A. J.	Co. C	Private
Wells, M. C.	Co. K	Corporal
Wells, P. V.	Co. E	Private
West, James	Co. D	Private
Weston, George H.	Co. E	Private
Whatley, Thomas J.	Co. D	Pvt.-Cpl.
Wheelan, John P.	Co. D	Private
Whelan, James	Co. H	Private
Whiley, J.		Private
Whitaker, J.	Co. F	Private
Whitaker, W. W.	Co. B	Private
White, Daniel	Co. C	Private
White, Garland A.	Co. D	Private
White, H.		Private
White, J. B.	Co. G	Private
White, J. M.	Co. B	Private
White, Leo	Co. H	Corporal
White, P. S.	Co. K	Private
White, Reuben	Co. B	Private
White, S. H.	Co. K	Private
White, W.	Co. B	Private
White, W. E.	Co. B	Private
White, W. J.	Co. B	Private
White, William R.	Co. A	Private
White, W. S.	Co. K	Private
White, William W. M.	Co. E	Private
Whitehurst, William	Co. A	Private

Name	Company	Rank
Whitley, J. J.	Co. C	Private
Whittle, John	Co. I	Private
Whitus, William R.	Co. A	Private
Wickham, James Charles	Co. G	Private
Wilf, James W.	Co. B	Private
Wilkinson, U.	Co. A	Private
Willey, Alexander	Co. A	Private
Williams, E. C.	Co. K	Private
Williams, Edward	Co. H	Private
Williams, Frank H.	Co. K	Private
Williams, Frank K.	Co. A	Pvt.-Cpl.
Williams, H.	Co. K	Private
Williams, J. H.	Co. A	Private
Williams, Joseph H.	Co. G	Private
Williams, J. W.	Co. E	Private
Williams, Peter	Co. E	Private
Williams, Peter	Co. H	Private
Williams, Robert M.	Co. A	Private
Williams, William	Co. F	Private
Williams, W. R.	Co. D	Private
Williamson, E. C.	Co. K	Private
Williamson, J. M.	Co. D	Private
Williamson, Sumpter M.	Co. A	Private
Willingham, William T.	Co. C	Private
Willingham, W. W.	Co. C	
Willis, J. J.	___	Private
Willis, L. C.	Co. F	Private
Wilner, J. B.	Co. F	Private
Wilson, B. H. G.	___	Private
Wilson, Charles	Co. G	Private
Wilson, E.	Co. A	Private
Wilson, E. J.	Co. C	Private
Wilson, J. Lewis	Co. A	Private
Wilson, Robert	Co. C/G	Private
Wilson, Samuel	Co. G	Private
Wilson, S. T.	Co. F	Private
Wimbush, J. H.	Co. F	Private
Winston, John A.	F&S	Colonel
Winters, Abram	Co. C	Private
Winters, Benjamin F.	Co. A	Private
Wise, Frank F.	Co. D	Private
Womac, N. P.	Co. C	Private
Womac, W.	___	Private
Wood, H.	___	Private
Wood, Henry C.	Co. E	Private
Wood, Hugh A.	Co. E	Private

Name	Company	Rank
Wood, W. H.	Co. I	Private
Woodruff, Luther	Co. F	Private
Woods, Charles B.	Co. D	Sgt.-2 Lieu.
Woods, J. B.	Co. D	Private
Woodward, T. B.	Co. H	Private
Wooley, H. A.	Co. F	Private
Wooly, B. E.	Co. B	Private
Wooten, J. T.	Co. F	Private
Wright, Albert E.	Co. E	Private
Wright, A. J.	Co. I	Private
Wright, B. D.	Co. C	Private
Wright, Henry	Co. C	Private
Wright, J. A.	___	Private
Wright, J. A.	Co. I	Private
Wright, J. B.	Co. D	Private
Wright, J. L.	Co. B	Private
Wright, John	Co. F	Sergeant
Wright, John	Co. F	Music.-Sergeant
Wright, Louis	Co. H	Cpl.-Pvt.
Wright, Reuben	Co. C	Private
Wright, W.	Co. B	Private
Wright, William	Co. F	Private
Wurniker, Wm.	Co. E	Private
Wyatt, Ira	___	Private
Wyers, John Henry	Co. A	Private
Wyncoop, J. W.	Co. E	Corporal
Yant, Francis M.	Co. D	1 Lieutenant
Yarbrough, John R.	Co. B	Private
Yarbrough, M. B.	Co. B	Private
Yearta, W. T.	Co. H	Private
Young, F. M.		Private
Young, George W.	Co. K	Private
Young, Henry C.	Co. K	Pvt.-Cpl.
Young, James	Co. K	Private
Young, Joe M. S.	Co. K	Private
Young, Joseph M. Jr.	Co. K	Private
Young, Wallace W.	Co. E	Private
Zell, E.	Co. D	Private
___, John	Co. H	Musician
Zelly, G.	Co. H	Private

APPENDIX B
PAROLES OF THE EIGHTH ALABAMA
INFANTRY REGIMENT C.S.A.

Emerich, John P.,	Lieutenant Colonel
Cleveland, M. S.	Adjutant
Royston, R. L.	Surgeon
Mordecai, W. W.	Captain
Knox, W. R.	Captain
Robison, G. T.	Captain
Fagan, W. L.	Captain
Harmon, J. B.	1st Lieutenant
Monroe, T. C.	1st Lieutenant
Killion, James	1st Lieutenant
Massey, M. V.	2nd Lieutenant
Gould, B. E.	2nd Lieutenant
Parsons, J. G.	2nd Lieutenant
Jones, S.	2nd Lieutenant
Gaddes, Robert	2nd Lieutenant
Massey, W. E.	Chaplain
Aumspaugh, J. H.	Q. M. Sergeant
Buell, D.	Ordnance Sergeant
Brown, J.	Hospital Sergeant
Smith, Geo. M.	Sergeant
Richardson, R. R.	Sergeant
Malone, M. A.	Sergeant
Brannan, J. W.	Sergeant
Henlein, F.	Sergeant
Milner, J. B.	Sergeant
Todd, J.	Sergeant
Page, N.	Sergeant
McCurdy, L. L.	Sergeant
Clourett, J.	Sergeant
Dix, F. B.	Sergeant
Ginn, A. V.	Sergeant
Spigener, G. M.	Sergeant

Lead, T. F.	Sergeant
Donovan, M. E.	Sergeant
Oaks, J. D.	Corporal
Floyd, M. C.	Corporal
Howard, J. W.	Corporal
Hartley, F. E.	Corporal
Dunn, J. W.	Corporal
Krause, A.	Corporal
Cherry, C.	Corporal
Goocher, W. J.	Private
Harbour, E. T.	Private
Harbour, J. R.	Private
Foster, M	Private
Graham, L.	Private
Hosley, G.	Private
Hippler, A.	Private
Lewis, F.	Private
Manning, W.	Private
Myers, J	Private
Padgett, W.	Private
Rutledge, J	Private
Spikes, J.	Private
Smith, J.	Private
Schneider, A.	Private
Taylor, A.	Private
Johnston, F. V.	Private
McLendon, J. J.	Private
Mills, L. W.	Private
Rollo, J. J.	Private
Sessions, J. J.	Private
Thornton, J. A.	Private
Wallace, W. F.	Private
Durden, J. W.	Private
Kirkland, J. S.	Private
Martin, W. D.	Private
Perkins, J.	Private
Wood, H.	Private
Warnicker, W.	Private
Baker, J.	Private
Braswell, B. B.	Private
Day, M.	Private
Dunlop, G. R.	Private
Foster, J. A.	Private
Hull, B. F.	Private

Hodge, W. L.	Private
Huff, J. M.	Private
Jones, J. A.	Private
Landford, J. B.	Private
Bledsoe, A. M.	Private
Bolling, J. T.	Private
Chandler, C. J.	Private
Fain, J. W.	Private
Fike, Jas. H.	Private
Fuller, R. P. T.	Private
George, M. D.	Private
Cooper, R. G. D.	Private
Darrah, H. F.	Private
Griffin, J. W.	Private
Russell, J. R.	Private
Reedy, J. L.	Private
Suttles, M. B.	Private
Schoelhoffer, P.	Private
Smith, G. W.	Private
Thompson, G. W.	Private
Watters, B. F.	Private
Young, J. M.	Private
Butler, J. M.	Private
Curtin, J.	Private, one horse
Crivaller, T.	Private
Mercer, J.	Private
Tompkins, J. L.	Private
Wright, J. A.	Private
Batton, T. H.	Private
Brannan, J. E.	Private
Cain, G. W.	Private
Carlen, M.	Private
Graham, J. A.	Private
Gore, J. M.	Private
Lofton, A.	Private
Leathers, A.	Private
McCormick, N.	Private
Pearce, W.	Private
Patterson, G. W.	Private
Ahren, P.	Private
Brown, A.	Private
Bowling, H.	Private
Izell, W. H.	Private
Lockridge, R. G.	Private
McVay, G. W.	Private
Palmer, P.	Private

Parramore, W. R.	Private
Pittman, G. P.	Private
Shirley, W.	Private
Meredith, T. J.	Private
Morris, J. T.	Private
Morris, J. R.	Private
Nalley, J. J.	Private
Oaks, J. M.	Private
Oaks, G. W.	Private
Proctor, C. W.	Private
Bush, J. H.	Private
Cariker, W. W.	Private
Richardson, T. J.	Private
Richardson, J. M.	Private
Downs, W. W.	Private
Dukes, W.	Private
Evans, B. R.	Private
Forbes, G. T.	Private
Gay, J. M.	Private
Harris, B. F.	Private
Martin, J. C.	Private
Kelly, M. J.	Private
Reneau, J. H.	Private
Swindel, D. W.	Private
Yabrough, M. B.	Private
Ashley, W. N.	Private
Burroughs, B.	Private
Draper, W.	Private
Marchand, P.	Private
Baker, J. W.	Private
Blake, W.	Private

List of Officers and Men of the Invalid Battalion commanded by Lieutenant Benjamin Bates:

Towers, J. D. M.	Co. B	8th Ala
Wise, F. F.		Private
Brown, J.		Private
Cooper, H.		Private
Cummings, J. W.		Private
Gill, J. K.		Private
James, H.		Private
Kirkland, B. J.		Private
Norris, M.		Private
Morgan, E. C.		Private
Truelove, E.		Private

Welsh, A. J. Private
Willingham, Wm. T. Private
Arnold, R. T. Private

Appendix C
Eighth Alabama Fort Delaware Prison Roster
Courtesy of Mr. Dan Cashin
Fort Delaware Society

Name	Alternate Names	Company	Notes
1. Abbott, John H.		Co. I	Gettysburg 7/5/63, Paroled 7/30/63 Enlisted 5/20/61 Wounded Gaines' Mill 6/27/62 Wounded Burgess Mill 10/27/64 Paroled Mobile AL 6/5/65
2. Barefield, Edmund		Co. A	Gettysburg 7/2/63 Wounded at Gettysburg Conscript Clifton AL 8/25/62 Trans. Pt Lookout 10/63 Chimborazo Hosp 3/64
3. Barathano J. E. H.	Bartlett, J. E. H.	Co. C (E)	Died 8/20/63
4. Bartlett, E. H.	Bartly, E. H.	Co. E	Died, 8/20/6
5. Berryfield. C		Co. A	Gettysburg 7/5/63 Trans. Pt. Lookout 10/26/63
6. Bice, J. A.			Dischg. FD hosp 2/6/65
7. Bice, James M.		Co. E	Released Pt. Lookout 6/14/64
8. Bice, John T.		Co. B to E	Gettysburg 7/2/63 to Ft. McHenry 7/4/63 to Ft Del 7/12/63 Released Pt Lookout 6/14/65
9. Bire, I. T.	Bice, (J.T.) (J.M.)	Co. E	To Ft. McHenry 7/7/63
10. Blair, James H.		Co. A	Seven Pines 6/62, Exchanged 8/5/64(62) Marion AL Hosp 5/8/61; Died at SC Hosp. Petersburg VA
11. Blake, Wm.		Co. B	Parole Appmtx. 4/9/65 Seven Pines 6/1/62 Exchanged 8/5/62 Wounded Gettysburg 7/4/63 Enlisted Wetumpka AL 5/17/61
12. Bennett, Jams M.	James W. Bennill, Benwill	Co. K	Died Ft. Del 9/20/63
13. Boley, W. H.		Co. B, D	Ft. Del Hosp 12/9/64
14. Bonnean, H. S.	Benneaw	Co. C	Exchanged 9/30/64

Name	Alternate Names	Company	Notes
15. Bonner, H. L.		Co. C	Trans. Pt. Lookout 10/20/63
16. Boone, L. H.		Co. C	
17. Bowley, W. H.		Co. B	Released FD 6/14/65
18. Bowlin, A.		Co. A	Joined 3rd MD US Cav.
19. Boykin, G.		Co. K	Gettysburg 7/2/63 Recd Ft. Del 7/6/63
20. Bradley, J. W.		Co. A	Parole 10/64 Gettysburg 7/2/63 Recd' 7/6/63 To USA smallpox hosp At Pt. Lookout 6/30/64 Enlisted Marion AL 5/8/61
21. Brannan, J. W.		Co. H	Exchanged 7/20/64 Wounded 7/3/63 Treated Letterman Hosp. Conscript Henry Co. AL 7/21/65? (63)
22. Brice, J. M.		Co. E	Gettysburg 7/2/63, Recd 7/6/63
23. Brown, Wm.		Co. G	
24. O'Brown, Wm.		Co. E	Gettysburg 7/5/63 Recd 7/12/63
25. Buck, H. W.		Co. H	KIA at Crater 7/30/64 Gettysburg 7/2/63. Wounded Recd 7/6/63 To Pt. Lookout 10/24/63. Exchanged 5/3/64. Wounded at Gains Mill 6/27/62. Enlisted Mobile AL 5/30/61
26. Burt, J. F.		Co. A	Died illness 11/30/64 Gettysburg 7/2/63 Recd 7/12/63. Illness, Exchanged 10/64 Enlisted Marion AL 5/8/61
27. Butler, J.E.		Co. D	Exchanged 4/1/64 Williamsport 7/6/63 Recd 7/12/63
28. Butler, L. E.		Co. D	4/17/64
29. Callahan Thos. C.		Co. K	Exchanged 2/13/65 Enlisted Perry Co AL 5/16/61 Wounded Gettysburg 7/2/63
30. Campbell, C.		Co. K	Joined US service
31. Candle, J. A.		Co. A	Gettysburg 7/2/63 Recd 7/6/63 Exchanged 9/30/63
32. Caneck,		Co. H	Exchanged 9/30/63 Gettysburg 7/2/63, Recd 7/6/63

Name	Alternate Names	Company	Notes
33. Carleton, W. E.		Co. K	Williamsburg 5/6/62 Exchanged Aiken's Landing 8/5/62 Gettysburg 7/2/63 Wounded, Enlisted Perry Co. Al 5/16/61
34. Cashin, John		Co. I	KIA Gettysburg 7/3/63 Seven Pines 6/1/62 Exchanged Aiken's Landing 8/5/62 Salem Church 5/13/63 wounded Enlisted Mobile AL 5/20/61
35. Cassidy, John		Co. I	Transferred to CS Navy Seven Pines 6/1/62; Exchanged 8/5/62
36. Cavalero			Sgt.
37. Clark, Edmond		Co. A	Machinist in Va. 9/2/64 Seven Pines 6/1/62 Exchanged 8/5/62 Enlisted Marion AL 5/8/61
38. Cobb, J. J.		Co. E	Hosp. 7/24/64
39. Cobini, Eugene A.		Co. H	At Crater Seven Pines 6/1/62 Exchanged 8/5/62 Sharpsburg 9/17/62 Exchanged same day Gettysburg 7/2/63 Wounded Exchanged as present At battle of Crater Enlisted Mobile AL 6/25/61
40. Cochran, J. W.	Cochran, John	Co. A.	Took Oath 5/65
41. Coggins, D. C.	Coggons, David C.	Co. C	Died of Chronic Diarrhea Ft. Del 9/7/63(10/17) Gettysburg 7/4/63 Recd 7/12/63 Enlisted Selma AL 5/10/61 Mounted orderly for Col. of regiment
42. Collins, Charles		Co. H	Joined 3 MD US Cav Gettysburg 7/2/63 Enlisted Mobile AL 1/1/63
43. Compton, A. H.		Co. C	
44. Conklin, J.			Sgt Paroled Ft. Del.
45. Coon, Jno.		Co. K	Gettysburg 7/2/63 Recd 7/6/63 Trans. 8/10/63 to Chester PA Hosp.

Name	Alternate Names	Company	Notes
46. Coone, John		Co. H	Died Chester Pa Hosp. Seven Pines 6/1/62 Exchanged Aiken's Landing 8/5/62 Conscript Camp Wells 6/18/62
47. Coville, David A.		Co. D	Took Oath Seven Pines 6/1/62 Enlisted Selma AL 5/10/62
48. Coyne, James		Co. I	Took Oath 8/10/62 Seven Pines Enlisted Mobile AL 5/20/61
49. Creech, A. C.	Creach	Co. H	Exchanged 10/64 Gettysburg 7/2/63 Conscript Camp Watts AL 9/5/62
50. Crutch, E. C.		Co. H	Gettysburg 7/2/63
51. Cuich, A.		Co. H	Hosp. 4/22-9/30/64
52. Cummings, F. P.		Co. K	Gettysburg 7/2/63 Exchanged 2/18/65 Wounded Gains Mill 7/27/62
53. Cutts	Cults	Co. E.	KIA Hanover Jct 5/24/64 Gettysburg 7/5/63 to Ft. Del 7/12/63 Exchanged 7/21/63 Enlisted Camp Watts AL 8/30/62 Wounded Gettysburg
54. Dayle, J.		Co. D	
55. DeBardeleban	DeBardlebrau, A. M. DeBauthbrau, A. M. Co. B		Parole Montg 5/19/65
56. Dix, F. T.	Dix, Frisby T.	Co. C	Exchanged 11/11/64 Gettysburg 7/3/63 Exchanged 11/11/64 Wounded at Gaines Mill 6/27/62 Enlisted Mobile AL 5/18/61
57. Duncan, Jas.	I.B.	Co. D	Died Ft. Del 8/7/63
58. Dunklin. J. B		Co. K	Died Ft. Del 8/7/63
59. Earnest, J. S.	J. H., Earnist, J. H.	Co. F	Took Oath 6/7/65
60. Edgar, Chas.		Co. D	Gettysburg 7/4/63 Recd 7/12/63
61. Edmonds, J. H.		Co. D	Died Ft. Del 8/28/63
62. Edwards, J.	James	Co. K	Released Oath 6/15/65 Captured near Fairfield 7/6/63 Recd 7/12/63 Hosp 3/29-4/14/64 Enlisted Marion AL 2/18/63
63. Edwards R. H.	K. H.	Co. D	Died Ft. Del 8/28/63

Name	Alternate Names	Company	Notes
64. Eldre, Daniel		Co. I	Took Oath 8/10/62
65. Ellis, E.	Edward	Co. D.	Oath? 12/64 Enlisted Selma AL 5/10/61
66. Engar, Charles		Co. D	Exchanged 2/18/65 Conscript
67. Fake, C. E.		Co. K	Gettysburg 7/3/63 Recd 7/12/63
68. Fike, Chas. E.		Co. K	Exchanged 2/18/65 Gettysburg 7/4/63 Pt. Lookout 10/63 Enlisted Perry Co. AL 5/16/61
69. Fisher, John		Co. G	Salem Church 5/3/63
70. Forman, Arthur		Co. I	Dischg. Phy. Dis 8/25/63 Seven Pines 6/1/62 Exchanged Aiken's Landing 8/5/62
71. Fowler, B. C.		Co. K	Gettysburg 7/5/63 Recd 7/12/63
72. Fowler, O. C.		Co. K	Paroled Selma 6/65 Williamsport 7/6/63 Exchanged 2/18/65 Regimental Wagoneer
73. Foy, Thomas		Co. C	Exchanged 2/18/65 Gettysburg 7/5/63 Wounded there Trans. Pt. Lookout 9/63 Wounded at Salem Church 5/3/63 Enlisted Mobile AL 5/18/61
74. Frith, Henry	Firth, H. H.	Co. K	Died Ft. Del 8/28/63 Gettysburg 7/2/63; Recd 7/6/63 Died pneumonia Enlisted Marion AL 2/15/63 Conscript
75. Fry, T.		Co. C	"Left"
76. Garrison, L. F.		Co. K	Gettysburg 7/5/63 Recd 7/12/63
77. Garrison, S. Frank		Co. K	Exchanged 2/18/65 Gettysburg 7/2/63, Wounded there; Enlisted Perry Co. AL 3/16/62
78. Gay, Thomas B.		Co. E	Died Pt. Lookout 12/63 Gettysburg 7/3/63 Wounded there Wounded Gaines Mill 6/27/62 Enlisted Mobile AL 5/6/61

Name	Alternate Names	Company	Notes
79. Geary, Cornelius		Co. I	Released 6/14/65 Gettysburg 7/3/63 Wounded there Wounded Salem Church 5/3/63
80. Gentry J. M.	John M.	Co. A	Died Pt. Lookout 1/16/64 Gettysburg 7/3/63 Recd 7/12/63 Enlisted Marion AL 8/8/61
81. Glary, Borden		Co. J	Released 6/15/65
82. Golding Patrick		Co. J	Released 6/14/65 Gettysburg 7/2/63 Wounded Gettysburg Ft. McHenry 7/14/63 Enlisted Mobile AL 5/20/61
83. Goldman R.	Goldsmith, R., Goldschmidt, Robert	Co. G	Released 5/10/65 oath
84. Gonyloes, A.		Co. D	7/2/63 Recd 7/6/63
85. Gratix, Joseph		Co. G	Paroled 2/18/65 Gettysburg 7/2/63 Wounded there Trans to Pt Lookout Wounded Gaines Mill 6/27/62 Enlisted Mobile AL 5/21/61
86. Gratting, Jas.		Co. G	Gettysburg 7/5/63 Recd 7/12/63
87. Gray, B. B.		Co. E	Gettysburg 7/4/63
88. Green, L.		Co. K	Dd. Gettysburg 7/5/63 Recd 7/12/63
89. Green, J. P.		Co. K	Parole Selma 6/65 Gettysburg 7/2/63 Wounded there Trans. Pt. Lookout 10/26/63 Exchanged 2/18/65
90. Griffin, Jas. H.		Co. D	Gettysburg 7/5/63 Recd 7/12/63
91. Griffin James A.		Co. D	Paroled 2/18/65 Gettysburg 7/3/63 Trans to Pt. Lookout 10/26/63 Conscript Lallapooson AL 8/20/62
92. Guary, C		Co. I	

Name	Alternate Names	Company	Notes
93. Guinn, Green A.	Gunn, G. A.	Co. D	Died Pt. Lookout 8/10/64 Gettysburg 7/3/63 Enlisted Selma AL 5/10/61
94. Hagan, P.	Hogan, Patrick	Co. C	Joined US 1st Conn –oath
95. Hamilton, J. L.		Co. G	"Left" Gettysburg 7/3/63 Recd 7/12/63 Trans Pt. Lookout 10/26/63
96. Hamrick, James	Hamsick, J.	Co. A	Exchanged 2/18/65 Williamsburg 5/6/62 Exchanged 7/62 Exchanged 5/6/64 Enlisted Marion AL 5/8/61
97. Harris, Walkins		Co. G	Joined US service Gettysburg 7/2/63 Recd 7/6/63
98. Haynes, Wm. L.		Co. F	Joined US service Seven Pines 6/1/62 Exchanged Aikens Landing VA 8/5/62 Spotsylvania CH 5/11/64
99. Henly, Edward Jr.,		Co. K	Released 6/14/65 Gettysburg 7/5/63 Wounded there Trans Pt. Lookout/ Elmira Prison 8/17/64 Enlisted Perry Co. AL 5/16/61
100. Herbert, Hillary A.		Co. F	Parole Greenville AL 5/65 Captain 5/21/61 Major 5/5/62 LtCol 5/3/63-11/2/64 Acting Col 5/3/64-5/6/64 Received Regt Compliment for Gallantry at Salem Church Seriously wounded at Wilderness 5/6/64 Sent home, retired 11/2/64 due to Permanent disability Captured Seven Pines 6/1/62 Exchanged 8/5/62
101. Hickman, J. H.		Co. D	Parole Richmond 5/1/65 Seven Pines 6/6/61 Exchanged 8/5/62

Name	Alternate Names	Company	Notes
102. Horton, James L.		Co. B	Died Richmond 1/20/65 Gettysburg 7/2/63 Exchanged 7/30/63 Conscript 4/5/62 from Wetumpka AL
103. Howard, Clayborne		Co. H	Parole disability 11/25/64 Salem Church 5/3/63 Conscript
104. Howell, A.		Co. H	Died Ft. Del 11/25/63 Gettysburg 7/4/63 Small pox while POW Conscript 8/20/62 Tallapoosa Co. AL
105. Hubbard, A. J.		Co. A	Exchanged 2/10/65 Gettysburg 7/3/63 Recd 7/6/64 Cpl/Sgt 4/1/63 Wounded and Captured Gettysburg
106. Huff, J. W.		Co. E	Exchanged 7/4/63 Gettysburg 7/3/63 Received 7/6/63
107. Huff, James M.		Co. K	Parole Appomtx, 4/9/65 Wounded and captured Gettysburg 7/3/63
108. Hursey, G. A.		Co. H	Died Pt. Lookout 11/14/63 Gettysburg 7/2/63 Recd 7/6/63 Wounded and Captured Gettysburg 7/3/63 Trans. Pt. Lookout 10/26/63 Wounded at Gaines Mill 7/27/62
109. Ieizand, J. L.		Co. F	Sgt. Hosp 7/24, 64
110. Ingram J. L.	Ingraham, Ingrahain, Ingrahaim	Co. F	Died Ft. Del 1/22/64
111. Insand, P.	Inzand, P., Jazand, P., Juisand, P., Juzand, Pierre	Co. E	Sgt Released 6/15/65
112. Inzand P.		Co. I	
113. Jackson, Henry		Co. C	Gettysburg 7/5/63 Conscript
114. Jarvis, J.	John W., Jarris, John W.,	Co. C	Died Ft. Del 2/21,22/64 Gettysburg 7/2/63
115. Jarvik, J. W.		Co. F	Died 10/26/63, Gettysburg 7/2/63 Inflamation of lungs
116. Jusand, P.		Co. F	Released 6/15/65
117. Kellerhan, T. C.		Co. C	Gettysburg 7/5/63 Recd 7/12/63

Name	Alternate Names	Company	Notes
118. Kent, Pierce		Co. I	Released 6/8/65, oath Wounded and captured Gettysburg 7/2/63 Wounded Gaines Mill 6/27/62
119. King, Anthony		Co. I	Parole disability 8/1/62 Wounded(loss of right Eye) and captured at Seven Pines 6/1/62. Given wounded parole. Discharged due to Physical Disability 8/1/62 Enlisted Mobile AL 5/20/61
120. King, J.		Co. G	Gettysburg 7/3/63 Recd 7/12/63
121. King, S. J			Parole 5/8/65 Wounded and captured Gettysburg 7/2/63 Exchanged 11/11/64 Trans. Pt. Lookout 10/26/63
122. Kirkland, A.	Abram	Co. E	Died Ft. Del 10/27/63 Gettysburg 7/2/63 Recd 7/6/63 Conscript Camp Watts AL 8/12/62
123. Knight, R.		Co. C	Died Ft. Del 9/21/63 Gettysburg 7/5/63
124. Lampson, E.		Co. E	Exchanged FD 8/13/63 Gettysburg 7/4/63 Exchanged from Ft.Del 8/13/63
125. Lanaham, J. P.		Co. I	Released 6/14/65, oath Gettysburg 7/3/63 Recd 7/12/63 Conscript 10/10/62 Camp Watts AL
126. Langford, J. B.		Co. K	Parole Selma 6/65 Gettysburg 7/2/63 Recd 7/6/63 Wounded and Captured Gettysburg To Ft. Del 10/27/63 Hosp Ft. Lookout 11/63 Enlisted Marion AL 2/7/63

Name	Alternate Names	Company	Notes

127. Leary, Pat		Co. I	Released 6/14/65
			Gettysburg 7/5/63
			    Recd 7/12/63
			    "Left"
			McHenry 7/7/63
			Wounded and captured
			Gettysburg 7/2/63
			Wounded Seven Pines 6/1/62
			Enlisted Mobile AL 5/20/61
			Name placed on Roll of honor

128. Lenaghan, J. P.		Co. J	Released 6/15/65 McHenry 7/7/63
129. Logan, E. M.		Co. A	Gettysburg 7/3/63 Recd 7/12/63
130. Logan Geo. W.		Co. A	Died 2/64 Gettysburg 7/3/63 Recd 7/12/63 Enlisted Marion AL 9/27/61
131. Logan, Henderson B.		Co. A	Died Richmond 4/3/65 Gettysburg 7/3/63 Recd 7/12/63 Enlisted Marion AL 5/20/61
132. Maher, Daniel		Co. I	Exchanged 8/5/62 Near Richmond 6/28/62 Exchanged 8/5/62 Enlisted Mobile AL 5/20/61
133. Marcus, Jas.	Mason, James	Co. K	Died Ft. Del 9/27,29/63 Gettysburg 7/3/63 Recd 7/12/63
134. Marritt, J. S.	J. G.	Co. D	Released 6/14/65 Gettysburg 7/3/63 Enlisted Mobile AL 8/26/62
135. Martin, B. F.		Co. K	Gettysburg 7/2/63 2nd Cp./Sgt 6/1/61 Enlisted Perry Co. AL 5/16/61
136. Martin, Bernard		Co. I	Dischg, probably Phys. Disability Seven Pines 6/1/62 Exchanged 8/5/62 Enlisted Mobile AL 5/20/61

Name	Alternate Names	Company	Notes
137. McCarron, John		Co. I	Sent to Elmira Seven Pines 6/1/62 Exchanged Aiken's Landing VA 8/5/62 Wounded and captured Gettysburg 7/4/63 Sent to DeCamp General Hosp, David Island NY Harbor; Exchanged at Camp Lee VA 9/63 Captured Wilderness 5/6/64
138. McCaserill, W		Co. C	Admit FD Hosp 1/24/65
139. McCaskil, W. E.	McCaskill, W. E.	Co. G	Released 6/14/65 Wilderness 5/10/64 Sent to Old Capitol Prison Wash DC Later to Ft. Del Conscript 10/12/62 Wilcox Co. AL
140. McCasker, H. J.		Co. G	Escaped Gettysburg 7/2/63 Recd 7/6/63
141. McCosker, Mathias L.			Gettysburg 7/2/63 Enlisted Mobile 5/21/61
142. McDevitt, Wm.		Co. I	Dischg. Phy. Disab. Wounded and captured Seven Pines 6/1/62 Exchanged Aiken's Landing 8/5/62 Enlisted Mobile 5/20/61
143. McDonald, Jas. P.	McDaniel	Co. F	Exchanged 11/1/64 Wounded and captured Gettysburg 7/2/63 Exchanged 11/1/64 Conscript 8/2/62 from Pike Co. AL
144. McDonald, J. W.		Co. F	Gettysburg 7/2/63 Recd 7/6/63
145. Menich, J. H.		Co. D	Gettysburg 7/3/63 Recd 7/12/63
146. Merrih, J.		Co. D	Admitted Hosp 1/14/65 Released 6/15/65
147. Merritt, J. S.		Co. D	Released 6/15/65 McHenry 7/7/63
148. Meyersburg, Louis	Myersberg	Co. I	Took Oath Wounded and Captured Gettysburg 7/3/63 Enlisted Mobile AL 5/20/61, Jewish drummer

Name	Alternate Names	Company	Notes
149. Moore, H. F.		Co. F	Gettysburg 7/3/63 Recd 7/12/63
150. Moore, J. F.		Co. F	Parole Pt. Lookout, 2/18/65 Conscript 8/11/62 Macon Co. AL
151. Moore, W. D.		Co. C	Trans. Pt. Lookout 10/26/63 Near Shipensburg PA 6/28/63 Recd 7/9/63
152. Moran, Francis		Co. I	Took oath Seven Pines 6/1/62 Enlisted 5/10/61 Mobile AL
153. Morman, George W.		Co. C	Died Tyhpoid Richmond 2/21/64 Seven Pines 6/1/62 Exchanged 8/5/62 Enlisted 5/18/61 Mobile AL
154. Morris, S.		Co. D	Exchanged 7/31/63 Gettysburg 7/2/63 Recd 7/12/63
155. Morris, W. L.		Co. B	Parole Montg 5/31/65 Gettysburg 7/2/63 Enlisted 5/31/61 Wetumpka AL
156. Morris, W. S.		Co. B	Admit. Hosp. 8/1/84
157. Morris, Zachariah S.		Co. D	Trans. to Elmira Wounded and captured Spotsylvania CH 5/12/64 Conscript from Marble Valley AL 9/2/63
158. Nall	Nail, R. N.	Co. K	Parole Salem AL 6/65 Wounded and captured Gettysburg 7/2/63 Exchanged 2/18/65 Enlisted Perry Co. AL 5/16/61
159. Neagle, John	Nagle	Co. F	Joined 1st Conn. oath
160. Nelson, John		Co. G	Released oath 5/10/65 Enlisted Mobile AL 5/25/61
161. Nelson T. A.	J. A.	Co. G	Gettysburg 7/5/63 Recd 7/12/63
162. Nesmith, O. W.	Oliver P., C. W.	Co. C, G, D	Died Ft. Del 8/29, 63
163. Neumar, James		Co. C	Joined 3rd MD Gettysburg 7/5/63
164. Neuman, T.	F., J.	Co. G	Joined 3rd MD Gettysburg 7/5/63 Recd 7/12/63
165. Norrison, W. R.	E.	Co. F	Joined 3rd MD

Name	Alternate Names	Company	Notes
166. O'Connor, Thomas	Olconnor, T.	Co. C	Died Ft. Del 8/13/63 Gettysburg 7/5/63 Recd 7/12/63
167. Padson, Felix			
168. Perry, B.		Co. K	Trans. Pt. Lookout 10/65 Gettysburg 7/3/63
169. Perry Edward		Co. F	Exchanged 2/18/65 Gettysburg 7/5/63 Exchanged 2/18/65
170. Pierce, Kent		Co. I	"Left" Gettysburg 7/3/63 Recd 7/12/63
171. Porter, Thomas W. D.		Co. D	Exchanged 8/5/62 Seven Pines 6/1/62
172. Powers M.	Michael, H	Co. C	Exchanged 2/27/65 Gettysburg 7/5/63 Recd 7/12/63
173. Quinn, Andrew		Co. I	Seven Pines 6/1/62 Exchanged 8/1/62 Pvt 5/20/61, 2nd Lt 11/13/62, 1st LT 7/3/63 Captain 12/27/63 Wounded Bristoe Station 10/14/63
174. Reed, J. F.		Co. B	Gettysburg 7/4/63
175. Richardson James Madison		Co. K	Dischg. Phy dis 10/25/62 Wounded and captured Seven Pines 6/1/62 Conscript 3/16/61 Perry Co. AL
176. Richardson, O.	Rickelson, O.	Co. D	Released 6/15/65 Gettysburg 7/3/63 Recd 7/12/63
177. Roley, W. C.		Co. B	Admit. Hosp. 3/26/65
178. Rothchilds, A.		Co. G	Died 7/17/63 of wound Seven Pines 6/1/62 Exchanged Aiken's Landing, 8/15/62 Cited for Conspicuous Bravery during battle Enlisted Mobile AL 5/25/61
179. Ryan, Wm. A.	W. A.	Co. E	Exchanged 7/27/63 From Johnson's Is. Gettysburg 7/4/63 Wounded at Frazier's Farm 6/30/62 Name placed on roll of Honor 5/6/62 2nd Lt for gallantry
180. Sanson, Thomas		Co. I	
181. Scharf, Henry		Co. G	Released 3/29/65 oath

Name	Alternate Names	Company	Notes
182. Sessions, J. J.		Co. F	Exchanged 4/27/64
183. Shader, B. H.		Co. E	Exchanged 7/30/ 63
184. Shadix, Benjamin H.	Shedix, B. H.	Co. E	Parole 7/30-31/63
185. Sharp, Henry	O'Sharp	Co. G	Exchanged 3/29, 65
186. Simons, A. C.		Co. F	Trans. Pt. Lookout 10/26/63
187. Singley, I. T.		Co. A	Trans. Pt. Lookout 10//63
188. Smelley, Thomas J.	Smiliy, Smelly, J. T.	Co. A	Exchanged 8/5/63
189. Smith, H. M.		Co. G	Parole Montg 6/5/65
190. Smith, W. W.		Co. G	
191. Spikes, J. S.		Co. G	Parole Appomtx 4/9/65
192. Sterling, Wm. R.	W. R.	Co. E	1st Lt. Johnson Isl. 7/27/63
193. Stewart, M.		Co. C	Died Ft. Del 8/12/63
194. Stringfellow, F. H.		Co. G	Joined 3rd MD Cav oath
195. Stryne, R.		Co. H	3rd MD Cav oath 9/63
196. Sudden, Alexander		Co. G	Johnson Is. 7/27/63
197. Sullivan, John		Co. I	Hosp. thru most of war
198. Summers G. W.		Co. I	
199. Summers, Wm.		Co. I	Exchanged 2/10/65
200. Swindal, John G.	J. C.	Co. B	Died Ft. Del, 12/5/ 63
201. Tarnmick, A.		Co. I	To Pt. Lookout 10/25/63 Gettysburg 7/1/63 Recd 7/6/63
202. Taylor, James A.		Co. G	Returned to duty 9/2/63 Gettysburg 7/3/63 to Ft. Delaware 7/31/63 Conscript.
203. Taylor, J. E.		Co. G	Exchanged 7/31/63 Gettysburg 7/1/63 Recd 7/6/63
204. Togin G.		Co. A	Gettysburg 7/5/63 Recd 7/12/63
205. Trindle, J. G.		Co. B	Died Ft. Del, 12/15/63 Gettysburg 7/5/63
206. Tyson, A. G.		Co. C	Exchanged 2/18/65 Gettysburg 7/1/63 Recd 7/6/63 Conscript from Coosa County AL 8/28/62
207. Wacher, George		Co. A	
208. Walker, Chas. F.	Wacker, C. F.	Co. G	1st LT Released 6/12/65
209. Walker, G. I.		Co. A	Joined US 3rd MD Cav
210. Ward, J. G.		Co. E	Released 6/15/65
211. Ward, J. J.		Co. E	Died Ft. Del 9/29/63 Gettysburg 7/5/63
212. Ward, James W.		Co. K	Died Ft. Del 9/29/63 Gettysburg 7/5/63
213. Ward, John J.		Co. E	Released 6/14/65
214. Ware, James		Co. F	KIA Antietam 9/17/62
215. Whalen, James	Whelan	Co. H	Deserted & joined CSN
216. White, P. S.		Co. K	Died Pt. Lookout 11/11/63

Name	Alternate Names	Company	Notes
217. Whitter, John	Whitler	Co. I	Exchanged 10/10/62
218. Wilf, J. W.	Wolfs	Co. B	Released 6/15/65
219. Williams, Edw'd		Co. H	
220. Williams, F. H.		Co. K	
221. Williams, Frank		Co. K	Wounded parole 5/3/63
222. Wood, H. A.		Co. E	Exchanged 11/1/64
223. Wright, Albert E.	A. E.	Co. E	Released 6/15/65, oath
224. Wright, J. B.		Co. D	Parole Pt. Lookout 2/18/65
225. Wright, John		Co. F	Musician, Arm lost 5/64
226. Wright, Reubin	K., R.	Co. C	Died Ft. Del 9/21/63
227. Wyncoop, J. W.		Co. E	Echanged 2/18/65
228. Yant, Francis		Co. C	1st LT
229. Young, C. H.		Co. K	Trans. Pt. Lookout 10/63
230. Young, H. C.		Co. K	Parole Selma 6/65
231. Young, H. H.		Co. E	Joined 3rd MD Cav 9/63
232. Young, Jas. C.		Co. A	Parole Selma 6/65
233. Young, S. C.		Co. K	Trans. Pt. Lookout 10/63
234. Young, W. W.		Co. K (E)	Joined 3rd MD Cav

Appendix D
Alternate Designation, Assignments, and Battles

Designations:
John A. Winston's Infantry
Young L. Royston's Infantry
John W. Frazer's Infantry
John P. Emrich's Infantry
Hillary A. Herbert's Infantry
Duke Nall's Infantry
Thomas E. Irby's Infantry
Thomas Phelan's Infantry

Assignments:

October 3, 1861	Fifth Brigade, Army of the Peninsula
January 31, 1862	Attached, Second Division, Department of the Peninsula
April 30, 1862	Pryor's Brigade, Center of Position, Army of Northern Virginia
May 21, 1862	Pryor's Brigade, Second Division, Army of Northern Virginia
July 23, 1862	Fourth Brigade, Longstreet's Division, Longstreet's Command, Army of Northern Virginia
September 20, 1862	Wilcox's Brigade, R. H. Anderson's Division, First Corps, Army of Northern Virginia
December 10, 1862	Wilcox's Brigade, R. H. Anderson's Division, First Corps, Army of Northern Virginia
June 1, 1863	Wilcox's Brigade, Anderson's Division, A. P. Hill's Third Corps, Army of Northern Virginia
May 1, 1864	Perrin's Brigade, Anderson's Division, Third Corps, Army of Northern Virginia
August 31, 1864	Sanders' Brigade, Mahone's Division, Third Corps, Army of Northern Virginia

February 28, 1865   Forney's Brigade, Mahone's Division, Third Corps, Army of Northern Virginia

Battles:

Siege of Yorktown VA	April 5-May 4, 1862
Evacuation of Yorktown VA	May 4, 1862
Battle of Williamsburg VA	May 5, 1862
Battle of Seven Pines (Fair Oaks)	May 31-June1, 1862
Seven Days Battles	June 25-July 1, 1862
Battle of Mechanicsville	June 26, 1862
Battle of Gaines' Mill, Cold Harbor, Chickahominy	June 27, 1862
Battle of Glendale, Frazier's Farm, Charles City Cross roads, New Market Crossroads, Willis Church	June 30, 1862
Battle of Second Manassas	August 16-September 2, 1862
Maryland Campaign	September 6-22, 1862
Maryland Heights	Sept 12-13, 1862
Siege Harper's Ferry	Sept 13-15, 1862
Battle of Antietam (Sharpsburg)	Sept 16-17 1862
Operations in Loudon, Fauquier and Rappahannock Counties VA	Oct 26-Nov 10, 1862
Battle of Fredericksburg VA	Dec 12-15, 1862
Chancellorsville Campaign	April 29-May 6, 1863
Engagement Fitzhugh's Crossing, Rappahannock River	April 29-30, 1863
Battle of Chancellorsville	May 1-5, 1863
Gettysburg Campaign	June 3-Aug 1, 1863
Battle of Gettysburg	July 1-3, 1863
Retreat to Near Manassas Gap VA	July 5-24, 1863
Skirmish, Funkstown MD	July 12, 1863
Engagement, Wapping Heights, Manassas Gap VA	July 23, 1863
Bristoe Campaign	Oct 9-22, 1863
Battle Bristoe Station VA	October 14, 1863
Skirmishes, Warrenton, Jeffersonton, Hazel River	Nov 8, 1863
Mine Run Campaign	Nov 26-Dec 2, 1863
Wilderness Campaign	May 4, June 12, 1864
Battle of Wilderness	May 5-7, 1864
Combat Laurel Hill VA	May 8, 1864
Battles, Spottsylvania Court House, Ny River, Fredericksburg Road	May 8-21, 1864
Combat, Po River VA	May 10, 1864
Assault on Salient Spottsylvania Court Hose	May 12, 1864
Operations on the line of the North Anna River	May 22-26, 1864
Operations on the line of the Totopotomoy River	May 28-31, 1864

Engagement, Cold Harbor VA	May 31-June 1, 1864
Battles about Cold Harbor VA	June 1-12, 1864
Battle of Bethesda Church	June 1-3, 1864
Siege Operations against Petersburg and Richmond	June 16-1864-April 2, 1865
Engagement Jerusalem Plank Road (Weldon R.R.)	June 22, 1864
Explosion, Petersburg Mine & Assault on Crater	July 30, 1864
Battle of Weldon RR, Globe Tavern, and Black's Station	Aug 18-21, 1864
Battle Ream's Station	Aug 25, 1864
Battle of Poplar Springs Church, Pebble's Farm, Pegram's Farm, Chappel House, Laurel Hill	Sept 29-Oct 2, 1864
Engagement, Boydton Plank Road (Hatcher's Run)	Oct 27-28, 1864
Battle Hatcher's Run, Armstrong's Mills etc	Feb 5-7, 1865
Appomattox Campaign	March 28-April 9, 1865
Assault and Capture of Petersburg lines	April 2, 1865
Surrender, Appomattox Court House VA	April 9, 1865

Appendix E
Transcribed Company Notes from
National Archives Microfilm
Eighth Alabama Infantry CSA

Captain Royston's Company of Alabama Rangers
  Young L. Royston Commanding
                Record of Events
Called into service of the Confederates States in the Provisional Army under Provisions of the Act of Congress passed February 1861 by the Honorable L. P. Walker, Secretary of War on the 8th day of May 1861 for the term of the continuance of the war unless sooner discharged.
  Certificate of Mustering Officer 21 May 1861
              Henry B. Kelly 1st LT CS Inf.
  Subsequently to become Company A 8th Alabama Infantry

Company A
Company Muster Roll May 8 to June 30 1861
Stationed Yorktown VA
                Record of Events
This company was tendered to and received into the Confederate States service May 8, 1861 for the war. Received marching orders May 16, 1861 and forthwith proceeded from their rendezvous point in Perry Co. AL to Richmond VA where it was ordered to Gloucester Point where it remained engaged in fortifying and defending said Point till 13 June when it was ordered to this place where it has been much of the time say about twenty days employed in making entrenchments and also that this company with others of said 8th Alabama Regiment and under the command of General Magruder marched near and by New Port News, then and now in the enemy's possession. The command encamped near Young's Mill and there remained until ordered to return to their regiment and its encampment near Yorktown. This company was employed three days in making fortifications.

Company A
Company Muster Roll July & Aug 1861
Stationed near Yorktown VA
                Record of Events
This company arrived at Gloucester Point May 28 1861, and remained there about 27 days. It was then transferred to Yorktown July 1, 1861. It marched with the Army

of General Magruder down the peninsula within a short distance of Hampton Old Point and New Port News being absent about ten days having marched about forty seven miles during this time. About Aug. 4, 1861, it marched again down the peninsula being part of the Army of General Magruder a distance of about thirty miles and was on duty near Hampton at the burning of said town being absent about ten days.

Company A
Company Return Jan 1862
Harrods Mills VA

Company A
Company Return Sept & Oct 1863
Near Brandy Station VA

Record of Events

This company since Aug 5, 1863 has been doing picket duty at Rapadan Bridg. On the 8th it took up a line of march in the direction of Madison Court House. Then on to Culpeper Court House, thence to Warrenton, thence to Bristoe Station where it was ordered into the line of battle. The enemy retreated it was ordered to take up a line of march for the bridge on the Rappahannock crossing the river. It went into came near Brandy Station, where it remained doing guard duty and drilling October 31, 1863

Thos. R. Heard
Capt. Co. A. 8th Ala Reg.

Company A
Company Muster Roll Sept Oct 1864
Stationed Near Petersburg VA

Record of Events

Since last muster this company has been stationed near Petersburg and has been in all engagements that the regiment has been in.

M.V.Massey
Lt. Commanding Co. A 8th Ala Reg.

Company A
Company Record May 8, 1861 to December 31, 1864
Stationed Petersburg VA
Dated 31 Dec 1864

Historical Memoranda

This company was originally called "Alabama Rangers' was organized at Perry Co. AL on May 8, 1861 by Capt. Young L. Royston. Left Marion May 16 And arrived Richmond May 27th and was mustered into the service of the Confederate States for the war on May 22, 1862 at Montgomery AL by Capt. Young L. Royston.

This company remained in Richmond two days was sent then to Gloucester Point near Yorktown where it remained there drilling and constructing Fortifications until 15 June when it was moved across the river to Yorktown and incorporated into the 8th Alabama Regiment Col. Jno. A. Winston commanding as Company A camped on the river and remained there doing garrison duty and building fortifications until 9 October when it removed to Big Bethel 12 miles southward. Took several marches during the autumn time frame toward Hampton and New Market and finally build winter quarters at Harwood's Mills nine miles from Yorktown. Upon McClellan's advance up the peninsula, this Company (with the regiment) fell back to the river defenses and occupied a portion of the line near Wynn's Mills. Remained there doing heavy garrison fatigue and picket duty under almost constant artillery fire of the enemy until 3 May 1862 when the Army retired from Yorktown. On May 5, at Williamsburg, the company was engaged, lost two killed and eight wounded. It also participated in the battles of Seven Pines, Gaines' Mill, Fraziers Farm, 2nd Manassas, Sharpsburg, and Fredericksburg, losing many of its best officers and men. It wintered near Fredericksburg doing heavy and continuous picket duty at Banks Ford on the Rappahannock and was poorly provided with shelter from the winter.

During the campaign of 1863 this company was actively engaged in the battles of Chancellorsville, Gettysburg, and Bristow Station, and it was also present at the hostile demonstration at Mine Run in November. Spent the winter of 63/64 near Orange Court House picketing near the Rapidan Bridge. Was very comfortably quartered and enjoyed a tolerable quiet winter. During the campaign of 1864 this company participated in forty seven engagements and has been stationed for weeks at a time exposed to continuous artillery and musket fire. In common with the other companies of the regiment and brigade, it has suffered severely as a glance at the historical table will show. Of the original number at its first organization of 97, only 18 are now on the muster roll. Too many of its finest and best man have fallen to allow particular mention here. This company has been comfortably quartered three miles from Petersburg on the Boydton Plank Road since November and has performed regular picket duty on the lines.

(END OF COMPANY A)

Company B
Company Muster Roll May 17 to 30 June 1861
Stationed Near Yorktown VA

Record of Events

This company under the name of the "Governor's Guard" was offered to the Secretary of War at Montgomery Alabama May 13th 1861 and was reported ready to march. It was accepted on the same day and received orders to hold itself in readiness to move.

On May 17th ordered were issues to the Captain to come down the river to Montgomery by steamer enroute to Richmond, and in the week of their being no steamer for that day he caught the first boat down the river. The company was held in its barracks awaiting river transportation until the morning of May 20th in which day it was transported by wagon to Montgomery and left the same evening for Richmond, where it arrived on the 23rd of May and went into camp at the Fairfield Race Course. On the 27th of May it was mustered into the service of the Confederates for the War by Capt. Scott. Immediately after the mustering the company moved to Gloucester Point VA in obedience to ordered received May 26th. The company crossed the York River and joined the eight Alabama companies forming the 8th Alabama Regiment Col. J. A. Winston commanding. Since June 14th the company has been engaged in company and battalion drill and throwing up entrenchments.

On June 21st, the company marched with the Alabama battalion in the direction of Fort Monroe for bivouac at various places between Yorktown and Hampton and then returned to Yorktown on the 25th of June.

Private W. P. Cairs being unable to travel was left behind, but he rejoined the company at Gloucester Point later that month. Nine dollars and fifty cents is due him from the Confederate states for transportation.

Private G. W. Campbell enlisted in his company for the war on June 21st and was mustered into the service of the Confederate States by Lieut. Col. Frazier at Yorktown on July 13th. Due him for transportation is $35.75.

Company B
Company Muster Roll July-Aug 1861
Stationed Near Yorktown

Record of Events

This company since its last muster has been stationed at Yorktown with the exception of about two weeks spent in open camp on the Peninsula. The health of the company has only been moderate. The company has been engaged in drill, throwing up entrenchments, clearing woods, and dragging guns upon the works.

Company B
Company Muster Roll Sept Oct 1863
Stationed Near Brandy Station

Record of Events

Since last muster this company has been encamped near Orange Court House Virginia and engaged in doing picket duty at Rapidan Station. At 8 October when we left and marched to Bristow Station and stopped three or four days, then marched back to the south side of the Rappahannock River and went into camp near Brandy Station 18th October 1863 having marched about 100 miles.

Company B
Company Muster Roll Jan-Feb 1864
Stationed Near Orange Court House VA
Record of Events

This company was last mustered near Orange Court House 31 Dec 1863 and since that time has been doing picket duty at Rapidan Station. The Company reenlisted unconditionally for the war on the 29th day of January 1864.

Company B
Company Muster Roll March April 1864
Stationed Near Orange Court House VA
Record of Events

Since last muster this company has been encamped near Orange Court House Virginia. Has marched to Madison Court House and back on 1st of March 1864 a distance of 36 miles.

Company B
Company Muster Roll Sept Oct 1864
Stationed Near Petersburg VA
Record of Events

Since last muster this company near Petersburg and has been in one engagement with the enemy on October 2nd 1864.

Company B
Company Return January 1862
Stationed at Harwood's Mill

Company B
Record of Company B "Governor's Guards" from Coosa Co. AL for May 13, 1861 to Jan 1865 near Petersburg dated January 18, 1865
Historical Memoranda

Recapitulation	
Total Commissioned Officers	9
Total Enlisted Men	114
Aggregate	123
Deduct Casualties	-66
Aggregate Remaining	57

Killed	22
Died of Disease	23
Died of Wounds	1
Resigned	2
Dropped	2
Retired	0
Discharged	10
Transferred	5
Deserted	1
Missing by capture/otherwise	0
Total Casualties	66

(END OF COMPANY B)

Company C
Company Muster Roll May 23 to June 30 1861
Record of Events

This company was accepted on May 18th 1861. They left Mobile Alabama on the 23rd and arrived Richmond Virginia on the 27th and were mustered into service on the 28th.

We left Richmond on June 13th and arrived at Yorktown on the 14th of June.

On the 27th of June we left Yorktown and moved toward Bethel. On the 28th we moved on in the same direction. On the night of the 28th about eleven o'clock we moved on to Bethel and thence on near Newport News and thence on to the Smith place and thence on about six miles toward Warwick Court House where we stopped about two o'clock after a march of about thirty two miles through mud and rain a good portion of the time at double quick. The men were much fatigued. Many of them lost their blankets, their shoes and other things on the march. On the night of the 29th we moved to Young's Mill, where we remained until July 4th. We then moved to Harwood's Mill where we remained til the 6th and then returned to Yorktown.

The disciple is moderate. The men are true and brave and many of them fine marksmen.

Company C
Company Muster Roll July Aug 1861
Stationed Near Yorktown VA
Record of Events

George B. Batchellar was discharged June 16th 1861 by Ridge and Inspector General Cooper.

Company C
Company Return Jan 1862
Stationed Near Harwood's Mill

Company C
Company Muster Roll Sept Oct 1863
Stationed Near Brandy Station VA
Record of Events
This company has been on picket duty at Rapidan Bridge from 13th Sept 1863 to 8th October 1863 when ordered to march on to Culpeper via Madison Court House. We pursued the enemy to Manassas and were the first to arrive at Bristow Station on the 14th of October. Left Bristow Station on the morning of the 18th and marched to Brandy Station where it is now encamped.

Company C
Company Muster Roll Jan Feb 1864
Stationed Near Orange Court House VA
Record of Events
Since last muster this company has been doing picket duty at Rapidan Station.

Company C
Company Muster Roll March & April 1864
Stationed Near Orange Court House VA

Company C
Company Muster Roll Sept & Oct 1864
Near Petersburg VA
Record of Events
This company since last muster has been in the trenches before Petersburg up to the 27 of October and then it was withdrawn to go to battle of Burgess Mills. October 27, 1864 The company lost in the engagement—one man wounded.

Company C
Record of Company C for May 18, 1861 to December 31, 1864 shows stationed at Boydton Plank Road Petersburg and dated January 1, 1865
Historical Memoranda
This company was organized at Mobile AL May 7, 1861 under the name of the "Alexander Stephens Guards." The company was received into the Confederate Service on the 18th of May 1861 at Richmond Virginia. Mustered by Lt. Scott. Upon organization of the Eighth Alabama Regiment it was allocated to this command as Company C. The regiment was organized then and were ordered to report to General Magruder who was here commanding at Yorktown VA. When we arrived on June 15th 1861 the regiment was commanded by Col. John A. Winston. After staying at this place for three months we were moved down the Peninsula to Bethel Church to do outpost duty. We started to build winter quarters, but received orders to fall back to Harwood's Mill and build winter quarters. We got the quarters about the first of February, and then we have to go

on scouting parties and were doing outpost duty all the time into Geo. B. McClellan's advance up the Peninsula in the campaign of 1862. We fell back from Harwood's Mill to Wynn's Mill of our outer defenses of Yorktown. We remained in the trenches at Wynn's Mill 26 days during the bombardment. Then we evacuated to the place where we participated in the Battle of Williamsburg on May 5th 1862. We then fell back to Richmond, suffered very severe at the Battle of Seven Pines. After the wounding of General Joseph E. Johnston we fell back again to Richmond. We went back to our old camps and were there about three weeks during the time; General Robert E. Lee took command of the Army on June 25th 1862. We left camp again and moved down the Mechanicsville turnpike road toward the Chickahominy Bridge. We crost the bridge the night of June 25th and encamped in the woods on the side of the hill for the night. In the morning we were ordered into the line of battles and the enemy commenced to shell up. We were ordered to support Tim Price's Brigade which was then moving forward to engage the enemy but a dense fog settled on the earth and we were prevents from making the attack and the Yankees fell back to Gaines Mill. We attacked them in the evening and routed them making them disbandon.

We then went to Frazier's Farm and engaged the enemy on the 30th of June took eight pieces of artillery and drove them from the battlefield.

At the battle of Malvern Hill we were held in reserve and were not engaged. We then moved to Charles City Court House and encamped there for a few days. We then came back to our old camp around Richmond.

We were in the first invasion of Maryland, were at the surrender of Harper's Ferry, present at 2nd Manassas. We had three men wounded but were not engaged until the Battle of Sharpsburg. We had nine men at the time all made the first charge-two of then got killed and six wounded leaving only one man in the company. We were present at the battle of Fredericksburg. Suffered seven at the Battle of Gettysburg. We were at Bristow Station and had been present for the Campaign of General Grant since he crossed the Rapidan River

Recapitulation	
Total Commissioned Officers	8
Total Enlisted Men	131
Aggregate	139
Deduct Casualties	-93
Aggregate remaining	43
Killed	20
Died of Disease	7
Died of Wounds	5
Resigned	2
Retired	2
Discharged	20
Transferred	4
Disabled	28
Missing by capture/otherwise	5

Total	-93
Aggregate wounded	49
Aggregate Disabled	2
Captured	15
Exchanged	4
Escapes	0
Died	2
Oaths to US	4
Not Returned	5

(END OF COMPANY C)

Company D
Company Muster Roll May 10 to June 30, 1861
Stationed—Not Stated

Company D
Company Muster Roll July-August 1861
Stationed—Not Stated

Company D
Company Muster Roll Sept-Oct 1861
Stationed Near Brandy Station
Record of Events
The company was in camp near Orange Court House during the month of September and did picket duty at Rapidan Station on October 7th and broke camp and participated in the last campaign to Manassas.

Company D
Company Muster Roll Jan & Feb 1864
Stationed Near Orange Court House VA
Record of Events
Since last muster this company has been in winter quarters near Orange Court House Virginia and has done picket duty at Rapidan Station.

Company D
Company Muster Roll March & April 1864
Stationed Near Orange Court House VA
Record of Events
Since last muster this company has been in camp near Orange Court House Virginia and has done picket duty at Rapidan Station

Company D
Company Muster Roll Sept & Oct 1864
Stationed Petersburg VA

Record of Events

Since last muster the company has been in the trenches in front of Petersburg and participated in the engagement on Boydton Plank Road October 27, 1864

Company D
Company Return January 1862
Stationed—not stated

(END OF COMPANY D)

Company E
Company Muster Roll May 18-June 30, 1861
Stationed Near Yorktown

Record of Events

April 5, 1861 organized in Mobile and the company was accepted on 20 April by Governor A. B. Moore, On May 6, the officers were ordered to be ready for early marching orders and were commissioned. On May 18, the company received orders to report to General Lee in Richmond Virginia, arriving there on the 24th and were mustered into the Confederate States service by Capt. John Scott May 29, 1861.

On June 11 ordered to form part of the 8th Ala regmt. Under Col. John A. Winston and were ordered to Yorktown VA and once there were employed erecting defensive works and made demonstrations against the enemy at Hampton, Newport News and Fortress Monroe. Are the best drilled in the regiment. Men are tough and healthy.

Company E
Company Muster Roll Sept & Oct 1863
Stationed Near Brandy Station

Record of Events

Since last muster this company has been doing picket duty on the Rapidan River for about a month then took up a line of march toward Manassas when we overtook the enemy. This company was under a very heavy shelling from the enemy. The company lost three men wounded. The enemy fell back the same night. We camped near Bristow Station for two days. We then took up a line of march for Brandy Station where we are now encamped.

Company E
Company Muster Roll Jan-Feb 1864
Stationed Near Orange CH
Record of Events
Since last muster the company has been doing picket duty near the Rapidan River.

Company E
Company Muster Roll March & April 1864
Stationed Near Orange CH
Record of Events
Since last muster this company has been doing picket duty and throwing up fortifications near the Rapidan River.

Company E
Company Muster Roll Sept & Oct 1864
Stationed Near Petersburg
Record of Events
Since last muster this company has been engaged in the battles on the Weldon Railroad with the regiment and has been doing picket duty on the line and has had three men wounded.

Co. E.
Company Return Jan 1862
Stationed Near Harwood's Mill

Co. E
Company Muster Roll May 6, 1861 to Dec 31, 1864
Stationed Near Boydton Plank Road Petersburg VA dated Jan 1, 1865
Historical Memoranda
This company was organized at Mobile May 6, 1861 under the name Hamp Smith Rifles and was mustered into the Service of the Confederate States at Richmond June 5, 1861 by Lt. Scott CSA. Upon the organization of the 8th Ala Regmt. It was allotted to this command as Company E. No sooner than the regiment was organized it was ordered to report to General Magruder who was then commanding at Yorktown VA. Here we arrived 15 June 1861. The regiment being commanded by Col. Jno. A. Winston. After staying at this place for three months during which time we have been engaged in building fortifications, we moved down the peninsula to the vicinity of Bethel, where we built huts and winter quarters. We remained here during the winter of 1861-1862 doing outpost duty and going on scouting expeditions and it was while on one of those expeditions we encountered a similar part of the enemy and thus became engaged in our maiden battle Dec 22, 1861. Upon McClellan's advance up the peninsula,

we fell back to Wynn's Mill, a point on the defenses of Yorktown where we remained doing garrison duty until May 3, 1862 when the army evacuated the position. On the retreat to Richmond we fought the Battle of Williamsburg, May 5, 1862, reaching the former place on May 29th. At the battle of Seven Pines on June 1, Gaines Mill June 27, and Frazier's Farm June 30, 1862 we were engaged and suffered twenty in lost of killed and wounded as the table will show. We followed the Army in the first Maryland campaign, participated in the Battle of Manassas No. 2 Aug 30 1862, and Sharpsburg Sept 17, 1862 and we constituted a portion of the command which invested Harper's Ferry being present at the surrender of this place which occurred Sept 15, 1862. We were present but not taking part in the battle of Fredericksburg Dec 13, 1862. This being the last battle of the campaign and the season having far advanced we remained for the winter at Banks Ford on the Rappahannock Rive engaged in doing picket duty. This was severe as the men being poorly clad and sheltered from the weather. Upon the appearance of good weather also affirmed our foe on May 3 we fought at the battle of Salem Church, in which the company was engaged. After this follows the mission at the Pennsylvania campaign in which we participated being present July 2 and 3 at the battle of Gettysburg. In this engagement the company suffered heavily in killed, wounded and missing. In this we lost two Lieutenants wounded and captured. Upon the Army falling back to VA we encamped for a short time at Orange Court House until General Lee's advance in October where we fought the battle of Bristow Station October 14, 1863. This company being engaged later in the season we were present but not engaged at Mine Run, and during the winter of 1863-64 we were encamped at Orange Court House, but upon Grant's advance we broke up camp May 5, 1864 and since which we have been kept actually engaged having participated in no less than seventeen general engagements and numerous skirmishes and marches too numerous to mention. At present this company is encamped on the Boydton Plank Road near Petersburg VA having been relieved from the trenches on Nov 1, 1864 where we had been confined since June 17, excepting such time as were taken out and put into engagements.

Recapitulation	
Total Commissioned Officers	7
Total Enlisted	146
Aggregate	153
Deduct Casualties	-101
Aggregate Remaining	52
Killed	17
Died of Disease	10
Resigned	2
Retired	5
Dropped	2
Discharged	7
Transferred	16
Dispatched	27

Missing by capture/otherwise	1
Total Casualties	101
Aggregate wounded	57
Aggregate disabled	8
Captured	20
Exchanged	7
Escaped	0
Died	0
Oath to US	3
Total	10
Not Returned	10

(END OF COMPANY E)

Company F
Company Muster Roll May 21 to June 30, 1861
Stationed Near Yorktown

Company F
Company Muster Roll July Aug 1861

Company F
Company Return January 1862
Stationed Near Harwood's Mills

Company F
Company Muster Roll Sept Oct 1863
Stationed Near Brandy Station
                    Record of Events

This company left Orange Court House on 8 October in line of march to Bristow Station. Was in engagement at Bristow Station on 14 October 1863 and no casualties occurred in this company. This company now being very comfortable encamped near Brandy Station on the Orange and Alexandria Railroad

D. B. Thornon
Lieut. Commanding

Company F
Company Muster Roll Jan Feb 1864
Stationed Near Orange Court House
Record of Events
This company has been very comfortably quartered since last muster near Orange Court House VA and occasionally performing picket duty on the Rapidan River.

Company F
Company Muster Roll Sept Oct 1864
Stationed Near Petersburg VA

(END OF COMPANY F)

Company G
Company Muster Roll June 8 to June 30, 1861
Stationed Near Yorktown
Record of Events
We were accepted and ordered to march to Richmond on May 25, 1861 as soon as ready being occupied and delayed until 30 May 1861 in fitting out the company with uniforms, knapsacks, cartridge and cap boxes and then we left mobile on the 30th arriving at Richmond on the night of June 5, 1861.

Mustered into service 8 June 1861 and ordered to Yorktown VA on 12 June arriving on the morning of June 13.

Details from the company have been made daily for general guard service and camp guard duty and fatigue duty on the breastworks.

Company G.
Company Muster Roll July and August 1861
Stationed Near Yorktown
Record of Events
We were ordered to march toward Bethel on 24 July 1861 and returned to camp at Yorktown on 29 July.

On August 2 we again received marching orders and marched to Wall's Farm, camped there till the 5th. In the evening we marched to Bethel. In the evening of the 6th we again marched toward Newport News and Hampton; returned to Bethel on the 8th. In the evening of the 10th marched back to Wall's Farm, camped there till the morning of the 13th when we returned to camp at Yorktown.

Company G
Company Muster Roll Sept & Oct 1863
Stationed Near Brandy Station
Record of Events

This company was last mustered near Orange Court House VA while doing picket duty on the Rapidan River; took up line of march in pursuit of Meade arriving at Bristo Station, formed line of battle but did not become engaged with the enemy. Lay in line of battle while troops were destroying the Orange and Alexandria Railroad, formed line of march on the morning of 18 October and camped near the Rappahannock Railroad bridge that evening having marched a distance of 32 miles. Crossed the river on pontoons and company camped on land owned by John Minor Botts.

Company G
Company Muster Roll Jan Feb 1864
Stationed Near Orange Court House VA
                    Record of Events
This company has been in winter quarters, doing picket duty since last muster.

Company G
Company Muster Roll March & April 1864
Stationed Near Orange Court House VA
                    Record of Events
This company has been in winter quarters doing picket duty since last muster.

Company G
Company Muster Roll Sept & Oct 1864
Stationed Petersburg VA
                    Record of Events
Since last muster this company has been engaged in the defense of Petersburg VA; also in one engagement losing four men wounded.

Company G
Company Return January 1862
Harwood's Mills York Co. VA

(END OF COMPANY G)

Company H
Company Muster Roll May 30 to June 30, 1861
Stationed Near Yorktown
                    Record of Events
On the 18th day of May 1861 we received marching orders to report to the city of Richmond VA, left the city of Mobile on 30 May 1861 in pursuance of said orders which period was as early as possible to said orders.
The orders from the war department specify that we should leave for Richmond as soon as organized and prepared. We were not organized and

prepared before 30 May and then the government contemplated paying us for our services for the times required to prepare ourselves for actual duty from 18 May to 30 May 1861. We therefore received this pay under protest.

We were mustered into the service of the Confederate States on the 8th of June 1861 and on the 12th we reached Yorktown VA at which place we have been stationed since except while on two different tour of duty in the neighborhood of Newport News both of which were without interest except the latter during which time the town of Hampton was burned.

             Jno. D. Collier
             2nd Lieut. Co. H

Company H
Company Muster Roll July & Aug 1861
Stationed Near Yorktown

Company H
Company Return January 1862
Stationed Near Harwood's Mills VA

Company H
Company Muster Roll Sept Oct 1863
Stationed Near Brandy Station VA
        Record of Events

  This company was stationed near the Rapidan Bridge during the month of September doing picket duty, left there on 8 Oct and move with the Army to Bristow Station, where they arrived 14 Oct. On that day lost one private killed and one non commissioned officer, and one private wounded by the explosion of a shell from the enemy's batteries into our lines: remained there for three days, and then marched for this place arriving here on the 20th where we have been drilling.

             W. H. Dunn
             LT Commanding Co. H 8 Ala Reg.

Company H
Company Muster Roll Jan & Feb 1864
Stationed Near Orange CH Va
        Record of Events

  Since last muster the company has remained in came near Orange Court House doing picket duty on the Rapidan River

Company H
Company Muster Roll March April 1864
Stationed Near Orange Court House VA
Record of Events
Since last muster the company has remained in camp near Orange Court House VA doing occasional picket duty on the Rapidan River.

W. W. Mordecai
Capt. Comd. Co. H

Company H
Company Muster Roll Sept Oct 1864
Stationed Near Petersburg VA
Record of Events
Since last muster the company has been in the trenches around Petersburg doing garrison duty and participated in the battle of Burgess Mill on the Boydton Plank Road October 27, 1864

W. W. Mordecai
Capt. Comd. Co. H

Company H
Record of Captain W. W. Mordecai's Company H 8 Regmt Ala Vols. From 17 May 1861 to 31 Dec 1864 on the Boydton Plank Road near Petersburg VA January 1, 1865.

Historical Memoranda

This company was organized in Mobile Alabama May 17, 1861 under the name "Mobile Independent Scouts" and was mustered in the service o the Confederate States at Richmond Virginia June 8, 1861, but Lt. Scott CSA. Upon the organization of the Eighth Alabama Regiment it was allotted to the command as Company H. No sooner was the regiment organized than it was ordered to report to General Magruder who was then commanding at Yorktown Va. Here we arrived on 15 June 1861, the regiment being commanded by Col. John A. Winston. After staying at this place for three months during which time were engaged in building fortifications, we moved lower down the peninsula to the vicinity of Bethel where we built huts and went into winter quarters. We remained here during the winter of 1861-1862 doing outpost duty and going on scouting expeditions and while on one expedition we encountered a similar part of the enemy and thus became engaged in our maiden battle December 22, 1861.

Upon G. McClellan's advance up the peninsula we fell back to Wynn's Mill, a point in the defenses of Yorktown, where we remained doing garrison duty until 3 May 1862 when the Army evacuated the position.

On the retreat to Richmond we fought at the Battle of Williamsburg on 5 May 1862, reaching the former place on 29 May. At the battle of Seven Pines June 1, Gaines Mill 27 June, Frazier's Farm 30 June 1862, we were engaged and suffered severly in loss of killed and wounded as the table will show. We followed the Army in its first Maryland campaign participating in Manassas No. 2 Aug 30, 1862 and Sharpsburg Sept 17, 1862 and so constituted a portion of the campaign which invested Harper's Ferry being present at the invasion of this last named place which occurred on the morning of September 15th. We were also present but taking no part in the battle of Fredericksburg on Dec 13, 1862. This being the last battle of the campaign and the season being far advanced we remained for the winter at Banks Ford on the Rappahannock River engaged in doing picket duty. This was severe upon the men being poorly clad and sheltered from the weather. Upon the appearance of good weather on May 3, 1863 fought in the battle of Salem Church in which the company was engaged.

After this followed the memorable Pennsylvania campaign in which we participated and engaged in the battle of Gettysburg on July 2 and 3. In this engagement the company suffered heavily in killed and wounded. Among the former were Lt. Scott and Sergt W. H. McGraugh then whom the two bravest men ever lived. Upon the Army falling back to Virginia we were encamped for a short time at Orange Court House til General Lee's advance in October when we fought at the battle of Bristow Station October 14th, 1863. The company being engaged later in the season was present though not engaged at Mine Run. During the winter of 63/64 we were encamped at Orange Court House Va, but upon General Grant's advance broke camp May 5, 1864 and since that time we have been kept actively engaged having participated in no less than seventeen general engagements and innumerable skirmishes and marches too numerous to mention. At present the company is encamped on the Boydton Plank Rd. near Petersburg Va. Having been relieved from the trenches on November 1, 1864 where we have been confined since June 17 except at times as we were taken out and put into engagements. During the campaign the company lost many of its best and bravest members among whom were Sgt. Reipschlager killed June 23rd and Private Jno. Sproul killed June 23 1864.

Recapitulation	
Total Commissioned Officers	7
Total Enlisted Men	128
Aggregate	135
Deduct Casulaties	-94
Aggregate Remaining	40

Killed	29
Died of Disease	10
Died of Wounds	14
Resigned	2
Retired	0
Discharged	12
Transferred	14
Deserted	14
Missing by capture/otherwise	0
Total casualties	94

Aggregate Wounded 56
Aggregate Disabled 2

Captured 24

Exchanged 15
Escaped 0
Died 5
Oath to US 1
Total 21

Not returned 3

(END OF COMPANY H)

Company I
Company Muster Roll May 20 to June 30, 1861
Stationed—Not Stated

Company I
Company Muster Roll July & Aug 1861
Stationed Near Yorktown
                    Record of Events
This company has been usually at Yorktown except when below on this peninsula. It has done efficient work on the defenses both in Yorktown and below and always was efficient in the discharge of the duties of good soldiers.

Company I
Company Muster Roll Sept & October 1863
Camped Near Brandy Station Va
                    Record of Events
This company has done picket duty from Sept 13 to October 8 at Rapidan Bridge when ordered to march to Culpeper by way of Madison Court House, was engaged in the pursuit of the enemy towards Manassas; had an officer wounded at Bristow Station on the morning of the 18th of October and are now encamped near Brandy Station Va.

Company I
Company Muster Roll Jan Feb 1864
Stationed Near Orange Court House Va.
                    Record of Events

Since last muster this company has been doing picket duty at Rapidan Station.

Company I
Company Muster Roll March April 1864
Stationed Near Orange Court House Va.
Record of Events
This company left camp on the morning of March 1, 1864 at 2 o'clock AM. Marched to Madison Court House a distance of about twenty miles and returned to camp on the evening of 2nd of March since which time we have been doing occasional picket duty at Rapidan Station.

Company I
Company Muster Roll Sept Oct 1864
Near Petersburg Va.
Record of Events
Since last muster this company has been doing picket duty in front of Petersburg Va. And was engaged with the enemy on the Plank road October 27th losing one man wounded.

Company I
Company Return Jan 1862
Harwood's Mills Va.

Company I
Record of May 20, 1861 to Jan 1, 1865
Petersburg Va.
Dated Jan 1 1865
Historical Memoranda
This company was originally named the "Emerald Guards" and was organized by Captain Patrick Loughry in Mobile City, State of Alabama May 20, 1861; Left for Richmond Va. June 3, 1861 and arrived Richmond June 8, 1861 where it remained for four days and left for Yorktown Va on 12 June 1861, arriving Yorktown Va on 13 June 1861 and went into camp and was engaged in drilling and throwing up fortifications. The regiment being then organized and commanded by Col. John A. Winston. This company marched from Yorktown to Harwood's Mills where it lay in the woods one day and took up march at 10 o'clock at night for Young's Mill going by Newport News and arriving at Walls Farm the next evening, rested one day, marched to Young's Mill, formed a line of battle and awaited the enemy. Left for Harwood's Mill, next day and marched half way, and was ordered back, then again to Harwood's Mills where we remained three days more thence to Yorktown, where we remained in camp for sometime, the above march commenced on 1 July and ended on the 8th. Left Yorktown for wall's Farm enroute to Hampton, back to Bethel, thence to Walls Farm, thence to Yorktown, remaining in camp some time. Started for Harwood's Mills, then to Bethel and Back to Harwood's Mills where we went into winter

quarters and remained until McClellan's army appeared and fell back to Wynn's Mill, lay in the woods for 28 days, fell back to Richmond with General Joseph E. Johnston's army, was engaged in the battle of Williamsburg, was engaged in the series of battles around Richmond. Marched to Manassas and joined the battle. Thence to the Potomac crossing the river and marching to Frederick Maryland, thence to Boonesboro, thence to Sharpsburg, Maryland. Participated in that battle and fell back to Washington Springs near Winchester. Camped there for about six weeks. Marched to Culpeper Court House by Front Royal, Flint Hill and camped near Culpeper Court House about three weeks. Marched to Fredericksburg and camped at Banks Ford, done picket duty all winter. Left camp about 3 April 1863 marched to Chancellorsville and back to Banks Ford and was engaged in the battle of Salem Church May 3, 1863. Went back to camp, done picket duty to June 14. Left for Gettysburg PA June 14, reaching there July 1, 1863. Participated in the battles of both days, left battlefield July 4th, marched to Potomac and crossed thence to Culpeper Court House, camped there for some days, marched from there to Rapidan crossed and encamped near Orange Court House doing picket duty. Left for Bristow Station 8 October 1863, from thence back to Rappahannock River thence to Orange Court House, built winter quarters, done picket duty on the Rapidan River. Marched to Mine Run, back to Orange Court House, remaining in camp sometime. Marched to Madison Court House and had to camp. Left camp 5 May 1864 and marched to Wilderness and participated in the battle of 6 & 7 May thence to Spotsylvania Court House and was in battle on the 12th of May thence to Petersburg participating in all the battles with Grant's army.

Recapitulation		
Total Commissioned Officers	8	
Total Enlisted Men	141	
Aggregate	149	
Deduct Casualties	-99	
Aggregate Remaining	50	
Killed	43	
Died of Disease	2	
Died of Wounds	12	
Resigned	3	
Retired	4	
Discharged	17	
Transferred	9	
Deserted	8	
Missing by capture/otherwise	1	
Total casualties	99	
Aggregate Wounded		140
Aggregate Disabled		24
Total		164

.Captured	46
Exchanged	26
Escaped	0
Died	1
Oath to US	3
Total	30
Not Returned	16

(END OF COMPANY I)

Company K
Company Muster Roll May 25, 1861-June 30, 1861
Stationed Near Yorktown
Record of Events
    Left Radfordsville AL 25 May arrived Montgomery 27 May
    Left Montgomery 31 May for Richmond arrived Richmond 4 June
    Left Richmond for Yorktown 12 June arrived 13 June
    Remained in Yorktown till 30 June
    Mustered into Service on 9 June 1861 at Richmond by Capt. John Scott
    On 9 July marched off to Camp Davis near Richmond
Capt. D. Nall
Commanding Co. K 8th Ala Reg

Company K
Company Muster Roll July & Aug 1861
Stationed Near Yorktown
Record of Events
    Aug 2 marched from Yorktown to Walls Farm via Warwick
    Aug 5 marched from Walls Farm to Bethel, Aug 8, 1862 in evening marched about five miles toward Hampton
    Aug 9 marched at 7am for Hampton went within a few miles of Newport News
    Aug 10 marched back to Bethel
    Aug 13 left Bethel for Walls Farm
    Aug 15 arrived at Yorktown
    During the march, the men and regiment were in excellent spirits

Company K
Company Muster Roll Sept Oct 1863
Near Brandy Station
Record of Events

This command was camped near Orange Court House until Sept 14 when it moved down near Rapidan Station and where it camped until October 8 doing field duty and strengthening the position by cutting rifle pits.

On 8 Oct it took up line of march via Madison Court House passed north of Culpeper Court Hose by Warrenton to Bristow Station where it arrived 14 Oct and was under heavy shelling for about 20 minutes and had one man slightly wounded.

On 18 October it recrossed the Rappahannock and camped near Brandy Station

D. Nall
Capt. Cmdg. Co. K
8th Ala Reg.

Company K
Company Muster Roll Jan & Feb 1864
Near Orange Court House
Record of Events
This company since last muster has been stationed near Orange Court House Virginia and it has been doing picket duty at Rapidan Station.

Company K
Company Muster Roll March & April 1864
Near Orange Court House
Record of Events
Since last muster this company has been stationed near Orange Court House doing picket duty.

Company K
Company Muster Roll Sept & October 1864
Near Petersburg
Record of Events
Since last muster this company has been in the trenches near Petersburg doing picket duty and has participated in the battle of 27 October.

Company K
Company Return Jan 1862
Harwood's Mills Va.

(END OF COMPANY K)

Appendix F
Transcribed Field and Staff Notes
From National Archives Microfilm
Eighth Alabama Infantry CSA

Field and Staff Muster Roll Sept & Oct 1863
Near Brandy Station Virginia

Record of Events

This regiment was encamped near Orange Court House until 8 October when it stared on the march and arrived at Bristow Station on October 14, though not engaged in the battle lost by shells one killed and seven wounded. Now encamped near Brandy Station

Field and Staff Muster Roll Jan and Feb 1864
Near Orange Court House

Field and Staff Muster Roll March and April 1864
Near Orange Court House

Field and Staff Muster Roll Sept and October 1864
Near Petersburg Virginia

Historical Memoranda

1861 This regiment composed of ten companies, five from Mobile, two from Perry County, one from Dallas Co., one from Coosa Co. and one from Butler Co. was the first that entered the service for the war from the State of Alabama. The regiment was organized in Richmond on the 10th day of June 1861 and John A. Winston Ex Governor was appointed as Colonel. On the 11th we left Richmond for Yorktown and reached there on the 13th and camped on the beach below the town where we remained during the summer and part of the fall. Whilst here the regiment made several marches to the vicinity of Hampton and parts of it were engaged in three slight engagements. Amongst the killed were Capt. Loughry Co. I, Capt Summers of Co. C, Lt. Kennedy Co. H, Lt. Scott Co. H, Lt. McGrath Co. I, were mentioned in the report for their gallantry. Lt. Col H. A. Herbert was wounded and captured. After this engagement we returned to our camp and were soon transferred to General Wilcox' brigade composed entirely of Alabamians. Col. John A. Winston resigned on 16 June 1862 when command devolved upon Col. Y. L. Royston. When the great battles of Richmond commenced, the regiment though it moved several times, did not become engaged until 27 June 1862 at the battle of Gaines' Mills. In this engagement the regiment lost about 400 on the field. We lost one hundred forty nine killed and wounded.

Among the killed were Capt. Phelan Co. A, Lts. Maynard and Loyall of Co. B; Jenson of Co. G, and Lane of Co. F all brave and meritorious officers. Capt. Hannon of Co. B and Lt. Bennett of Co. K received wounds of which they afterward died both gallant and efficient officers. Corporal J. P. Harris of Co. K was appointed on the field as Color Sergeant for gallantry in carrying the colors after Sgt. Saxton of Co. I, a brave soldier was killed. On the 29th of June the regiment marched to the Richmond side of the Chickahominy towards the battlefield of the 29th Fraser's Farm. This action was fought on the 30th. Our loss in killed and wounded was sixty-more than half the number carried into the fight. Col. Y. L. Royston was here severely wounded. Private Ryan Co. E was afterwards appointed Lt. for gallantry in this engagement. After this engagement, the regiment remained in camp near Richmond under the command of W. F. Cleveland Jr., until the beginning of the Maryland campaign when Major H. A. Herbert having been exchanged took command. We left Richmond for Gordonsville on Aug 10th. From Gordonsville, we marched with Longstreet's Corps of which we formed a part of the Aug 31 battlefield at Manassas No. 2. Our loss in this engagement was seventeen killed and wounded. We then crossed the Potomac near Leesburg on the 6th of September and were present at and took part in the engagement of Harper's Ferry. From this place we marched to the battlefield of September 17th—Sharpsburg. Our loss in this battle was seventy eight killed and wounded out of one hundred twenty in the fight. The following men were distinguished for gallantry: Sgt Robinson Co. B, now Captain; Sgt B. E. Gould Co. G, now Lt., Sgt. Geo Batch Co F, now 1Lt., Sgt C. F. Brown Co. D now 1Lt. Privates Bolger Co. B, McClosky, P. Smith and C. Rowe of Co. G, T. Russell Co. H, and J. C. Callahan Co. C.

On the night of the 18th the army fell back and we crossed the Potomac River at Shepherdstown and marched to the neighborhood of Martinsburg at which place Col. Royston rejoined the regiment and being the senior field officer took command of the brigade. On the 27th of September we moved to within six miles of Winchester where we remained until 30 October. We then moved to Culpeper Court House which place we reached on the 2nd of November and remained till the 19th on which day we set out for Fredericksburg arriving at Price on Nov. 22. At this place most of the 300 conscripts which had been assigned to our regiment reached us. We remained in camp here until the Dec 12 battle of Fredericksburg in which our loss was one man wounded. When the battle of May 3, 1863-Chancellorsville-commenced we were assigned to guard Banks Ford, and hence were not engaged until at Salem Church on May 3. Our loss in this action was forty four killed and wounded. Col. Y. L. Royston was wounded and permanently disabled. Capt. Mordecai, Lts. Rice and Sterling were mentioned for gallantry. On the 14th of June we started on the Pennsylvania campaign and were not engaged in any fight or skirmish until the battle of July 2-3—Gettysburg, in which we lost two hundred sixty two killed, wounded and missing our of four hundred and twenty in the fight. Of twenty six officers, seventeen were killed and wounded. Among the killed were Capt. C. P. B. Branegan, Lts. B. J. Fuller, Geo. Schwartz, gallant and efficient officers. Capt. Livingston a brave and faithful officer and Lt. R. R. Scott died of wounds received here. The Color Sgt L. P.

Radsdell, Privates Rothchilds Co. G, Jas. Reynolds and R. J. Heard Co. K, Sgt Bulger Co. B were conspicuous for bravery and daring. On the return from Gettysburg we had a skirmish at St. James College near Hagerstown Maryland in which one man was wounded.

From this place we recrossed the Potomac and marched to Bunker's Hill where we rested for several days. We then marched to Culpeper Court House and again rested for several days from which place we marched to Orange Court House and remained doing picket duty until October 11th on which day we took up the line of march toward the battlefield of Oct 11th—Bristow Station. Our loss in this battle was one killed and seven wounded. We then returned to Orange Court House where we built winter quarters and remained during the winter. On November 30, 1863, we were engaged in the skirmish at Mine Run in which our loss was one man wounded. On the 29th of Jan 1864 we re-enlisted for the war unconditionally. The re-enlistment was conducted entirely by the non-commissioned officers and privates. We then marched in February to Madison Court House Virginia to meet an advance of the enemy but as he did not remain to give us battle, we returned to our camps after a march of several days in the midst of winter. General Wilcox having been promoted, General Perrin of South Carolina was assigned to the brigade. Col. Y. L. Royston being disabled, Ltc. Herbert had command of the regiment and on May 5th we opened the campaign marching down the Fredericksburg and Orange Plank Road to the Battle of the Wilderness 6 & 7 May. Our loss in the two days was forty six killed, wounded and missing. Among the wounded were Ltc. Col. Herbert, Capt. Nall, Capt Lea successively in command of the regiment, thereby making the command devolve upon Capt. W. W. Mordecai.

Left his place on 8 May for Spotsylvania Court House and same day fought May 8 at Bradshaw's Farm. We reached Spotsylvania Court House on the 9th at which we engaged at the 11th and 12th Battle of Spotsylvania Court House. In this engagement our loss in killed, wounded, and missing was twenty six. General Perrin was here killed. We remained at this place till 21 May when we marched to the 24 May battle of Hanover Junction. Our loss was 8 killed, wounded and missing. From this place we marched to the battlefield of June 1st-Tottottopotomy Creek. Our loss was eight killed, wounded and missing. From this place we marched to battlefield of June 3-Cold Harbor. Our loss was fifteen, killed and wounded. From this place we marched June 13th to White Oak Swamp. Our loss two wounded. From this place we crossed the James River. We took position in the line at Battery No. 30 near Petersburg where we remained until the battle of June 22 "Enemy Left Flank" in which our loss was twenty seven killed, wounded and missing. One the next day we marched to the battle of the 23rd June-Gurley's Farm—our loss one killed and two wounded. On the night of the 23rd we returned to our original position at Battery No. 30 where we remained until the battle of 29th June at Reams' Station on the Weldon Railroad. Our loss was five killed, wounded or missing. On the night of 29th June we returned to our original position on the lines in front of Petersburg where we remained until the battle of July 30th—the Crater—our loss was eighteen killed and wounded. After this engagement we again returned to our original position at Battery No. 30 and remained until Aug 14th when we marched to the north side of the James River to the Aug 16th battle of Deep Bottom. Our loss was six killed, wounded and missing. After this engagement we returned to our original position at Battery No. 30 where we remained until the battle of Aug 21 at Weldon Railroad. Our loss was eleven killed wounded or missing. Here our gallant brigade commander General J. C. C. Sanders fell mortally wounded. Also Capt. Mordecai in command of the regiment was wounded. We returned to our old position Battery No. 30 remaining there till the battle of Aug 25 at Reams' Station. At this place we were held in Reserve, loss nothing. After this engagement, we returned to Battery No. 30, our original position and remained there until mid October when we relieved Finnegan's Brigade at Battery No. 27 to our left and remained in the new position until October 27th Battle of Burgess Mill. Loss was seven wounded. We marched back again to our position a Battery No. 30 and remained in camp till 12 November when we moved to the right of our lines in front of Petersburg and built winter quarters in which we are now staying. On the 6th of December we commenced the march after Warren and his raiders. This march lasted seven days and was one of the worst that this regiment ever before experienced. It was through heat, cold, rain, hail and snow. The limited space would not permit anything more than bare mention of the most prominent parts of the history of the regiment and companies. Below find the details. It is proper to state that most of the deserters from the regiment are still in the Confederate States Service.

Recapitulation	
Total Commissioned Officers	102
Originally Enlisted Men	879
Recruits Received	440
Aggregate	1421
Deduct Casualties	-921
Aggregate remaining	500
Killed	226
Died of Disease	151
Resigned	24
Retired	29
Discharged	145
Transferred	98
Missing by capture/otherwise	41
Total Casualties	921
Aggregate wounded	734
Aggregate Disabled	85
Captured	259
Exchanged	124
Died	24
Oath to US	26

Total	174
Not returned	85

8th Regiment Alabama
Regimental Return Dec 1861 dated Jan 6, 1862
Stationed at Harwood's Mills Va.

Record of Events

From October 31 was encamped at Bethel till Dec 9 when we marched to Harwood's Mills remaining ten days. Then on Dec 18th we marched back to Bethel, bivouacking and marching every day on foraging and scouting expeditions. On Dec 22 a detachment of the regiment under Col. Winston's command marched towards the New Market Bridge and seeing a party of the enemy pursued them over a small creek and engaged them in a skirmish. Co. I lost one man and one wounded. Company H lost two men wounded. We captured one prisoner of the 20th New York regiment. Our men behaved gallantly and left in good order. On Dec 27th we moved back to Harwood's Mills and engaged in building winter quarters.

The cause of the delay in sending these returns was an alary given and the regiment was lying in ambush al day waiting for further orders, a few miles from our present camp.

8th Regiment Alabama
Regimental Return January 1862 dated Feb 4, 1862
Stationed at Harwood's Mills Va.

8th Regiment Alabama
Regimental Return February 1862 dated March 31, 1862
Stationed at Harwood's Mills Va.

Last Recapitulation

Total Commissioned Officers	19
Enlisted Men	6
Aggregate	25
Deduct Casualties	-15
Aggregate remaining	10

Killed	1
Died of Disease	0
Died of Wounds	0
Dropped	1
Resigned	3
Retired	2

Discharged	0
Transferred	8
Deserted	0
Missing by capture/otherwise	0
Total casualties	15
Aggregate Wounded	11
Aggregate Disabled	15
Captured	4
Exchanged	1
Escaped	0
Died	0
Oath to US	0
Total	1
Not Returned	3

Roster
March 25, 1865
Remarks

Adj't & Insp. Genl's Office
Richmond

Col.
    It is desired that this blank be filed with the names of the officers of your regiment, at its entry into the confederate service, and returned to this office within ten days of its receipt.
    Note all changed among the officers, with exact dates of each change, and whether by death, resignation, promotion or otherwise.
    Also the names of officers succeeding to the vacancies and whether by election, promotion or appointment; if the latter by whose authority and generally whatever may be necessary to complete the history of your command

                      Jno. Blair Hoge AAG

There is no record of the Regiment to be had, everything belonging to the Adjutant's Office was lost in the late valley campaign, and there is no one that can assist me in making such a record for I am a Lieutenant commanding the regiment.

                      Very respectfully yours,
                      J. S. Gilbert

Appendix G
Bibliography

Manuscript Collections

P. G. T. Beauregard Papers, New Orleans, LA: Tulane University.

P. G. T. Beauregard Papers, Baton Rouge, LA: Louisiana State University,

P. G. T. Beauregard Papers, Springfield, IL: Illinois State Historical Society.

Confederate Records, Eighth Alabama Infantry Microfilm, Washington, D. C.: National Archives.

Elias Davis Papers, Southern Historical Collection, Chapel Hill, NC: University of North Carolina.

Hilary A. Herbert Papers, Southern Historical Collection, Chapel Hill, NC: University of North Carolina.

R. E. Lee Papers, Richmond., VA: The Virginia Historical Society.

Papers of James Longstreet, 1821-1904, Special Collections Library, Durham, NC: Duke University.

Moseley Family Papers, Decatur, AL: Morgan County Archives

John Caldwell Calhoun Sanders Papers in the Collection of Papers of William Henry Sanders, Montgomery, AL: State Department of Archives and History.

Papers of James Ewell Brown Stuart, San Marino, CA: The Huntington Library.

Papers of Thos. H. Watts, Governor of Alabama, Montgomery, AL: Department of Archives and History.

Cadmus Wilcox Papers, Washington, D. C.: The Library of Congress.

Papers of John Anthony Winston, Governor of Alabama, Montgomery, AL: State Department of Archives and History.

Newspapers

    Montgomery (AL) Weekly Advertiser, April, 20, 1864.

    Richmond (VA) Daily Dispatch, August 23, 1864.

    Macon (MS) Beacon, April 1876.

Primary Sources: Articles by Participants in the War Between the States

    Alexander E. Porter, "The Great Charge and Artillery Fighting at Gettysburg," Battles and Leaders of the Civil War, Vol. 3, New York: Castle Books Inc., 1956.

    Alexander, E. P., "Records of Longstreet's Corps, Army of Northern Virginia, The Seven Days Battles," Southern Historical Society Papers, Vol. I, January to June, 1867, New York: Kraus Reprint Co., 1977.

    Allan, Colonel William, "Relative Strength at Second Manassas," Southern Historical Papers, Vol. VIII, New York: Kraus Reprint Co., 1977.

    Author Unknown, "The Defense of Fort Gregg," Southern Historical Society Papers, New York: Kraus Reprint Co., 1977.

    Author Unknown, "The Opposing Forces at Petersburg and Richmond," Battles and Leaders of the Civil War, Vol. 4, New York: Castle Books Inc., 1956.

    Author Unknown, "University of North Carolina in the Civil War," Southern Historical Society Papers, Vol. XXIV, New York: Kraus Reprint Co., 1977.

    Barnwell, Robert W. "The Battle of Seven Pines," Confederate Veteran, Vol. XXXVI, No. 2, February 1928.

    Beauregard, G. T., "Four Days of Battle at Petersburg," Battles and Leaders of the Civil War, Vol. 4, New York: Castle Books Inc., 1956.

    Charles, R. K., "Events in the Battle of Fredericksburg," Confederate Veteran, Vol. XIV, No. 2, February 1906.

    Clark, George, "Chancellorsville and Salem Church," Confederate Veteran, Vol. XVIII, No. 3, March, 1910.

Clark, George, "From the Rapidan to Petersburg: Wilcox' Alabama Brigade in that Memorable Campaign," Confederate Veteran, Vol. XVII, August, 1909.

Clark, George, "Wilcox's Alabama Brigade at Gettysburg," Confederate Veteran, Vol. XVIII, No. 5, May, 1909.

Couch, Darius N., "The Chancellorsville Campaign," Battles and Leaders of the Civil War, Vol. 3, New York: Castle Books Inc., 1956.

Demott, John D., "The Cause of the Silent Battle," Battles and Leaders of the Civil War, Vol. 2, New York: Castle Books Inc., 1956.

Draper, Joseph, "Who Fought in the Battle of the Crater," Confederate Veteran, Vol. VII, November 1900.

Featherston, Capt. John C., "The Battle of the Crater As I Saw It," Confederate Veteran, Vol. XIV, January 1906.

Floyd, N. J., "Concerning the Battle of the Crater," Confederate Veteran, Vol. XVI, April, 1908.

Galloway, G. Norton, "Hand-to-Hand fighting at Spotsylvania," Battles and Leaders of the Civil War, Vol. 3, New York: Castle Books Inc., 1956.

Grant, U. S., General Grant on the Siege of Petersburg," Battles and Leaders of the Civil War, Vol. 4, New York: Castle Books Inc., 1956.

Hill, Daniel H., "Lee Attacks North of the Chickahominy," Battles and Leaders of the Civil War, Vol. 2, New York: Castle Books Inc., 1956.

Hill, Daniel H., "McClellan's Change of Base and Malvern Hill," Battles and Leaders of the Civil War, Vol. 2, New York: Castle Books Inc., 1956.

Hogan, H. R., "Battle of Frazier's farm—A Correction," Confederate Veteran, Vol. I, No. 11, November, 1893.

Hogan, N. B., "Gains' Mill," Confederate Veteran, Vol. VI, No. 12, December 1898.

Hunt, Henry J., "The Third Day at Gettysburg," Battles and Leaders of the Civil War, Vol. 3, New York: Castle Books, 1956.

Houghton, Charles H., "In the Crater," Battles and Leaders of the Civil War, Vol. 4, New York: Castle Books Inc., 1956.

Johnson, Joseph E., "From Manassas to Seven Pines," Battles and Leaders of the Civil War, Vol. 2, New York: Castle Books Inc., 1956.

Law, E. M., "From the Wilderness to Cold Harbor," Battles and Leaders of the Civil War, Vol. 3, New York: Castle Books Inc., 1956.

Longstreet, General James, "Battle of Seven Pines—Report of General James Longstreet," Southern Historical Society Papers, Vol. III, New York: Kraus Reprint Co., 1977.

Longstreet, James, "The Battle of Fredericksburg," Battles and Leaders of the Civil War, Vol. 3, New York: Castle Books Inc., 1956.

Longstreet, James, "Lee's Right Wing at Gettysburg," Battles and Leaders of the Civil War, Vol. 3, New York: Castle Books Inc., 1956.

Longstreet, James "The Seven Days Battles Including Frayser's Farm," Battles and Leaders of the Civil War, Vol. 2, New York: Castle Books Inc., 1956.

McIntosh, David Gregg, "The Campaign of Chancellorsville," southern Historical Society Papers, Vol. XL, New York: Kraus Reprint Co., 1977

McMahon, Martin T., "Cold Harbor," Battles and Leaders of the Civil War, Vol. 3, New York: Castle Books Inc., 1956.

Perry, General William F., "Reminiscences of the Campaign of 1864 in Virginia," Southern Historical Society Papers, Vol. VII, New York: Kraus Reprint Co., 1977.

Phillips, B. F., "Wilcox" Alabamians in Virginia," Confederate Veteran, Vol. XV, No. 11, 1907.

Porter, Horace, "Five Forks and the Pursuit of Lee," Battles and Leaders of the Civil War, Vol. 4, New York: Castle Books, 1956.

Powell, William H., "The Battle of the Petersburg Crater," Battles and Leaders of the Civil War, Vol. 4, New York: Castle Books Inc., 1956.

Purifoy, John, "Assault of Anderson's Division, July 2, 1863," Confederate Veteran, Vol. XXXI, No. 10, October 1923.

Rogers, George T., "The Crater Battle," Confederate Veteran, Vol. III, March, 1895.

Smith, Gustavus W., "Two Days of Battle of Seven Pines (Fair Oaks)," Battles and Leaders of the Civil War, Vol. 2, New York: Castle Books, Inc., 1956.

Stewart, Lt. Col. William H., "The Charge of the Crater," Southern Historical Society Papers, Vol. XXV, New York: Kraus Reprint Co., 1977.

Talcott, T. M. R., "The Third Day at Gettysburg," Southern Historical Society Papers, Vo. XXV, New York: Kraus Reprint Co., 1977.

Thomas, Henry Goddard, "The Colored Troops at Petersburg," Battles and Leaders of the Civil War, Vol. 4, New York: Castle Books Inc., 1956.

Todd, Westwood A., "Reminiscences of the War Between the States," Southern Historical Collection, Chapel Hill, NC: University of North Carolina.

Vance, S. W., "Heroes of the Eighth Alabama Infantry," Confederate Veteran, Vol. VII, November 1899.

Watson, Walter E., "Sailor's Creek," Southern Historical Society Papers, New York: Kraus Reprint Co., 1977.

Wilcox, Cadmus M., "General C. M. Wilcox on the Battle of Gettysburg," Southern Historical Society Papers, Vol. IV, New York: Kraus Reprint Co., 1956.

Wilcox, Cadmus M., "General C. M. Wilcox on the Battle of Gettysburg," Southern Historical Society Papers, Vol., VII, Kraus Reprint Co., 1977.

Wilcox, General C. M., "Cadmus Wilcox on the Battle of Gettysburg," Southern Historical Society Papers, Vol. VI, New York, Kraus Reprint Co., 1977

Willcox, Orlando B., "Actions on the Weldon Railroad," Battles and Leaders of the Civil War, Vol. 3, New York: Castle Books Inc, 1956.

Williams, Major J. H. "Wilcox' Brigade at Gains' Mill," Confederate Veteran, Vol. VIII, No. 10, October, 1900.

Other Primary Sources: Books/Pamphlets

Author Unknown, Eighth Regiment Alabama Volunteer (Infantry), Montgomery, AL: 1866, Introduction and edited by William Stanley Hoole, Confederate Regimental Series No. 10, University, AL: Confederate Publishing Co., 1985.

Brock, R. A. editor with an Introduction, Paroles of the Army of Northern Virginia from the Duplicate Originals in the archives of the Southern Historical Society, Vol. XV, Richmond, VA: Southern Historical Society, 1887.

Chestnut, Mary Boykin, A Diary from Dixie, edited by Ben Ames Williams, Boston, MA: Houghton Mifflin Co., 1949.

Evans, Clement A., editor, Confederate Military History Extended Edition, Wilmington NC: Broadfoot Publishing Co., 1987, reprint of the Confederate Publishing Co. edition of 1899.

Freeman, Douglas Southall, Lee's Dispatches Unpublished Letters of General Robert E. Lee C. S. A. to Jefferson Davis and the War Department of the Confederate States of America 1862-1865 from the private collection of Wymberley Jones deRenee of Wormsloe, GA, New Edition, New York: G. P. Putnam's Sons, 1957.

Longstreet, James P., From Manassas to Appomattox, Memoirs of the Civil War in America, New York: Smithmark Publisher Inc., 1992 version.

McClelan, Baily George, I Saw the Elephant, Company D, 10th Alabama, edited by Norman E. Rourke, Shippensburg, PA: White Mane Publishing Co. Inc., 1995.

Mosby, John S., Stuart's Cavalry in the Gettysburg Campaign, New York: Moffat, Yard & Co., 1908.

Patterson, Edmund DeWitt, Yankee Rebel The Civil War Journal of Edmund DeWitt Patterson, edited by John G. Barrett, Knoxville, TN: University of Tennessee, 2004, originally published in 1966 by the University of North Carolina Press.

Sorrel, G. Mosley, recollections of a Confederate Staff Officer, edited by Bell Irvin Wiley, Jackson TN: McCowat-Mercer Press, 1958.

U. S. Government, War of the Rebellion: A Compilation of the Official Records of the Union and Confederate Armies, Washington, D. C.: Government Printing Office, 1901.

Secondary Sources: Articles, Books, Notes, etc.

Author Unknown, Eighth Alabama Infantry Notes, Research Library, Antietam Visitors Center, National Park Service, Sharpsburg, MD.

Carmichael, Peter S., Lee's Young Artillerist, William R. J. Pegram, Charlottesville, VA: University of Virginia Press, 1995.

Codington, Edwin B., The Gettysburg Campaign, A Study in Command, New York: Charles Scribner's Sons, 1968.

Freeman, Douglas S., Lee's Lieutenants: A Study in Command, Vol. 3, New York: Charles Scribner's Sons, 1944.

Hassler, William W., A. P. Hill, Lee's Forgotten General, Chapel Hill, NC: University of North Carolina Press, revised, 1962.

Hattaway, Herman, Shades of Blue and Gray, Columbia, MO: University of Missouri Press, 1997.

Rhea, Gordon C., The Battle of the Wilderness May 5-6, 1864, Baton Rouge: Louisiana State University Press, 1994.

Sears, Stephen W., Chancellorsville, New York: Houghton Mifflin Co., 1996.

Stewart, Vaughn, et. al., The McClellan and Allied Families, 1985.

Thomson, Bailey, "John C. C. Sanders: Lee's 'Boy General'," Alabama Review, Vol. 32, April, 1979.

Tower, R. Lockwood, Lee's Adjutant, The Wartime Letters of Colonel Walter Herron Taylor, 1862-1865, Columbia, SC: University of South Carolina Press, 1995.

Wert, Jeffrey. General Longstreet, New York: Touchstone Books, 1993.

Other Heritage Books by Linda L. Green:

1890 Union Veterans Census: Special Enumeration Schedules Enumerating Union Veterans and Widows of the Civil War. Missouri Counties: Bollinger, Butler, Cape Girardeau, Carter, Dunklin, Iron, Madison, Mississippi, New Madrid, Oregon, Pemiscot, Petty, Reynolds, Ripley, St. Francois, St. Genevieve, Scott, Shannon, Stoddard, Washington, and Wayne

Alabama 1850 Agricultural and Manufacturing Census: Volume 1 for Dale, Dallas, Dekalb, Fayette, Franklin, Greene, Hancock, and Henry Counties

Alabama 1850 Agricultural and Manufacturing Census: Volume 2 for Jackson, Jefferson, Lawrence, Limestone, Lowndes, Macon, Madison, and Marengo Counties

Alabama 1860 Agricultural and Manufacturing Census: Volume 1 for Dekalb, Fayette, Franklin, Greene, Henry, Jackson, Jefferson, Lawrence, Lauderdale, and Limestone Counties

Alabama 1860 Agricultural and Manufacturing Census: Volume 2 for Lowndes, Madison, Marengo, Marion, Marshall, Macon, Mobile, Montgomery, Monroe, and Morgan Counties

Delaware 1850-1860 Agricultural Census, Volume 1

Delaware 1870-1880 Agricultural Census, Volume 2

Delaware Mortality Schedules, 1850-1880; Delaware Insanity Schedule, 1880 Only

Dunklin County, Missouri Marriage Records: Volume 1, 1903-1916

Dunklin County, Missouri Marriage Records: Volume 2, 1916-1927

Florida 1850 Agricultural Census

Florida 1860 Agricultural Census

Georgia 1860 Agricultural Census: Volume 1 Comprises the Counties of Appling, Baker, Baldwin, Banks, Berrien, Bibb, Brooks, Bryan, Bullock, Burke, Butts, Calhoun, Camden, Campbell, Carroll, Cass, Catoosa, Chatham, Charlton, Chattahooche, Chattooga, and Cherokee

Georgia 1860 Agricultural Census: Volume 2 Comprises the Counties of Clark, Clay, Clayton, Clinch, Cobb, Colquitt, Coffee, Columbia, Coweta, Crawford, Dade, Dawson, Decatur, Dekalb, Dooly, Dougherty, Early, Echols, Effingham, Elbert, Emanuel, Fannin, and Fayette

Kentucky 1850 Agricultural Census for Letcher, Lewis, Lincoln, Livingston, Logan, McCracken, Madison, Marion, Marshall, Mason, Meade, Mercer, Monroe, Montgomery, Morgan, Muhlenburg, and Nelson Counties

Kentucky 1860 Agricultural Census: Volume 1 for Floyd, Franklin, Fulton, Gallatin, Garrard, Grant, Graves, Grayson, Green, Greenup, Hancock, Hardin, and Harlin Counties

Kentucky 1860 Agricultural Census: Volume 2 for Harrison, Hart, Henderson, Henry, Hickman, Hopkins, Jackson, Jefferson, Jessamine, Johnson, Morgan, Muhlenburg, Nelson, and Nicholas Counties

Kentucky 1860 Agricultural Census: Volume 3 for Kenton, Knox, Larue, Laurel, Lawrence, Letcher, Lewis, Lincoln, Livingston, Logan, Lyon, and Madison

Kentucky 1860 Agricultural Census: Volume 4 for Mason, Marion, Magoffin, McCracken, McLean, Marshall, Meade, Mercer, Metcalfe, Monroe and Montgomery Counties

Louisiana 1860 Agricultural Census: Volume 1 Covers Parishes: Ascension, Assumption, Avoyelles, East Baton Rouge, West Baton Rouge, Boosier, Caddo, Calcasieu, Caldwell, Carroll, Catahoula, Clairborne, Concordia, Desoto, East Feliciana, West Feliciana, Franklin, Iberville, Jackson, Jefferson, Lafayette, Lafourche, Livingston, and Madison

Louisiana 1860 Agricultural Census: Volume 2

Maryland 1860 Agricultural Census: Volumes 1 and 2

Mississippi 1860 Agricultural Census: Volume 1 Comprises the Following Counties: Lowndes, Madison, Marion, Marshall, Monroe, Neshoba, Newton, Noxubee, Oktibbeha, Panola, Perry, Pike, and Pontotoc

Mississippi 1860 Agricultural Census: Volume 2 Comprises the Following Counties: Rankin, Scott, Simpson, Smith, Tallahatchie, Tippah, Tishomingo, Tunica, Warren, Wayne, Winston, Yalobusha, and Yazoo

Montgomery County, Tennessee 1850 Agricultural Census

New Madrid County, Missouri Marriage Records, 1899-1924

Pemiscot County, Missouri Marriage Records, January 26, 1898 to September 20, 1912: Volume 1

Pemiscot County, Missouri Marriage Records, November 1, 1911 to December 6, 1922: Volume 2

South Carolina 1860 Agricultural Census: Volumes 1-3

Tennessee 1850 Agricultural Census for Robertson, Rutherford, Scott, Sevier, Shelby and Smith Counties: Volume 2

Tennessee 1860 Agricultural Census: Volumes 1 and 2

Texas 1850 Agricultural Census, Volume 1: Anderson through Hunt Counties

Texas 1850 Agricultural Census, Volume 2: Jackson through Williamson Counties

Virginia 1850 Agricultural Census, Volumes 1-5

Virginia 1860 Agricultural Census, Volumes 1 and 2

West Virginia 1850 Agricultural Census, Volumes 1 and 2

West Virginia 1860 Agricultural Census, Volume 3